EMPOWERING PUBLIC SPEAKING

EMPOWERING PUBLIC SPEAKING

Deanna L. Fassett | **Keith Nainby**
San José State University | *California State University, Stanislaus*

cognella®
SAN DIEGO

Bassim Hamadeh, CEO and Publisher
Todd R. Armstrong, Publisher
Tony Paese, Project Editor
Abbey Hastings, Associate Production Editor
Jess Estrella, Senior Graphic Designer
Alexa Lucido, Licensing Manager
Natalie Piccotti, Director of Marketing
Kassie Graves, Vice President of Editorial
Jamie Giganti, Director of Academic Publishing

Copyright © 2021 by Deanna L. Fassett and Keith Nainby All rights reserved. No part of this publication may be reprinted, reproduced, transmitted, or utilized in any form or by any electronic, mechanical, or other means, now known or hereafter invented, including photocopying, microfilming, and recording, or in any information retrieval system without the written permission of Cognella, Inc. For inquiries regarding permissions, translations, foreign rights, audio rights, and any other forms of reproduction, please contact the Cognella Licensing Department at rights@cognella.com.

Trademark Notice: Product or corporate names may be trademarks or registered trademarks, and are used only for identification and explanation without intent to infringe.

Cover image: Copyright © 2019 iStockphoto LP/Rawpixel.

Printed in the United States of America.

cognella | ACADEMIC PUBLISHING
3970 Sorrento Valley Blvd., Ste. 500, San Diego, CA 92121

Brief Contents

CHAPTER 1
Public Speaking Is Constitutive — 2

CHAPTER 2
Public Speaking Is Relational — 22

CHAPTER 3
Public Speaking Is Responsive — 40

CHAPTER 4
Public Speaking Is Specific to Time, Place, and Purpose — 58

CHAPTER 5
Public Speaking Is Pedagogical — 80

CHAPTER 6
Public Speaking Is Structured — 106

CHAPTER 7
Public Speaking Is Informed — 124

CHAPTER 8
Public Speaking Is Performance — 142

CHAPTER 9
Public Speaking Is Impassioned — 170

CHAPTER 10
Public Speaking Is Accountable — 190

CHAPTER 11
Public Speaking Is Evolving — 214

CHAPTER 12
Public Speaking Is Empowering — 232

Contents

Preface xiii

CHAPTER 1
Public Speaking Is Constitutive 2

Our Introduction to Public Speaking 5
Communication, Including Public Speaking, Is Constitutive 9
    Communication Shapes and Creates Our Social Reality 10
Communication, Including Public Speaking, Is Relational 11
    Rhetoric Helps Us Think Critically About Communication in Our Lives 12
Empowering Public Speaking Is Socially Significant Advocacy 16
    Advocacy Entails Speaking Alongside Others to Amplify Their Voices 18
"Fight for Your Lives Before It's Someone Else's Job" 19
Concepts 20
Toward Praxis 20
Discussion Questions 21

CHAPTER 2
Public Speaking Is Relational 22

Public Speaking Emerges From and Shapes Interpersonal Relationships 25
    Public Speaking Is Not Just One Person Speaking at or to Many 26
    Public Speaking Is Cocreated By the Speaker and Listeners 27
    Public Speaking Should Be Respectful Between Speaker and Listener 28
Public Speaking Is More Like Posing Problems Than Banking 28
    There Is a Risk of Public Speaking Becoming Banking 29
    Teachers Should Be Problem Posers, Not Bankers 30
    Similarities Exist Between Teaching and Public Speaking 30
    Reflexivity Is Important in Problem Posing 31
    Public Speakers Are Actively Engaged in Praxis 32

Listening Must Be Critical and Compassionate   32
    Listen With Compassion   33
    Listen With a Critical Stance   33
    Communication Needs Reciprocity   34
Public Speakers Explore and Manage Their Fears   34
    Reframe the Fear of Public Speaking   36
"I Speak—Not for Myself, But for All . . ."   37
Concepts   38
Toward Praxis   38
Discussion Questions   39

CHAPTER 3
Public Speaking Is Responsive   40

Public Speaking Is Advocacy   42
    Rhetoric Is a Means of Persuasion   43
    Persuasion Entails Appeals to Ethos, Logos, and Pathos   45
    Persuasion as Advocacy Means Speaking **With** Others   45
Public Speaking as Advocacy Requires an Ethic of Care   46
    Reflexivity Relates to an Ethic of Care   47
Public Speaking Demands Careful Attention to Power   48
    Oppression Can Grow and Thrive Through Hegemony   48
    Hegemony Emerges From and Extends Unearned Privilege and Power   49
Audience Analysis Is Part of an Ongoing Dialogue   51
    Understand Audience Demographics   51
    Consider an Audience's Hierarchy of Needs   54
"Here in Newtown, I Come to Offer the Love and Prayers of a Nation"   54
Concepts   56
Toward Praxis   56
Discussion Questions   57

CHAPTER 4
Public Speaking Is Specific to Time, Place, and Purpose   58

Public Speakers Adapt to the Unique Circumstances of Speaking Occasions   60
    Speaking Occasions Are Defined by Their Relationship to Time   61
    Speaking Occasions Are Defined by Their Relationship to Community   63

Public Speakers Consider the Types and Purposes of Speeches in Each
   Speaking Occasion   64
   Informative Speeches Depend on a Present Community Relationship of
      Knowledge Levels   64
   Persuasive Speeches Depend on a Future Community Relationship of
      Possible Actions   66
   Ceremonial Speeches Depend on a Past Community Relationship of
      Esteemed Values   68
   Demonstration Speech Involves A Changed Relationship   68
Public Speakers Choose Topics That Are Well Suited for Particular
   Occasions, Purposes, and Audiences   70
   Undertake the Process of Brainstorming   70
   Undertake the Process of Topic Selection   71
   Undertake the Process of Narrowing a Topic   72
Public Speakers Develop a Thesis Statement That Guides the Structure
   and Focus of Their Speech   72
   An Effective Thesis Statement Is Precise   73
   An Effective Thesis Statement Is Unique   73
   An Effective Thesis Statement Is Direct   74
   A Thesis Statement Is Argumentative   75
   Thesis Statement Development Helps You Focus on Important
      Questions   75
"They're *Our Kids*. They're *Our Responsibility*. And It's Not Just Our
   Duty to Protect Them—It's *Our Right* to Protect Them"   76
Concepts   78
Toward Praxis   78
Discussion Questions   79

CHAPTER 5
Public Speaking Is Pedagogical   80

Public Speakers Set an Agenda for Audiences When They Speak   82
A Public Speaker's Role Relative to the Audience Shapes Their Efforts   83
   Informative Speaking Is Shaped by a Speaker's Credibility With Their
      Audience   85
   Informative Speaking Is Shaped by a Speaker's Relationship and
      Understanding of Their Audience   85
Public Speakers Enhance Their Credibility Through Careful
   Preparation   87
   Understand Your Role   88
   Understand the Importance of Syntax Structures   88
   Consider Speaker Credibility and Audience Learning Needs   89
   Identify Audience Members' Learning Needs   90
   Enhance Speaking Effectiveness Through Competence, Character, and
      Care   91

Public Speakers Practice Strategies to Attract and Retain Listeners' Attention   93
    Change the Frame for Your Audience   94
    Use an Attention Getter   95
Public Speakers Reshape Their Frames and Their Expectations   99
Public Speakers Advocate for Specific Transformations   100
    Doe's Impact Statement Pays Attention to Audience   101
    Doe's Impact Statement Changes Frames   102
    Doe's Impact Statement Has Credibility and Expertise   103
"Assault Is Not an Accident"   103
Concepts   104
Toward Praxis   104
Discussion Questions   105

CHAPTER 6
Public Speaking Is Structured   106

Structure Emerges From the Speaker's and the Listeners' Needs   108
Outlining Is a Helpful Means of Developing, Grouping, and Sequencing Your Main Ideas   110
    Develop Your Speech   111
    Group Your Ideas   113
    Order Your Ideas   114
You Can Strengthen Your Introductions, Transitions, and Conclusions for a Powerful Speech   116
    A Strong Introduction Establishes Your Relationship to the Topic and the Listener   116
    A Strong Transition Meaningfully Links Ideas Together and to Your Thesis   119
    A Strong Conclusion Leaves a Lasting Impression and Inspires Your Listeners to Action   120
"Let us remember . . . when displaced peoples ask, 'where do we go from here?', they are asking on behalf of us all."   121
Concepts   122
Toward Praxis   122
Discussion Questions   123

CHAPTER 7
Public Speaking Is Informed   124

Speakers Participate in Ongoing Conversations That Precede and Follow Them   126
    Speakers Must Practice Academic Integrity   128

The Speaker Has a Responsibility to Find and Critically Source
    Material   129
        Understand Different Types of Sources   130
        Evaluate the Quality of Sources   132
Speakers Have a Responsibility to Share Their Source Material   137
Speakers Help Create Reality as They Share Information   138
"No Longer Can We Compound Attacks on Truth With Our Silent
    Acquiescence"   139
Concepts   140
Toward Praxis   140
Discussion Questions   141

CHAPTER 8
Public Speaking Is Performance   142

Compelling Speakers Perform Their Speeches and Create Social
    Reality   144
        Speakers Participate With Their Audiences in Creating and Maintaining
            Social Reality   145
        Speakers Need to Be Intentional in How They Create Social Reality   146
Public Speaking Is a Distinct Form of Communication   147
        What Characterizes a Type of Communication as Public Speaking?   148
        Analyze the "Public" Tyson Was Addressing   150
        Public Speaking Is Situated Oral/Aural Communication   151
        Public Speech Relies on Timeliness   152
        Performance Speech Is Ephemeral   153
Public Speaking May Emerge From Different Modes of Delivery   154
        Extemporaneous Speaking Is Prepared and Practiced   155
        Time Is Important in Extemporaneous Speaking   156
        There Are Benefits and Drawbacks to Fully Memorized Speeches and
            Speaking From a Manuscript   157
        Impromptu Speaking Helps Novice Speakers Improve
            Public Speaking   159
Don't Let Public Speaking Anxiety Stop You From Your Best
    Delivery   161
The Speaker's Voice and Body Are Important Elements of Delivery   162
        Tyson Effectively Uses His Voice to Communicate   164
        The Speaker's Body May Meaningfully Complement Their Message   164
        Tyson Effectively Uses His Body to Communicate   165
Rehearsal Is an Essential Element of a Speaker's Success   166
"How Much Would You Pay for the Universe?"   167
Concepts   168
Toward Praxis   168
Discussion Questions   169

CHAPTER 9
Public Speaking Is Impassioned   170

Public Speakers Actively Construct Social Realities When They Speak   173
Public Speakers Frame the Speaking Situation Through Their Use of Language   175
    Understand the Rhetorical Frame   175
    Know the Differences Between Denotative and Connotative Meaning   176
Language Is Poetic   177
    Use Rhetorical Tropes   178
    Use Word Patterns in Rhetorical Schemes   179
Language Is Nuanced   180
    Nuanced and Inclusive Language Is Significant for Public Speakers   181
Public Speakers Advocate Through Their Uses of Language   182
    Assess the Rhetorical Strategies Used in de Blasio's Speech   183
    De Blasio's Speech Uses Inclusive Language   185
"It's All Our Problem—and Anyone Who Believes in the Values of This Country Should Feel Called to Action Right Now"   187
Concepts   188
Toward Praxis   188
Discussion Questions   189

CHAPTER 10
Public Speaking Is Accountable   190

Speakers Have a Responsibility to Use Reasoning Appropriately   192
Effective Speakers and Listeners Must Understand and Evaluate Different Forms of Reasoning   194
    Clarifying Reasoning Can Enhance an Argument   195
    Deductive Reasoning Helps Speakers Draw Conclusions From Evidence With Certainty   196
    Avoid Fallacies When Using Deductive Reasoning   197
    Inductive Reasoning Helps Speakers Draw Probable or Likely Conclusions   198
    Inductive Reasoning Can Be Based on Large Groups of Instances   198
    Inductive Reasoning Can Be Based on a Shared Relationship Between Instances   199
    Speakers Should Be Careful to Avoid Fallacies When Using Inductive Logic   202
    Causal Logic Can Offer Solutions to Problems, If Well Supported   203
    Distinguish Necessary, Sufficient, and Contributory Causes   205
    Strongly Defined Cause–Effect Relationships Can Help Speakers Avoid Fallacies   206
    Speakers May Also Reason by Making Meaningful Comparisons Called Analogies   206

Ethical, Inclusive Speakers Attend to Situated Reasoning 209
"We Must Account for That Inheritance" 211
Concepts 212
Toward Praxis 212
Discussion Questions 213

CHAPTER 11
Public Speaking Is Evolving 214

Communication Is Mediated—Often in Ways We Don't Notice 216
    CMC Is Meaningfully Different 218
    CMC Is Relevant for Public Speakers 220
    CMC Can Enhance the Reach and Impact of Public Messages 220
Traditional Public Speaking Concepts Both Deepen and Adapt in Mediated Contexts 223
    CMC Changes the Impact of a Speech Related to Space and Time 223
    Communication Expectations Are Evolving 225
Effective Speakers Communicate in Ways That Give Rise to Lasting Change 227
"It's About Keeping It Rolling Once You Go Home" 229
Concepts 230
Toward Praxis 230
Discussion Questions 231

CHAPTER 12
Public Speaking Is Empowering 232

Through Public Speaking, We May Empower Ourselves and Each Other 234
Empowering Public Speakers Practice and Encourage Reflexivity 237
    Practicing Reflexivity Provides Benefits 238
    What Does Becoming Reflexive Mean? 239
Empowering Public Speakers Practice Advocacy 240
    Practice Advocacy Through Reflexivity 241
    Practice Advocacy Through Dialogue 242
    Practice Advocacy Through Critical Literacy 243
    Practice Advocacy Through Alliance Building 244
"But I Am Hopeful. I Am Inspired" 244
Concepts 246
Toward Praxis 246
Discussion Questions 247

Glossary 249
References 257
Quotation Credits 263
Image Credits 265
Index 269

Preface

Books addressing public speaking often focus either on (1) a collection of skills that a prospective speaker can develop, keep in reserve as part of a communication repertoire, and then choose to apply, as they see fit, to a given opportunity established by a speaking context; or (2) a set of exemplary speakers and their accomplishments that can guide us, through study, to better understand effective speaking as an art. However, we, the authors of this book, find that what makes public speaking a compelling topic for us is a bit different: We are interested in how public speaking is a process that creates and sustains communities. We are most interested in the immediate, unpredictable, ever-evolving impact of public speaking on our lives as people who live in communities with others—communities that often demand intentional, difficult negotiations about how we should relate to one another and how we should share resources. Consider Greta Thunberg, who is perhaps an unlikely candidate as a world-transforming speaker given that she is a teenager as of this writing, that she was diagnosed with Asperger's syndrome at age 12, and that a primary focus of her activism (the "Fridays for Future" movement) involves urging other school-aged children to skip school). Yet she has "become the face of climate–change activism" and served as an invited speaker at a 2018 United Nations climate change conference, two distinctive accomplishments that attest to her persuasive power (Woodward and De Luce). Greta's example indicates that effective public speaking depends on speakers engaging others from their unique subject positions, in situated relation to particular communities, using the communication resources available to them, in response to shared perceptions of community needs.[1]

As an explicitly social-justice oriented introductory public speaking text, this book represents an important departure from conventional approaches. This departure stems from our central goal to foster readers' development as engaged speakers who appreciate the power of public speaking from two interrelated perspectives:

1. *We frame core dimensions of public speaking—such as audience and situation, topic selection, research, organization, supporting materials and delivery—as parts of widely established communication codes.* This frame supports students' practice of effective public speaking by foregrounding not only the constituent skills involved in effective public speaking, but also the ways that effective public speaking is a primary means through which particular people recognize and wield power at particular times, for particular reasons, in particular communities. This book thus highlights the unique importance

---

[1] Greta Thurnberg is *Time* magazine's 2019 Person of the Year (Alter, Haynes & Worland, 2019).

of public speaking in contemporary life as <u>both</u> a dimension of personal power (common to other public speaking texts) and a dimension of social, economic and cultural power (common only to other public speaking texts grounded in a "civic engagement" approach, and then with different values and emphases, as we explain below). In this way, we describe "the power of public speaking" as always more than a tool that can be taken up, or not, as speakers and audiences choose. In our book we treat this "power" as one communicative thread, among potential others, that students can trace in their own environments to more fully grasp how communication shapes social relations, identity development, and the sharing of scarce resources. Educators who expose the status of public speaking as a widely ratified code of power can help students to simultaneously acquire the capacity to effectively use the code and call into question the current social conditions created and sustained by this, and similar, codes (Delpit, 1995).

2 *We provide examples and discussions that raise the profile of public speaking as a socially significant act.* These examples and discussions promote exploration of how social, economic, and cultural power are historically rooted and are distributed among local communities rather than centralized within the resources of some alleged group of "those in power." We emphasize how each act of public speaking (re)makes the world by directing resources and by taking up power, even if the immediate (re)making appears localized in classrooms or similar speech communities. Through this approach, we treat socially significant public speaking as oriented not to civic engagement but to social transformation, because "civic engagement" connotes an existing speech community with mutually agreed upon rules for dialogue and change. Our focus on the historical and distributed roots of power, instead, encourages public speaking students to treat public speaking opportunities critically—i.e., to identify which speaking opportunities develop, for whom, in which communities, for which purposes, in the service of whose interests. Thus, we call upon students as present and future speakers to recognize and respect the differential access to power embedded in the concept of a "public speaker" when they themselves decide when, how and with whom to speak.

These interrelated perspectives on power and public speaking are unique to our textbook and are the rationale for its title: *Empowering Public Speaking* indicates that those who speak empower themselves and, perhaps, others through learning how to speak effectively; it also, simultaneously, indicates that the act of public speaking enfolds us in power relations that precede us and through which we are integrated as members of particular communities. *Empowering Public Speaking* adopts an advocacy position in how we discuss introductory communication concepts. We strive to extend the ways that existing public speaking texts implicitly normalize disciplinary discussions of public speaking; these discussions are, from our perspective, characterized by instrumental treatments of a set of established public speaking skills that, in and of themselves, serve as tools that students can master, include in their academic toolkits, and take up as needed. We contend that public speaking does not happen in sharply defined situations or well-formed speech communities and that, therefore, public speaking texts should begin with actual speakers' efforts to speak into the messy, incomplete, and often oppressive circumstances of the status quo. *Empowering Public Speaking* takes power, in the two overlapping senses described here, as its point of departure. The text is therefore an outgrowth and extension of relatively fresh research in critical communication pedagogy, through which curricular texts and pedagogical contexts are framed as responses (positively re-inscriptive of or negatively resistant to) a status quo marked by inequity.

Features and Benefits

This text introduces public speaking to readers as a socially (trans)formative communicative act, through which particular speakers utilize personal and public resources to shape our society according to particular purposes. Its sustained focus on power, privilege, and social transformation as necessary elements of any properly conceptualized speaking situation make it distinctive among other public speaking texts. Some specific features and benefits that flow from this approach include:

Attention to significant skills and concepts in public communication, engaged as readers might encounter them in situated contexts

- This textbook addresses concepts common to a broad array of public speaking texts, including, for example, listening (Chapter 2), audience analysis (Chapter 3), speaking situation (Chapter 4), topic selection (Chapter 4), organization and development (Chapter 6), research and evaluation of the credibility of source material (Chapter 7), and delivery (Chapter 8).

- Further, we introduce and accessibly define rigorous and contemporary concepts and vocabulary (such as "communication as constitutive" or "public speaking is ephemeral"), retaining the complexity of current communication studies research but sharing with readers in ways they will engage and retain it.

Issues-focused chapters

- Rather than organize this textbook through units driven only by public speaking curriculum concerns, we develop each of the concepts named above by exploring how a specific issue, and specific texts that have emerged in connection with this issue, reflect that concept. Such issues include the public communication surrounding events like the shooting at Sandy Hook Elementary School, including concomitant debates around gun control and mental health care access, or the recent rape of a 23-year-old female physiotherapy student in New Delhi that has become a catalyst for global and cross-cultural conversations about violence against women in India and around the world. Our rationale for this approach is twofold: First, it models the social justice orientation we advocate by engaging important issues in which public speaking concepts help speakers actively (re)make our world. Second, it embraces Freire's (1970/2003) call for problem-posing education, in which teachers organize curriculum not based on an established, abstract system of expertise but, instead, through how that curriculum links to immediately relevant concerns in students' lives.

Innovative sequencing of public speaking concepts

- Rather than moving, as more conventional public speaking texts do, from the self (concepts such as communication apprehension, listening, and ethics) to informative speaking to persuasive speaking, this book explicitly assumes from the outset that communication is neither neutral nor apolitical and that all public speaking, to some extent, is persuasive. To this end, we have structured the book to address *foundations and commitments* (our own, those of the discipline, those of our readers, those of the communities to which we belong or about which we care), *techniques and tactics* (including attention to power and privilege in the speech-making process, from topic selection and organization, to research and evaluation of source material, to delivery and response), and *challenges and changes* (which, instead of guiding students to static and fixed understandings of public speaking, helps students explore questions and contingent claims about public speaking as it will necessarily evolve with time).

Critical/cultural focus

- This book emerges from and embraces a critical pedagogy. Drawing from Paulo Freire's commitment to a problem-posing approach to teaching and learning, where students and teachers work together to build knowledge of a given phenomenon, we invite students to explore both public speaking concepts and contemporary and controversial public communication events in light of critical, social justice-oriented understandings of power and access, identity and dialogue.

Unconventional voice

- Rather than adopt a neutral or objective voice for this text, we engage in intellectually stimulating, appropriately argumentative, and accessible language and examples that help readers engage, apply, and challenge the text. By showing our seams, in a sense, we hope to invite students to participate in the process of knowledge construction that is the book and encourage them to question understandings of textbooks as neutral, impartial, and encyclopedic. This occurs through the use of first-person voice, personal examples, and by directly addressing readers. We identify a distinct social issue at the start of each chapter, then ground our exploration of relevant public speaking concepts in specific texts created by rhetors engaging this issue. In our opening chapter, for example, in exploring power, community, and advocacy, we consider the public speaking of Emma Gonzalez, a high school student who survived a February 2018 mass shooting as her school and, subsequently, became prominently associated with calls for government action to end gun violence in schools.

Expansive understanding of public communication

- Rather than limiting our textual analysis to traditional public address, we explore the broadening range of contexts that encapsulate core dimensions of public communication. These include social media (such as Facebook and Twitter) and internet-based broadcast platform posts (such as YouTube), as well as public performances (such as boycotts and altering or destroying of iconic images).

- In this book, we embrace our agenda-setting role as textbook authors. This shapes our personal writing voices and, especially, our selection of social issues as the anchor of each chapter. We hope that we model throughout the book our argument about the significance of our voices in public community. We also hope that this approach makes this book interesting to contemporary readers, for whom discourse is often personal and public at once.

Acknowledgments

There may be authors out there in the world who simply write without regard for whether there is an audience for their words. We are not those writers. This book is a collaboration in every sense of the word; without our colleagues, our students, and each other, this book would not exist. As our dear friend JTW would often say, there are those who find acknowledgments lovely and those who find them "icky"; if you're in the former, please read on, and, if you're among the latter, then you can safely turn the page, knowing that we appreciate everyone who has supported us in the long process of bringing *Empowering Public Speaking* to life, including you.

We'd first like to recognize our editorial and publishing support team. Todd Armstrong, Publisher, immediately caught our vision for this book, for which we are grateful. The entire Cognella team has been stellar, though we'd like to single out here: Abbey Hastings, Associate Production Editor, and Tony Paese, Project Editor, for their roles in helping bring this project to fruition. Laura Perry played an essential role in providing photo research for this project. Finally,

Elise Caffee should receive a medal for her grace and tact in helping us turn our—shall we say academic?—writing style into something a little more reader-friendly.

We are also proud to acknowledge here our reviewers, many of whom read multiple chapters multiple times. What we have written, and, really, who we are as educators and authors, is stronger for their generosity.

>Ahmet Atay, College of Wooster
>Andrea M. Baldwin, University of Houston-Clear Lake
>Brandon Gainer, De Anza College
>Kelly Glass, Gavilan College
>Katrina N. Hanna, Arizona State University
>Liliana L. Herakova, University of Maine
>Angela M. Hosek, Ohio University
>Juliane Mora, Gonzaga University
>Christine Pease-Hernandez, Slippery Rock University
>Sandra L. Pensoneau-Conway, Southern Illinois University, Carbondale
>Suzanne Pullen, San Francisco State University and University of San Francisco
>Robert J. Razzante, Arizona State University
>Armeda C. Reitzel, Humboldt State University
>C. Kyle Rudick, University of Northern Iowa
>Christina E. Saindon, Queensborough Community College—CUNY
>David P. Terry, Louisiana State University
>Satoshi Toyosaki, Southern Illinois University, Carbondale
>Adrienne Viramontes, University of Wisconsin-Parkside
>Julie L. G. Walker, Southwest Minnesota State University

We are also fortunate to have the support of colleagues at San José State University and California State University, Stanislaus, who understood that, as department chairs, sometimes we needed to close our office doors to write and who celebrated even the smallest accomplishments in this process with us.

We are especially thankful for our colleagues at San José State University for their work in developing instructional materials to accompany this text that are engaging, carefully designed, and consonant with the core principles of our argument: Laura Bell, Jemerson Diaz, Aggie Kuczera, Tiffany Martinez, Lindsay Walsh, Lucas Wang, and their mentor Tabitha Hart.

Finally, we recognize those closest to us, without whom none of this would be possible. Love is in the details, in the mundane as much as (and likely more than) the remarkable. We don't write for ourselves. We write for others, for those who are no longer with us, the ones who grow and change before our eyes, and those whom we have yet to meet.

Public Speaking Is Constitutive

In this chapter, we will work together to:

- Explore the relationship between public speaking and power
- Distinguish between communication as representation and communication as constitutive
- Identify contexts for public speaking as socially significant advocacy

> Six minutes, and about 20 seconds. In a little over six minutes, 17 of our friends were taken from us, 15 more were injured, and everyone, absolutely everyone in the Douglas community was forever altered...
>
> For those who still can't comprehend, because they refuse to, I'll tell you where it went. Six feet into the ground, six feet deep. Six minutes and 20 seconds with an AR-15, and my friend Carmen would never complain to me about piano practice. Aaron Feis would never call Kyra "miss sunshine," Alex Schachter would never walk into school with his brother Ryan, Scott Beigel would never joke around with Cameron at camp, Helena Ramsay would never hang around after school with Max, Gina Montalto would never wave to her friend Liam at lunch, Joaquin Oliver would never play basketball with Sam or Dylan. Alaina Petty would never, Cara Loughren would never, Chris Hixon would never, Luke Hoyer would never, Martin Duque Anguiano would never, Peter Wang would never, Alyssa Alhadeff would never, Jamie Guttenberg would never, Jamie Pollack would never.
>
> [4 minutes, 25 seconds pause]
>
> Since the time that I came out here, it has been six minutes and 20 seconds. The shooter has ceased shooting, and will soon abandon his rifle, blend in with the students as they escape, and walk free for an hour before arrest. Fight for your lives before it's someone else's job.
>
> (González, 2018)

Emma González was a student at Marjory Stoneman Douglas High School in Parkland, Florida, where in February 2018 a gunman opened fire on students and staff, killing 17 and injuring 17 more. As she sheltered in her school's cafeteria, González wasn't thinking about becoming the face of a movement: "I didn't know what was going on. . . . I didn't want to go on my phone to check and see if anything was real because I was in a complete state of denial" (Eller, 2018, para. 5). Yet 3 days later, she faced a crowd of hundreds on the steps of the federal courthouse in Fort Lauderdale and boldly proclaimed:

> Politicians who sit in their gilded House and Senate seats funded by the NRA telling us nothing could have been done to prevent this, we call BS.

Emma Gonzalez, Selections from "March for Our Lives Speech." Copyright © 2018 by Emma Gonzalez.

> They say tougher [gun] laws do not decrease gun violence. We call BS. They say a good guy with a gun stops a bad guy with a gun. We call BS. They say guns are just tools like knives and are as dangerous as cars. We call BS. They say no laws could have prevented the hundreds of senseless tragedies that have occurred. We call BS. That us kids don't know what we're talking about, that we're too young to understand how the government works. We call BS. (CNN Staff, 2018)

Emma González was and is empowered to speak on matters that affect us all, and so are you.

Public speaking doesn't always feel empowering, especially if a teacher or an employer is asking us to do it. Whether it's raising a hand in class to ask a question, presenting data to colleagues, or shouting into a megaphone in the pouring rain, public speaking can leave us feeling vulnerable and unheard. However, in the moment we decide to speak—when we take the floor—we do empower ourselves.

Power is not a possession, a tool we can wield whenever we want. Instead, power is something more fluid and complex. Power is relational. Understanding power—our own and others'—requires us to recognize the ways ideas and institutions operate through us as individuals in ways that may be harmful to us. When we can recognize power for what it is and act in ways

Choosing to speak in public can put us in a vulnerable position, but when we raise our hands in class and decide to take part in the discussion we are empowering ourselves.

Textbooks are not neutral or apolitical. They don't present reality in an objective or impartial way; they present what we think is valuable to our student readers.

that are consistent with our values, we can say we are empowered. This book is our effort to help you better recognize power in the communication around you and to practice communication in ways that help you initiate change. It is our hope that you will become more empowered as a result of reading this book and that you will be better prepared to enter into and to start conversations that will shape our lives for the better.

Our Introduction to Public Speaking

Before we go further, we must note that as the authors of this book, we are participating in a relationship with you, the reader, that is already imbued with power. Textbooks are not neutral or apolitical. Readers often assume that textbooks are like dictionaries or encyclopedias that *seem* to represent reality in an objective or impartial way. (Note that we are arguing here that even dictionaries and encyclopedias may hold a bias or perspective in what they value or choose to include or exclude.) This is *our* introduction to public speaking, and as the authors, we've chosen what to include based on what we feel would be most valuable for you, our reader. We hope that, like good teachers, we are showing you where to look but not what to see. However, we are particular people in the world, with identities and experiences that shape our worldviews, and inevitably that will affect our choices about examples, concepts, and even photographs or other features of the book like key terms and discussion questions. It is our hope that you will find our approach invitational and maybe even provocative, and we hope you'll bring your own identities, experiences, questions, and skepticism to your reading.

Your textbook authors, Deanna Fassett and Keith Nainby.

Please feel welcome to reach out to us with your questions and thoughts by e-mailing us at Deanna.Fassett@sjsu.edu and knainby@csustan.edu. Our conversations with you help us become better educators.

We will attempt to bring attention to power throughout this book in novel ways. In addition to inviting your direct communication, we will be writing in a style that is somewhat less formal than other books you've read (though, sadly, not as informal as really gripping fiction). This is to help you raise questions about what you're reading and to challenge us, so that you're not just accepting everything we write at face value. Every writer you read is **biased**; the word *biased* means favoring one perspective, focus, or outcome over others. Biases are based on existing perceptions or assumptions. What we hope to do here is remind you that we, the authors, are biased, that this is inevitable, that we may still share valuable insights with you, and that you should exercise your intellect to critically evaluate what you read. Our identities as authors are intertwined with forces of power that emerge from race (we are both White, though we work to be antiracist educators), class (we are both middle class, though Keith grew up working class), cisgender and heterosexual (though we hope to better understand the people we love who are gay, bisexual, transgender, gender fluid, and genderqueer), and ability (we are both currently able-bodied, though Deanna is a cancer survivor). We are both highly educated, but in the United States. This means that we have been taught communication and public speaking in a Western tradition. In this sense we are still learners, working to learn and incorporate non-Western and indigenous approaches to public speaking in our

> consideration. Not every idea is great, and when a group member suggests an idea that is considered less than ideal by other members, there is a tendency to evaluate the person rather than the idea. A more positive approach is to use **description**. Describing what is wrong with an idea gives the group member who introduced it the opportunity to clarify its presentation or to amend the idea for consideration by the group. Describing the idea may also encourage other group members to join in and help transform a poor idea into a better one. Thus, description is almost always preferable to evaluation because group members benefit when they know why an idea is rejected. **Evaluation**, or using language that criticizes others and their ideas, simply humiliates the person who offered the idea, and is likely to result in a defensive relationship and a defensive group climate.
>
> ## Problem Orientation
>
> To make the most of group situations, members need to exhibit the spirit of group participation and democracy. Taking a **problem orientation** approach, group members strive for answers and solutions that will benefit all group members and satisfy the group's objective. The opposite of problem orientation is **controlling behavior**. A group member using controlling behavior assumes there is a predetermined solution to be found. Alternately, asking honest questions like "Is the budget we're working with $250,000?" is

We have included bold face terms throughout the text to help you find concepts and definitions without a lot of hassle, but we worry that this tool will require you to do less work in processing our text and you will appreciate it less. This in an example of how we, as authors, will inevitably write in ways that are contradictory or paradoxical to our goals.

teaching and speaking. This is all to say that there are many different ways to explain how to be a compelling speaker, and what you are reading here is our way. You will add to this story in your own ways.

As authors, we will inevitably write in ways that are contradictory or paradoxical. Take, for example, our use of boldfaced terms throughout the book. We have included these because they can help you navigate the contents of this book to find concepts and definitions without a lot of hassle. However, as educators, we worry that removing the mental friction that comes from having to revisit a chapter and read it more than once will make reading the book less rewarding for you in the long run. We hope that naming this tension for you here brings it to mind when you read any textbook.

We will write in ways that are at times more casual, but we will also support our insights by referencing trustworthy source material. These moments will feel significantly more formal because they will be accompanied by academic citations in APA style. You read the first of these at the end of the opening speech example: "(González, 2018)." You'll be able to find this source material in the references by looking at the author name (González) and, if necessary, the year. These moments aren't meant to interrupt your reading. Instead, these citations are how we as educators and researchers have learned to show our work, support our positions, and invite you into the process of building an informed argument.

We imagine the readers of this textbook to be diverse in all the ways that humans can be diverse. How do you think this perspective will shape the way we have written this book?

We believe that opening up the book in this way, by showing you that we are making particular and intentional choices as writers, will help you think about how teachers, researchers, writers, and others decide what is worth your time and energy to study and practice. And we believe that opening up the book in this way will help you imagine yourself as a speaker and a writer, as someone who persuades, and as someone who is nestled in relationships that are affected by power. Our goal is to imagine you both as broadly and as intricately as possible (yet another paradox, perhaps). We imagine that you might be reading this book as someone enrolled in an introductory communication course, but we don't want to assume students are the only people reading this book. We imagine that you are learning public speaking, and that you have some interest in using this skill to navigate classes you're taking. We expect that you intend to use these skills in your work (and perhaps even in work you can't imagine yet). We also know that you will need these skills in your lives more broadly, in your neighborhoods and in your communities, to speak your truth to those in power. Finally, we imagine you as readers to be diverse in all the ways that humans can be diverse—in ethnic and racial background, economic class, gender and sexual orientation, age and ability, faith, political perspective, educational background, geographic location, and so on. With this in mind, we intentionally use *they* as a generic pronoun to refer to people of any gender or gender expression.

We imagine all of our readers, both generally and particularly, in dialogue with us about communication as powerful and empowering. With this introduction, we will invite you into an exploration of the power of communication to create the reality around us—from ourselves to our relationships, our communities, and our cultures. This is not only a philosophical insight;

it is also a personal and shared responsibility that will shape how you engage in public speaking as a speaker and listener. You may not yet know where you will make a difference with your words, but you undoubtedly will.

Communication, Including Public Speaking, Is Constitutive

Most of us learn at a young age that words represent things, and that communication is basically a process of sending and receiving messages. The old rhyme "sticks and stones may break my bones, but names will never hurt me" springs to mind. This makes it seem like words are of little consequence, not as sharp or as hard as stone. This is a misleading statement, and it is further amplified by popular images and stereotypes of communication in general, and public speaking in particular, as monological and unidirectional. Yet the words we use are more than containers for ideas. Words

The word "coffee" sometimes means an actual cup of coffee and sometimes the word "coffee" just stands for the drink you may be holding in your hand. When we talk about communication as representation we are talking about the way words can be symbols or representations for things in the world.

shape and build our realities, our possibilities for interaction with ourselves, others, and our environment. Think, for example, of the new words that evolve to articulate the new experiences we share, such as *mansplain*, *coparenting*, *false flag*, or *lactivism*. Sometimes new words such as *date rape* or *sexual harassment* help us better name, recognize, and act on abuses of power.

Communication as representation is a model or way of thinking that invites us to see words as symbols or representations for things in the world, such as the word *coffee* standing in for the drink you may be holding in your hand. This model has been helpful in teaching scholars and students of communication that language and gestures can be arbitrary, abstract, and ambiguous. To say that a word or gesture is **arbitrary** means that we could, if we agreed to do so, choose a different word to represent the same thing or concept. We could, for example, choose to refer to coffee as *joe*, *kahvi* (Finnish), or even *burnt tea* or some such. Admittedly, it would be difficult to change a well-established word, though this does happen. It may seem silly to call coffee something other than whatever members of our community typically call coffee, but consider how we have contested or arguable understandings of words like *patriotic* or *justice*. To say that a word or gesture is **abstract** means that a word is not the thing itself. You cannot drink the word *coffee*, nor is the word *run* the act of running. The word stands in for or represents the item, idea, or experience (though, as we'll argue here, it does so much more). Finally, words and gestures are always to some extent **ambiguous**. The word *coffee* can evoke, variously, the type of roast, a hot or cold drink, something bitter that you may not like, and so on. What you imagine when you say the word *coffee* may not be exactly what your listener imagines, though there will likely be some overlap. Here it may help to consider that words have both denotative and connotative meanings. A **denotative meaning** of a word is what you would find in the dictionary. It denotes or specifies an official meaning for the word. However, any given word also has a **connotative meaning**, which may be highly personal or individual. Denotatively, a cat is a feline—a small, often domesticated, carnivorous animal. Connotatively, a cat may evoke fear, affection, or indifference, and you may think of a particular cat in your world or even a 1960s "hip cat."

> "Our concepts structure what we perceive, how we get around in the world and how we relate to other people. Our conceptual system thus plays a central role in defining our everyday realities."
>
> —George Lakoff & Mark Johnson

Communication Shapes and Creates Our Social Reality

Communication may always be to some extent representational, but that is not all it is.

To say that **communication is constitutive** is to argue that communication shapes and even creates our social reality. In this model, our words do not simply *represent* individuals, organizations, and cultures. Instead our words *make* those individuals, organizations, and cultures. Here it may help to think of names. When a baby is born, they receive a name, one that will inevitably shape and define them. Names often carry expectations—of your gender, your ethnicity, or your generation. Consider how challenging it can be to change your name. If the difficulty doesn't lie in changing how you see yourself, then perhaps it lies in transforming how others have seen you. When you change your name, you must address not only all the feelings leading you to want to make the change but also the feelings of your parents who named you and the loved ones who experience your name and you as intertwined. Further, there are all the layers of legal and institutional communication that may make this process challenging. To officially change your name, you must work with county, state, and federal government offices, to say nothing of executing the change with schools, banks, doctors, and even social media platforms. It is also important to consider where there are established and easy pathways for name change (such as when a woman marries a man) and when name changes are fraught, difficult, or exclusionary (such as when someone wishes to choose a name that better matches their gender identity). Our names, like other words, reflect *and* shape reality.

It is not that surprising that popular understandings of language and communication still imply that words mainly represent things or ideas. The very structure of our language encourages this. In their germinal text, *Metaphors We Live By*, authors George Lakoff and Mark Johnson (1980) illuminate how language is essentially **metaphorical**. By this, they mean that we often use one concept to understand and explain another. They offer the example of argument as war: Here we use the metaphor of war to identify and better understand different aspects of the experience of argument. Think of how we have to "fight" for our ideas or defend them from attack. These sorts of expressions evolve from the metaphor of argument as war. To show how the metaphorical quality of our words can make it harder or easier to observe different aspects of experience, Lakoff and Johnson offer a different metaphor: Argument as dance. Reimagining argument as dance helps us see our differences in collaborative, invitational ways, as a necessary back-and-forth that can be beautiful rather than hostile, where everyone plays an important role, but where no one is necessarily a loser.

This perspective helps illustrate how language does not simply follow thought, as if we package our ideas into words that we can send easily to our listener or reader. Instead, language co-occurs with or even precedes our ideas, with our communication choices making some ideas possible and not others. Take, for example, a speaker's use of the term *illegal alien*. Not only does this language choice imply a particular power relationship, it reinforces it too. Compare this term to *undocumented immigrant* or even a term like *Dreamer*. Each term both indicates and creates a different way of understanding someone and therefore a different relationship with that someone. Each is partial and incomplete.

To say that communication is constitutive implies an ethical stance. If communication both illuminates and obfuscates, or hides, understandings, if it opens some conceptual (and actual) doors and closes others, then we must bring a more nuanced understanding of ethics to our communication. Instead of ethics being limited to well-chosen words—for example, to include people rather than exclude (though it does involve this)—ethics must as well include a dimension of accountability for what our communication creates in the world.

Communication, Including Public Speaking, Is Relational

When she accepted the Nobel Prize in Literature, Toni Morrison (1994), author of classics like *The Bluest Eye* and *Beloved*, observed, "language doesn't represent violence, it is violence; it doesn't represent the limits of thought, it limits thought" (p. 16). Here Morrison not only establishes

In accepting the Nobel Prize in Literature, Toni Morrison explained how important it is to understand that there are very real consequences of our actions and inactions, our voices and our silences. We have a responsibility as communicators and humans.

CHAPTER 1 | PUBLIC SPEAKING IS CONSTITUTIVE | 11

communication as constitutive but also reveals the ethical imperative in such an understanding. As communicators, whether we are speaking to our family members, into an ethereal social media platform, or to a crowd gathered on the courthouse steps, we must know that there are very real consequences of our actions and inactions, our voices and our silences. Morrison argues something more complex than a rebuttal to the old "sticks and stones" rhyme. She wants us to understand that words are not just representations or symbols of violence, they are violence in their own right—to both the speaker and the listener. Consider exclusionary language. Racist, sexist, (cis)heterosexist, ageist, ableist, theist, or other oppressive language not only reflects or mirrors violence in the world, it enacts its own violence by marginalizing, dehumanizing, and silencing others. Further, use of oppressive language violates not only its target but also the people who bear witness to it and those who utter it. If we only know argument as war, we will miss the nuanced understandings another metaphor would offer. Similarly, if we only understand marginalized groups of people in terms of stereotypes and narrow worldviews, we will continue to participate in the disenfranchisement and dehumanization of others.

In other words, we are inextricably intertwined in our communication with others. Our motives and intentions matter. The outcomes of our communication matter. Our successes and our mistakes matter and have consequence not only for ourselves but for others around us. Because communication—from whispers to howls and even our silence—creates us and our relationships from the interpersonal to the global, we must communicate in ways that invite care, reflection, insight, and change.

Our responsibility to one another as communicators becomes all the more important when we consider that our communication is often explicitly or implicitly persuasive. For some of us, this may be surprising—especially with respect to moments when we see our communication as casual or spontaneous. We may think of persuasion as something we do when we argue: We fight for a particular position and furnish evidence in a purposeful way to convince someone. But, again, thinking back to Lakoff and Johnson's theory that our understandings of persuasion will be inevitably metaphorical, perhaps persuasion is not always so adversarial. Our communication also has a reciprocal, back-and-forth quality that requires participation from others. It is always relational. Our communication shapes our perceptions of ourselves as well as others' perceptions of us and our shared reality. We persuade ourselves, and we persuade each other. In that persuasion, we become something new—perhaps a different person, a community, or a political or social movement.

Rhetoric Helps Us Think Critically About Communication in Our Lives

Communication studies scholars study **rhetoric** or persuasion in all forms in order to better understand how language shapes and defines us and our world. What do you think of when you hear the term *rhetoric*? Do you think of politicians going on about ideas about which they may have little conviction or commitment? Do you think of spin doctoring—attempts to manipulate or turn public understandings of an event to someone's advantage? Do you think of famous speeches and maybe the scholars who analyze them? Public speaking teachers in Western cultures often begin the study of rhetoric with ancient Greece. In ancient Greece, citizens represented themselves in courts of law, giving rise to the Sophists, who were in some sense our earliest public speaking teachers. Sophists such as Gorgias and Protagoras felt that perception and how an individual articulates their experience affects our understanding of truth (and even what counts as truth). Believing that "nothing exists outside the human senses" and "man is the measure of all things," the Sophists advanced a practical understanding of persuasion: We simply cannot know what *actually* happened, when someone's understanding of actions and events is inherently partial and incomplete. Every experience is filtered through humans, who are inevitably imperfect.

Public speaking teachers in Western cultures often begin the study of rhetoric with ancient Greece—particularly studying Plato and his student Aristotle.

The Sophists' understanding of rhetoric stands in direct contrast to Plato's. Plato, perhaps best known as a student of the classic Greek philosopher Socrates, was dismissive of Sophistry, believing instead in the importance of systematic philosophical examination and attempts to better know an external, verifiable reality (what we might think of as *The Truth*, as opposed to multiple contingent and arguable truths). Plato described rhetoric or persuasion as "mere cookery, a habitude or a knack" (see Plato's Gorgias, for e.g.). In other words, Plato argued that rhetoric was more a matter of style than substance, giving rise to perceptions of rhetoric as manipulation.

It is Plato's student Aristotle who gives the field of communication studies perhaps its most often-cited definition of rhetoric. Believing that it was important for everyday citizens (and not just philosophers) to have an effective means of discerning truths, Aristotle developed the first comprehensive book on rhetoric, titled *Rhetoric*. In it, he defines rhetoric as "uncovering, in any given situation, the available means of persuasion" (Rapp, 2010; Sachs, 2008). Aristotle's definition has been and remains immensely helpful to the analysis of communication, helping people to become better producers, consumers, and evaluators of messages.

"Education is the most powerful weapon which you can use to change the world."

— Nelson Mandela

CHAPTER 1 | PUBLIC SPEAKING IS CONSTITUTIVE | 13

Aristotle's definition of rhetoric, by challenging us to think of anything as potentially persuasive, helps us think critically about communication in our lives. Let's take a minute to analyze his definition here. *Uncovering* refers to the work of careful analysis and investigation, taking nothing for granted. "In any given situation" means anything might be persuasion, from a politician's joke to the structure and plan of a city. "The available means of persuasion" refers to the tools someone can use to convince us. As part of his definition, Aristotle identified three types of artistic proofs or persuasive appeals to a listener: ethos, pathos, and logos.

Artistic appeals involve the intentional and artful use of language to persuade. **Ethos** refers to a speaker's efforts to appear credible: qualified, trustworthy, and confident. For example, the speaker may call on or cite other sources in a speech or share their own prior experience with the topic. When González, in the speech quoted at the start of this chapter, indicates that she herself was present at a shooting and offers audience members exact statistical figures ("17 of our friends were taken from us, 15 were injured"), she is developing an ethical connection with these audience members by assuring them that she is a highly credible, trustworthy speaker on this topic. **Pathos** refers to a speaker's efforts to draw on listeners' emotions, helping them connect with a person or issue in personal ways. For example, this might include sharing an extended and emotionally fraught story. González appeals to pathos when she says, "Everyone who was there understands. Everyone who has been touched by the cold grip of gun violence understands. For us, long, tearful, chaotic hours in the scorching afternoon sun were spent not knowing." Finally, **logos** refers to the speaker's efforts to demonstrate the sound logic or reasoning of the speech. For example, the speaker would work to establish the connective tissue between evidence and the conclusions they've drawn from that evidence,

Classroom teachers use a combination of ethos, pathos, and logos to establish credibility and to persuade students to pay attention to what they are saying..

demonstrating unequivocally for the listeners that the argument is valid. González's use of a logical appeal is especially nuanced and compelling, in our estimation. When she says, "Six minutes and 20 seconds with an AR-15, and my friend Carmen would never complain to me about piano practice" and follows this with the names of each of the other victims of the shooting, she is subtly but very effectively making a logical, causal connection between the rapid-firing capacity of the weapon and the long-lasting impact of such a weapon on those it affects.

To better understand ethos, pathos, and logos, it may help to consider the communication that occurs in the classroom. Your teacher very likely engages in a number of behaviors to establish credibility, even beyond reminding you of their qualifications. They might refer to other trusted sources, speak *with* you instead of *at* you, and/or dress in particular clothing. You may find that your teacher uses emotional appeals in the classroom as well. For example, they might share examples that help illustrate the importance or value of the skills they're teaching you, such as a story about a student whose careful mastery of public speaking led to a successful career as a local public official or a story that illustrates the power of public speaking to effect material change in people's lives. Finally, your teacher is likely to demonstrate valid reasoning, for example, when they show a causal relationship between length of time practicing for a speech and a sense of self-confidence on speech day, or when they draw the comparison between learning to speak in public and training to run a race.

It is also highly likely that you engage in some form of all three persuasive appeals in order to convince listeners in your life. In this same classroom example, for example, in order to make your best case for a deadline extension, you would want to show your teacher that you're trustworthy and deserving of the exception (ethos); that you would be appreciative because you care about learning the content of the class; that you wouldn't usually ask but you're struggling with a difficult situation that is interfering with your ability to complete the assignment in a timely way (pathos); and finally, that you have sound reasons (logos) for requesting the extension (that you would be better able to show your best work because you could give the assignment the time and attention it deserves). Your argument will be strongest when you engage in all three appeals. Think of how you decide where to make a donation of time or money. Chances are, while you may be moved by particular examples that evoke an emotional response, you are likely more persuaded by results, by evidence that your time and/or money will make a real difference.

Aristotle gives us a very practical approach to creating and evaluating persuasion in our lives. That we can analyze communication (whether a press conference or a first date's clothing choices) for how it shapes our perception and understanding of reality is significant. Communication shapes and creates our social reality, and it is our responsibility to creatively, critically, and compassionately explore that process. Otherwise we risk complacency and manipulation.

One of the most accomplished and well-known Roman orators, Quintilian, defined rhetoric as a good [person] speaking well (Golden, 2011; Quintilian, 1856). This, again, reminds us of the ethical dimension of public speaking and offers us a powerful way of evaluating it. To say communication is constitutive is analogous to saying we are what we eat. We build realities through our language choices, shaping both understandings and actions. So, to be an effective communicator, you must be more than technically skilled—you must also have a moral compass, a sense of what is meaningful and just, and a sense of how your communication affects others and yourself for better and for worse.

Empowering Public Speaking Is Socially Significant Advocacy

Whether or not we are aware of it, the communication that moves in and through us is inevitably persuasive, knitting together or pulling apart ways of seeing and being. Each utterance, whether word or gesture, advocates for a particular version of reality; it names what we love or uphold and what we choose to neglect. This is true whether we are communicating in the streets or in our homes, places of worship, places of employment, or classrooms. Therefore, it is important to make the most of every opportunity to be heard.

Our goal in this book is to help you become an empowered and empowering public speaker. By this, we mean that we would like to support you as you become more attentive to power as it is created and challenged in communication. When you speak, you are empowered to name what is important, for you and for your listeners. This means that you must consider whether you are

In your public speaking class you may be required to participate in a debate. If you are going to argue for ten minutes to/with 20–30 people, and want your discussion to be socially significant, your listeners must either agree (or come to agree during the course of your speech) that this is time well-spent.

addressing issues of **social significance** (and for whom). One way to think about social significance is to address its different parts. Socially significant communication would address topics that are relevant or meaningful for some culture or group. This requires you to understand to whom you are speaking and why or to what end. You will need to consider how your focus, your argument, and your examples draw together these listeners in support of some common goal or objective (whether that is to learn more, have a lighthearted moment of celebration, or make a change).

We would also like for you to consider the role of power in social significance. How does your communication strengthen or weaken power within and for a particular group of people? Let's imagine that you have 10 minutes in which to speak with a group. In this example, let's assume this is a public speaking class, and you may choose, within some set of parameters (such as that the speech must be persuasive), what you plan to discuss. If you are going to argue for 10 minutes to/with 20 to 30 people, to be socially significant, your listeners must either agree (or come to agree during the course of your speech) that this is time well spent. Socially significant speeches help listeners become more informed and better understand some aspect of their lives so that they can act in ways that improve their own and others' lives. Socially significant speeches help nurture your own and your listeners' sense of **agency**. Agency refers to a person's ability to feel as though they can take action in the world that is meaningful. They see themselves as having the understanding, skills, and resources to make a positive difference. In our classroom example, it means that you've chosen to speak on something about which you know and care deeply and that will excite your listeners to think, feel, know, and/or do something that matters.

Kamala Harris speaks to a crowd of supporters at a Democratic Rally. Political speeches, like the ones Kamala Harris might give, are socially significant and help listeners become more informed and better understand ways that they can improve their own and others' lives.

CHAPTER 1 | PUBLIC SPEAKING IS CONSTITUTIVE

Let's take social significance and this sense of power a step further: Instead of speaking in a classroom, let's imagine you have been invited by a group to speak on a topic (issue, skill, or process) that matters to them. In such settings, you will likely share what you know and help others through your insight and expertise. It can be very useful to both you and your listeners to understand what has motivated your invitation to speak. Here it can help to consider the role of power beyond your own and your listeners' sense of personal empowerment by exploring the power relationships involved in the speaking opportunity. Are you speaking as part of a desire to be employed by that group (as in a job interview), and do you feel as though you can speak candidly to the group? Has someone required this group to have additional training and that's why you're there (at the request of someone with power over the listeners)? Is this group looking to make a change in their process? Who has been included with your invitation? And who has been excluded? How are members of this group positioning your talk with respect to their own beliefs, values, and frustrations? Do you want to play the role they've assigned you? Or do you want to resist or complicate their expectations? These questions can help you consider how your own and your listeners' sense of agency may be constrained.

Advocacy Entails Speaking Alongside Others to Amplify Their Voices

Thinking carefully about power in communication also helps us embody an understanding of public speaking that is **advocacy**. More than just arguing or making a request, advocacy

Emma Gonzalez and her peers at Parkland have spoken to many different audiences about gun legislation. They understand that through their voices and actions they have the ability to enact change. Other students around the country have been mobilized because of their examples. Your voice can join theirs in the classroom, at the lunch table, or on the train. How will you use it?

entails speaking alongside others so as to amplify their voices. It is often the case that those in power do not need advocacy—their voices carry because they are woven into the fabric of our lives, from laws and institutions to stereotypes and expectations. We would like to challenge you to think about whose voices need and deserve amplification in our world. Socially significant topics aspire to create spaces for speakers and listeners to join others in discussing matters that are marginalized or overlooked and yet important to us all. This can include learning from and with others who have been affected by unique or incompletely understood lived experiences (such as living in shelter housing following a natural disaster or living with a particular physical condition like an addiction), government legislation (regarding, for example, immigration or firearms possession), or corporate or organizational policy (including, for example, actions around privacy, sustainability, or free speech).

> "Everyone has the right to freedom of opinion and expression; this right includes freedom to hold opinions without interference and to seek, receive and impart information and ideas through any media and regardless of frontiers"
>
> —United Nations

Agency matters because, through it, we effect material change. One type of change involves development of or revision to the policies and procedures that governments and other organizations create and enforce. In such conversations, you and your listeners may hold an organization accountable, and in influencing policy, you make that change for others beyond yourselves. Another type of change involves interpersonal justice, where you work in small ways, one person and one conversation at a time, to change someone's mind or behavior. As you learn the concerns that the marginalized voices in your world would like amplified, your voice can join theirs in the classroom, at the lunch table, or on the train. In these moments, your sense that you can make a difference can open spaces for you and the people you meet to explore their assumptions, stereotypes, prejudices, and biases. Through your agency, you and others make a difference.

"Fight for Your Lives Before It's Someone Else's Job"

It's difficult to imagine exactly what Emma González and her peers were thinking and feeling as they sheltered in place in their school cafeteria. What does seem clear is that this terrible tragedy changed her, turning her sense of agency toward action in the world. While she has spoken for many audiences, the speech that frames this chapter (and book) illuminates how what we say matters. Our words are action in the world. But, all the more remarkable in this speech, González proves that our silences communicate in powerful ways.

In the months since the Parkland shooting, González and her peers have spoken to many different audiences (from legislators to the media to parents and near-voting-age youth) about gun legislation. They have taken up this fight—what will you fight for?

Concepts

abstract 9
advocacy 18
agency 17
ambiguous 10
arbitrary 9
artistic appeals 14
biased 6
communication as representation 9
communication is constitutive 10
connotative meaning 10
denotative meaning 10
ethos 14
logos 14
metaphorical 11
pathos 14
rhetoric 12
social significance 17

Toward Praxis

1. **Reflection:** When have words or gestures changed you or defined you? When was this helpful? When was this harmful?

2. **Discussion:** Consider everyday examples of language shaping and defining or limiting our actions. What cultures were central or normative? What cultures were marginalized? How so?

3. **Action:** Reflect on an issue of social significance. How has understanding of that issue been defined by contested, misleading, or dehumanizing language? Find occasions in your everyday communication to surface unspoken or unreflective assumptions, clarify key terms, or intentionally underscore the personhood of people speaking into and/or affected by the issue.

Discussion Questions

1. In what ways has naming shaped you? In what ways have you embraced and/or resisted these expectations?

2. How do you typically use textbooks and features like boldfaced terms or discussion questions? How do books, assignments, and other instructional materials enhance or interfere with your learning?

3. Where do you find persuasion in your lives? Think broadly to include this textbook, your classroom, or even your city as an argument. Explore those different settings for Aristotle's persuasive appeals.

CHAPTER 2

Public Speaking Is Relational

In this chapter, we will work together to:

- Explore how public speaking is a creative response to specific concerns, interests, and commitments shared by specific communities

- Reflect on and practice learning as an active process for all those participating

- Identify the responsibilities of speakers and listeners

> Dear brothers and sisters, do remember one thing. Malala day is not my day. Today is the day of every woman, every boy and every girl who have raised their voice for their rights. There are hundreds of human rights activists and social workers who are not only speaking for human rights, but who are struggling to achieve their goals of education, peace and equality. Thousands of people have been killed by the terrorists and millions have been injured. I am just one of them. So here I stand... one girl among many.
>
> I speak—not for myself, but for all girls and boys.
>
> I raise up my voice—not so that I can shout, but so that those without a voice can be heard.
>
> Those who have fought for their rights:
>
> Their right to live in peace.
>
> Their right to be treated with dignity.
>
> Their right to equality of opportunity.
>
> Their right to be educated.
>
> (Yousafzai, 2013)

2014 Nobel Peace Prize recipient Malala Yousafzai was just 15 years old when she was shot in the head by a Taliban gunman while she was taking the bus home one day after school. After repeated threats on her life were published in newspapers, posted to Facebook, and slid under her door, Taliban leaders determined that the best way to silence Yousafzai was to murder her. In the years before the shooting, at a young age, Yousafzai had become known in Pakistan and around the world for her activism. She had communicated publicly and often, in social media and public gatherings, challenging governments to provide equal access to education for both girls and boys. Her message is consistent and clear—that education is an essential human right.

Education is a human right we can and should demand on behalf of ourselves and others, but we can sometimes lose sight of this message if we've been privileged to have access to education in our own lives. Our awareness often requires a personal connection; as Yousafzai has observed, "When someone takes away your pens you realize how quite important education is" (Yousafzai & Lamb, 2013, p. 134). The education of all children—girls in particular—has become a global concern because it is a means of reducing poverty, improving public health, and engendering problem-solving and critical-thinking skills (Kristof & WuDunn, 2009). Yet when many, relatively speaking, affluent Westerners think of public speaking,

---

Malala Yousafzai, "Speech at the Youth Takeover of the United Nations." Copyright © 2013 by Malala Yousafzai.

> "Courage is rightly esteemed the first of human qualities, because, as has been said, it is the quality which guarantees all others."
>
> —Winston Churchill

especially if they are required to take such a course as part of general education requirements, they tend to think of it as a kind of hurdle to clear or, perhaps more optimistically, as something that will be good for them (even if they would rather not take the course). Yousafzai's example, however, stands as a reminder of public speaking's power to transform ourselves, our communities, and our cultures.

Because we are often first exposed to public speaking as part of a classroom lesson, where we are challenged to introduce ourselves or persuade our classmates to take a particular course of action on an issue, it is easy to become jaded to its power. Yet Yousafzai's story, along with so many others you'll see in this book, illustrates that speaking up and speaking out is transformative. People encountered the power of Yousafzai's words—through her blogs, her appearances on television, and her public presentations before world leaders—and have been moved to action. As just one example, UN Special Envoy for Global Education Gordon Brown launched a petition in Yousafzai's name, calling on world leaders to educate the approximately 58 million out-of-school children worldwide (Office of the UN Special Envoy for Global Education, 2014). Without education, these children and the countries to which they belong (not just in the developing world, but in the United States and elsewhere) are subject to economic, health, and social crises. Yousafzai's words, as amplified by a number of public speaking engagements, have heightened global awareness of a problem that affects us all.

Public figures like Yousafzai are without question compelling individuals, whether or not we agree with them. They possess passion and drive, and their communication leaves us changed in some way. The distinctive passion and drive demonstrated by such communicators often means we focus on the individual speaker—on the message and its outcome. When we focus on the individual speaker, we risk neglecting the ways in which public speaking is inherently **dialogic** and **interpersonal**. Dialogic means that two or more people are engaged in a mutual sharing of ideas. Interpersonal means that this mutual sharing of ideas depends on the particular histories and perspectives of each person in dialogue. It may not seem obvious at first how public speaking shares these qualities, given the common image of one active speaker addressing a large group of passive listeners. In this chapter, we will explore how public speaking reflects dialogic and interpersonal qualities when it is effective.

In what follows, we will first explore public speaking as **relational**—created at the intersection of personal and communal interests. It is advantageous for public speakers to see ourselves as educators—as people who work with others to create knowledge. For this, we will need to explore some foundational concepts from critical, social justice–oriented approaches to teaching. In particular, we will learn more about Brazilian educator Paulo Freire, *Pedagogy of the Oppressed* (1993; arguably his most significant publication), and the distinction he draws between **banking** and **problem posing**. For Freire, so-called banking education approaches treat teachers as experts who share their knowledge with passive students who lack knowledge and who gradually become more and more knowledgeable through the actions of teachers sharing their knowledge. In contrast, Freire describes an alternative educational approach he calls problem posing, in which students' existing knowledge and experiences help motivate their active learning as they work together with teachers to solve problems that enhance their ability make sense of the world. We will also discuss the role of listening in becoming an effective and meaningful public speaker. Finally, we will address how to cope with our own fears and challenges as empowered and empowering public speakers.

Public Speaking Emerges From and Shapes Interpersonal Relationships

Our own personal understandings of public speaking—what it is, what it looks like, who engages in it, and why they engage—are shaped by our past experiences with, and our expectations and stereotypes of public speaking. It matters who introduced us to public speaking. The way in which we were prepared for our earliest public communication made that process exciting, intimidating, meaningful, or mundane. For instance, research suggests that teachers who experience anxiety about speaking in public tend to teach younger students, whom they may find less threatening and more approachable (McCroskey & Richmond, 1991). It is possible, then, that one or more of your teachers modeled public speaking anxiety with you, affecting your perceptions of and attitudes toward public speaking (McCroskey, Anderson, Richmond, &

Your own experience with public speaking has been shaped by your past experiences with, and your expectations and stereotypes of public speaking. Who introduced you to public speaking? What did you learn about public speaking from them?

Wheeless, 1981). It is also entirely possible that you have routinely encountered gregarious and outgoing public speakers in your life, leading you to embrace and pursue opportunities to speak. It is also possible that the prominent speakers in your life seemed like naturally gifted or "born" public speakers, rarely nervous and somehow above the need to prepare and practice.

Public Speaking Is Not Just One Person Speaking at or to Many

Similarly, we routinely consume images of public speaking in the media that show it at its most stereotypical (e.g., speakers reading from their PowerPoint slides, drinking alcohol, or imagining that their listeners are naked to quell their anxiety) or at its most rarefied and refined (e.g., the pitch-perfect closing statements on a legal drama or a speech to the country by a fictional president after an alien invasion). These images and experiences may subtly reinforce our expectation that public speakers are isolated individuals who craft a message entirely on their own and with limited or little regard for the people in their world. A good example of this is when teachers ask students to bring objects for show and tell or to present their final papers for class. Such assignments, while giving students an opportunity to practice public speaking skills, may subtly undermine the role of the listener in public speaking. In these sorts of speaking occasions, the speaker chooses something to talk about simply because the teacher required it. This results in communication that is **monologic**—communication that suggests that only one person's voice is present and matters. While we will likely all be called to give a public presentation because

The use of "show and tell" in a classroom setting sometimes reinforces our expectation that public speakers are isolated individuals. These assignments give students an opportunity to practice public speaking skills but de-emphasize the role of the listener. Effective public speakers should be responsive to the needs and interests of others.

26 | EMPOWERING PUBLIC SPEAKING

someone else requires it, more often, speakers who create lasting change do so because they have effectively addressed an issue of importance to a group of people. Furthermore, we would argue that the students who tend to perform best in public speaking classrooms are those who find their own purpose and meaning in the exercise before them, rather than only responding to a teacher's request. This is to say that effective public speakers are varied and diverse, made rather than born, and responsive to the needs of others.

Public Speaking Is Cocreated By the Speaker and Listeners

But once we get past the surface view of public speaking, beyond the image of one person speaking *at* or *to* many, we can better explore how it is, at its core, **dialogic**. To refer to public speaking as dialogic is to say that the meanings produced in this communication are cocreated by the speaker and the listeners. Communication studies teachers have long argued that public speaking is really more of an enlarged conversation (Winans, 1915). Even if the tables of contents of many public speaking textbooks suggest that a speaker must first choose a topic and then analyze the audience in order to better adapt that topic to their needs and interests, the reality is that in most public speaking settings, consideration of the audience occurs alongside (and sometimes before) a speaker's choice of topic. In any given instance of communication, speakers typically consider their purpose for speaking—their reason for speaking and the goal(s) they hope to achieve. For example, as a college student, you might have reason to convince your teacher to change how classroom activities are conducted during class meetings. Maybe you would like more time to work in groups, or you would like to have the chance to get feedback on your own work from the instructor during class time. Your idea most likely emerged from your interactions and experiences with your classmates, which led you to

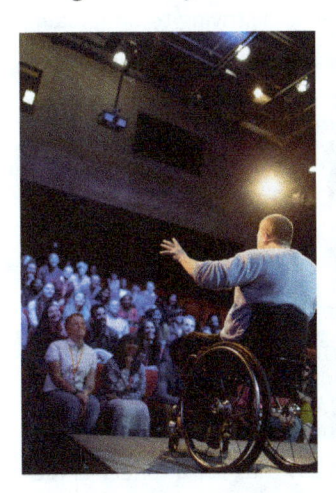

Speakers must consider their audience for their message and how they'll adapt that purpose or message for a particular audience, using particular persuasive and stylistic choices. These two audiences have unique needs and purposes that a speaker must learn and understand before speaking to them.

CHAPTER 2 | PUBLIC SPEAKING IS RELATIONAL | 27

> "I am driven by two main philosophies: know more today about the world than I knew yesterday and lessen the suffering of others. You'd be surprised how far that gets you."
>
> —Neil deGrasse Tyson

propose this idea, and you'll need to anticipate your instructor's reservations and motivations so that you can convince this person to give your idea a try. The same is true for convincing your investors that your business plan is profitable and sustainable or your child that your given disciplinary choice is fair and reasonable.

Public Speaking Should Be Respectful Between Speaker and Listener

Public speaking as **dialogic communication** emphasizes this relationship between speakers and listeners. Philosopher Martin Buber (1970/1996) described **dialogue** as a respectful engagement between speaker and listener characterized by remaining open-minded even (and perhaps especially) when they don't agree. Buber took care to distinguish between what he referred to as an "I/it" relationship and an "I/thou" relationship. The first, "I/it," presumes superiority on the part of the speaker, rendering communication top-down, self-centered, and manipulative. We may feel echoes of this perspective when we think, "I—the speaker—am giving a speech to it—the audience." In this perspective, the individual people in all their nuance don't matter, only the "it"—the idea of an audience—does. The second, "I/thou," recognizes the agency of both parties, asking both to understand themselves as they attempt to understand each other. We may think of this perspective in this way: "I—the speaker—am engaging in relationship with you—the *people* in the audience. In this way we must build understanding together." We recommend approaching public speaking as dialogic communication by cultivating an appreciation for and a willingness to persist in the tension between standing your own ground and remaining true to your own heartfelt commitments and also becoming fully open to the other and striving to understand your listeners' perspectives (Spano, 2001). This is important to us as teachers who care deeply about critical, social justice–oriented, relational approaches to teaching and learning.

Public Speaking Is More Like Posing Problems Than Banking

Brazilian educator Paulo Freire is certainly among the world's foremost theorists of education. In *Pedagogy of the Oppressed,* Freire (1970/1993) makes a powerful observation about education, that it is suffering from a kind of "**narration sickness**" (p. 52). By narration sickness, he means that educators have tended to focus on transmission of knowledge rather than helping students join in the process of knowledge construction. This is to say that, for a variety of reasons (including the pervasive disenfranchisement of teachers and teaching as a profession and the reliance on standardized testing as a means to measure success, especially in the United States), teachers may concentrate on stuffing chunks of information into students rather than

Just like good teachers don't just concentrate on stuffing chunks of information into students, good public speakers understand that they are creating a dialogue between themselves and their audience. Notice how the teacher in this photo is developing a relationship wih the students he is speaking to? How might this idea transfer over to a public speaking situation?

working with students to build knowledge and make it relevant and actionable together. When teachers focus primarily or exclusively on filling students up with information as though they are empty vessels (or accounts), without regard for their own insights and experiences, then education contributes to dehumanization, disengagement, disinterest, and disenfranchisement. This perspective implies that knowledge is fully formed and easily transferrable from one person to another like currency. This dehumanizing approach to teaching and learning is what Freire describes as **banking**. Here the teacher makes a deposit into the learner, who then withdraws (summarizes or regurgitates) that information on command.

There Is a Risk of Public Speaking Becoming Banking

Public speaking, like teaching, runs the very real risk of becoming banking in the sense Freire describes. If, as speakers, we think of ourselves as simply pouring information into our listeners, as if they do not actively contribute to the meaning-making process, then at best we do not achieve a shared or common goal; at worst we manipulate or neglect them. All too often students feel pressured into selecting speech topics that seem like good speech topics to them (e.g., abortion, capital punishment, gun control), when they have not yet considered whether the topic is meaningful to their particular audience. Without the audience to serve as "a kind of magnetic field which exerts an organizing or focusing force on our words" (Elbow, 1998, p. 191), these sorts of speeches can miss their mark. On the one hand, that might not seem so bad:

Teachers and public speakers are alike in fundamental and important ways. And teachers are public speakers each time they address their classes.

What does it matter if we craft a speech that doesn't necessarily meet an audience's needs or extend their understanding of a phenomenon or inspire action in their lives? It's only a few minutes of their time. Freire would argue that even those few minutes matter very much if they inadvertently teach an audience to see themselves as passive consumers of knowledge, or as captives who learn (or relearn) to check out of material they see as irrelevant.

Teachers Should Be Problem Posers, Not Bankers

Freire (1970/1993) encourages us to understand teachers not as bankers but as midwives, as caring people who help others transform themselves. We can think of this capacity to transform ourselves, learn, grow, and effect change in our lives and in the world as **agency**. Students as agents are not passive recipients of teachers' wisdom but active collaborators with teachers in making knowledge real and relevant for themselves and others. It is the job of the teacher to help students identify (or pose) problems in their lives for which additional learning might offer ways of understanding and solutions. In this way, their roles change to teacher-student and student-teacher (Freire, 1970/1993), each learning from and listening to each other. **Problem posing** is, therefore, a process of working together to identify and change what is dehumanizing in our lives.

Similarities Exist Between Teaching and Public Speaking

While there are important distinctions we could make between teaching and public speaking, they are alike in some fundamental and important ways (and indeed, teachers are public speakers each time they address their classes). Both teachers and speakers bear a responsibility to establish themselves as credible and trustworthy. They must acknowledge their qualifications and be candid about what they do and do not know about a given subject or issue. Further, they must anticipate that their listeners harbor not only misunderstandings about that subject or issue but also insights and experiences worthy of their attention, if not their respect. In order to engage in problem posing in or out of the classroom a speaker must work to better understand their listeners and their needs, fears, and desires. Dialogue—open and thoughtful exchange between speakers and listeners—can make this possible. Whereas dialogue is impractical (not every speech can be an interactive back-and-forth between speaker and listeners), speakers can aspire to dialogic communication. Dialogic communication describes our efforts to engage one another in ways that recognize that the people listening to us are intelligent, powerful, and thoughtful people in their own right. While not a dialogue per se, it opens the possibilities for dialogue.

"Education either functions as an instrument which is used to facilitate integration of the younger generation into the logic of the present system and bring about conformity or it becomes the practice of freedom, the means by which men and women deal critically and creatively with reality and discover how to participate in the transformation of their world."

— *Richard Shaull*

Reflexivity Is Important in Problem Posing

Dialogic, problem-posing communication challenges speakers to be reflexive. **Reflexivity**, in Freire's sense, is the capacity to see ourselves as part of the problem, issue, or situation we are working to describe. Speakers who are reflexive are aware of how they are implicated in the issue they are addressing, and that their communication shapes their own and others' understandings of and actions with respect to that issue. To be implicated means that we each play a role in not only a problem but also its solution. Reflexive speakers are often credible as well as knowledgeable about their topic and how they shape it for others; however, credible speakers are not always reflexive. For example, a speaker may give an informed and compelling speech about the importance of aggressively pursuing terrorist cells in Afghanistan, but to be reflexive, they must consider how their words affect others—how those words empower or disempower others and how they shape their own and others' actions in the world. If we act on your words, what will the consequences be, and for whom? How are these consequences more or less obvious to us depending on our cultural position? What does it mean to advocate war on someone else's soil? How do such actions exacerbate global inequities, violence, and instability? Whose interests do our arguments serve? Our own? The people of Afghanistan? Oil companies? Halliburton and other private contractors? Even when we intend to speak to patriotism or protection in ways that make sense to us and our immediate audience, we may miss how we are serving power interests that are far more complex, interwoven, and global. Our words as (in)actions have implications for ourselves and for others, long beyond when we speak them.

Public Speakers Are Actively Engaged in Praxis

Our communication is **constitutive**. *Constitutive* means that our communication does not simply label the world we find around us; instead, our communication is the means by which we access the world around us and recognize it as meaningful for ourselves and for others. How we choose our words, when and with whom we share them, and even our silence creates the world around us, inviting us into some relationships and actions in the world and making others seem difficult or impossible. Freire (2005) reminds us that we all have the capacity for **praxis**: "reflection and action on the world in order to transform it" (p. 51). As public speakers, we are actively engaged in praxis—reflecting and acting with others on some aspect of our world such that we can change and improve it for someone. It is important that we remember that, even in some classroom somewhere, even on some assignment, our words matter. The classroom is not the place where we wait for our lives to begin; our lives in the classroom are vivid and real, and they affect others. The classroom can be the place where we cultivate our ability to be leaders: thoughtful and bold, curious and informed, receptive and collaborative.

Listening Must Be Critical and Compassionate

It's a safe bet that listening is the most commonly overlooked and underdeveloped communication skill. Very few of us receive explicit instruction in how to listen well (Coakley & Wolvin, 1997), despite the critical role of effective listening in settings from the living room to the classroom to the boardroom. We usually spend quite a lot of time listening, and how well we

Listening is an overlooked and underdeveloped communication skill. But, think about all of the places listening might be critically important in someone's life: business meetings, classrooms, doctors offices, hospitals, airplanes, courtrooms, etc.

EMPOWERING PUBLIC SPEAKING

do it absolutely affects how others perceive our performance at school (Conaway, 1982) and at work (Haas & Arnold, 1995).

Part of the challenge in learning to listen well is to remember that **listening** is an active process of making meaning rather than a passive process of receiving information. Communication is, at its essence, collaborative; without a listener, a speaker is lost. This is why communication studies professors routinely discuss and explore listening, heightening our awareness of listening as a process that we can influence by reflecting on it carefully so that we will do it well. While it can be so tempting to sit back and soak in a class discussion, it is important to remember that we must actively engage a speaker's ideas in order to challenge them, reject them, and/or make them our own.

Listening well is more than simply being able to accurately restate what you have heard. Listening well involves communicating that you understood not only the content but the intent of a message and that you have integrated that information meaningfully with respect to a broader context—whether of an issue or within your life. Let's take each of those in turn.

Listen With Compassion

Listening well entails empathy and acknowledgment of why someone has chosen to speak; the effect of those words on the speaker, you, and others; and your responsibility to respond candidly but also compassionately. Listening and responding with **compassion** requires tempering our inclination to judge, pausing to consider the conditions that made a given speaker's utterance possible and, if possible, trying to intimately imagine those conditions in our own lives. This can be especially challenging when someone shares something that is difficult for us to hear, perhaps because it makes us feel uncomfortable or angry. In *The Courage to Teach*, Parker and Scribner (2007) put it this way:

> When the going gets rough, turn to wonder. If you feel judgmental or defensive, ask yourself, "I wonder what brought her to this belief?" "I wonder what he's feeling right now?" "I wonder what my reaction teaches me about myself?" Set aside judgment to listen to others—and to yourself more deeply. (p. 18)

Compassionate listening can help us learn about others and ourselves, as well as help us appropriately frame any feedback we intend to give to the speaker, shaping it in such a way that they can hear and make meaning from it.

Listen With a Critical Stance

Listening well also entails a **critical** stance. By *critical*, we mean listening to and thinking about a speaker's ideas so that you evaluate their merit, recognizing what the speaker has done well and where the speech may still be lacking. Too often, when we think of the term *critical*, we think of it as harsh and negative, focused on identifying problems. What if we were to think of *critical* as appraising? Listening critically in this way would mean respecting (though not necessarily agreeing) with a speaker's intent, considering the merits of the argument and offering an honest response that, where appropriate, respectfully identifies issues, questions, and concerns the speaker needs to know in order to learn and grow. In this sense, critical listening also means a willingness and desire to look beyond the structure of a message to the content of that message and the effects that communication might have on the world. Take, for example, a speech addressing the implications of the rise in White nationalism in the United States and around the world. Critical compassionate listening requires more than checking to see whether there is a thesis in the introduction and transitions between the main ideas. Critical compassionate listening means challenging ourselves to recall and engage historical context, to meaningfully acknowledge our roles in the fraught and painful outcomes of racism in the United States and elsewhere, and to act in ways that build alliances and effect humanizing change (Warren & Hytten, 2004).

Communication Needs Reciprocity

Any given communication utterance is potentially a learning moment if we recognize it as such. As speakers, we have the responsibility to listen to the people who will be most affected by our messages; as listeners, we have the responsibility to respond to speakers so that we may affect them in turn. This requires not only curiosity and intelligence but also sensitivity and empathy. The process of compassionate critical listening reminds us that it is important to engage in someone's ideas fully and respectfully. Respect, therefore, means being willing to help another person learn and grow. Respect is not pretending that a speaker's communication is flawless and powerful when it is not, nor is it deriding and demeaning someone who is learning how to frame and articulate their thoughts. Communication as a process of cocreation of meaning requires each of us to enter into sustained and thoughtful contact with one another. This **reciprocity**, or mutual interdependence, may make us feel vulnerable as speakers and listeners, but it needn't make us feel weak or small.

Public Speakers Explore and Manage Their Fears

> The terrorists thought they would change our aims and stop our ambitions, but nothing changed in my life except this: Weakness, fear and hopelessness died. Strength, power and courage was born. I am the same Malala. My ambitions are the same. My hopes are the same. My dreams are the same.

> Dear sisters and brothers, I am not against anyone. Neither am I here to speak in terms of personal revenge against the Taliban or any other terrorist group. I'm here to speak up for the right of education of every child. I want education for the sons and daughters of all the extremists especially the Taliban.
>
> (Yousafzai, 2013)

Many of us have heard that Americans fear public speaking more than death itself. This is a provocative claim, based on a single 1973 market research study (the Bruskin Report, which was, to some extent, replicated by Dwyer & Davidson, 2012). While the study did not actually ask people to rank their fears or to name their top fear (it merely noted that the largest percentage of respondents indicated a fear of speaking in public), that this claim has found so much traction in popular media sources tell us something about Americans and **communication anxiety**. Communication anxiety is a feeling of aversion to engaging in communication with others; for many people, this feeling of aversion is specific to a certain type of communication, such as speaking in public to an assembled audience. That as many as 70% of Americans report public speaking anxiety (Richmond & McCroskey, 1998) is fascinating, considering how pervasive free speech is as a cultural narrative.

As many as 70% of U.S. Americans report having public speaking anxiety. Even some people who regularly speak in front of millions of people get anxiety. Would it surprise you to know that President Abrahm Lincoln had public speaking anxiety? In addition, singer and songwriter Adele suffers from panic attacks, social phobia, and severe stage fright. Adele had to quit touring for a time as she found the anxiety and panic unbearable.

CHAPTER 2 | PUBLIC SPEAKING IS RELATIONAL | 35

Malala Yousafzai confronted two deeply rooted fears—public speaking and death—and emerged triumphant. In an interview with Michel Martin of NPR in 2014, Yousafzai described it this way:

> I have already seen death, and I know that death is supporting me in my cause of education. Death does not want to kill me. Before this attack, I might have been a little bit afraid how death would be. Now I'm not because I have experienced it. So they cannot make me stop to continue my campaign.

Reframe the Fear of Public Speaking

Yousafzai's comments underscore an important aspect of how even everyday people might confront their fears and thrive in the face of public speaking anxiety: Our purpose and mission drives us forward and motivates us to speak. That message is more important than our individual fears and frustrations. It is important to reclaim public speaking from stereotypes and images, reframing it as an opportunity to engage in praxis, to reflect on our world with others and change it with them for the better. Speaking in public amplifies our voices and perhaps also our fears—that we might not be prepared enough, that others might not accept us as credible, that others might notice our fears. However, it is possible to reframe these fears as anticipation, as an acknowledgment of how powerful communication can be in transforming our lives. While **reframing** is not as simple as changing the frame

Like Yousafzai we can learn to speak and listen from the heart. Public speaking, if it is done well, has the ability to transform.

EMPOWERING PUBLIC SPEAKING

that surrounds a painting (or the image you're sharing on Instagram or Facebook), it is the process of turning an idea or an experience into something else. In this case, you can reframe your fear by changing it into an opportunity—something powerful and meaningful. Taken in this light, even if the fears don't feel especially empowering, they indicate a respect for communication and what we can achieve through it. Don't let fear stop you from speaking. Invite that fear to become something more powerful, something that challenges to do more and be more in the world.

"I Speak—Not for Myself, But for All . . ."

Like Yousafzai, we can learn to speak from the heart. This is a matter of speaking our truth and listening to the truths of others. To do so requires courage and a willingness to be vulnerable. As Palmer (2011) describes,

> "Heart" comes from the Latin cor and points not merely to our emotions but to the core of the self, that center place where all of our ways of knowing converge—intellectual, emotional, sensory, intuitive, imaginative, experiential, relational, and bodily, among others. The heart is where we integrate what we know in our minds with what we know in our bones, the place where our knowledge can become more fully human. Cor is also the Latin root from which we get the word courage. When all that we understand of self and world comes together in the center place called the heart, we are more likely to find the courage to act humanely on what we know. (p. 6)

Speaking (and listening) from the heart requires courage, but it also gives us courage. While that might not totally eliminate the worries we have when entering a public speaking occasion, it can give us strength.

Your words give rise to our shared social reality, in ways that may be helpful or harmful. In this sense, you are speaking not only for yourself but also for others. Are you representing those others well? Is your communication making a world that is more just and humane for them and for you?

Concepts

agency 30
banking 24
communication anxiety 35
compassion 33
constitutive 32
critical 33
dialogic 27
dialogic communication 28
dialogue 28
interpersonal 24

listening 33
monologic 26
narration sickness 28
praxis 32
problem posing 24
reciprocity 34
reflexivity 31
reframing 36
relational 24

Toward Praxis

1. **Reflection:** Consider a time when you did not speak up about something you cared about deeply. What stopped you? What would you do differently if you could? What or who could have helped you find courage in that moment?

2. **Discussion:** How do you know when someone is speaking from the heart? How does it make you feel as a speaker? How does it make you feel as a listener? How can we encourage ourselves and others to speak from the heart?

3. **Action:** Take stock of the issues that concern you most in the world. What role do you play in perpetuating or challenging these issues? How knowledgeable are you about them? Where in your community can you speak into these issues? Explore these as potential topics for upcoming speaking engagements.

Discussion Questions

1. What do you imagine when you think of a public speaker? Is it a politician? Is it a protester? Is it a student in front of a classroom podium?

2. What kind of learner are you? What do you see as your role in making meaning in the classroom?

3. Do you feel nervous when speaking in public? What do you do to manage those fears?

CHAPTER 3

Public Speaking Is Responsive

In this chapter, we will work together to:

- Explore public speaking as "speaking with" rather than "speaking for" others
- Establish a credible public speaker as attentive to power and privilege
- Define and identify approaches to understanding an audience's needs, values, and goals

> We gather here in memory of 20 beautiful children and six remarkable adults. They lost their lives in a school that could have been any school in a quiet town full of good and decent people that could be any town in America.
>
> Here in Newtown, I come to offer the love and prayers of a nation. I am very mindful that mere words cannot match the depths of your sorrow, nor can they heal your wounded hearts.
>
> I can only hope it helps for you to know that you're not alone in your grief, that our world, too, has been torn apart, that all across this land of ours, we have wept with you. We've pulled our children tight.
>
> And you must know that whatever measure of comfort we can provide, we will provide. Whatever portion of sadness that we can share with you to ease this heavy load, we will gladly bear it. Newtown, you are not alone.
>
> (Obama, 2012)

What happened on December 14, 2012, in Newtown, Connecticut, was quite simply a nightmare realized. In less than 5 minutes, 20-year-old Adam Lanza murdered 20 children and 6 staff members at Sandy Hook Elementary before taking his own life. Even after an extensive analysis by experts, his motives remain unclear (Office of the State's Attorney, 2013). The challenges for a president under those circumstances are considerable, including honoring the dead, consoling citizens both directly and indirectly affected by the tragedy, and offering some assurances that there are actions we can take as a nation to prevent such tragedies from occurring again. Reportedly, the actions and aftermath at Sandy Hook Elementary were some of the most difficult days of Barack Obama's presidency, made all the more complex by the four mass shootings that had taken place during his first 4 years in office (Adams, 2012). When people chose to listen to the president's speech, they could have been seeking solace, understanding, direction, or advocacy, illustrating the complex influences an audience might have for any public speech. The president chose to share his grief with his listeners, but he also chose to engage the public debate on gun legislation. As a result, this particular speech has become an example of not only how speeches do not fall cleanly into particular speech types (such as ceremonial or persuasive speaking) but also how meeting an audience in dialogue is critical to public speaking success.

In this chapter, we first explore public speaking as **advocacy**—as **speaking with** instead of **speaking for** particular communities. Speaking *for* is parallel to the banking model of education we discussed in the previous chapter in that a speaker can approach a public speaking opportunity as if they are already as knowledgeable as they need to be on their topic, as if their task is merely to share this knowledge with a passive, waiting audience. In contrast, speaking *with* a particular community is parallel to the problem-posing model of education also discussed in the previous chapter, in that a speaker can approach a public speaking opportunity as a means of deepening their understanding of the current conditions of a community and a chance to work together with that community to support its growth. To this end, public speaking is an ethical response that informs and is informed by our efforts to listen to and empathize with others. Public speaking as an ethical response always exists in relation to the status quo, so it is always an act that demands careful attention to power and must always reflexively examine the privilege of one's speaking position. Next, we consider **audience analysis** as a meaningful process of learning the needs, values, and goals of groups about which we care and whom we respect. In this way, audience analysis is always, necessarily, attentive to power and privilege, and credibility is inextricably connected to a speaker's own reflexivity.

Public Speaking Is Advocacy

The public speaking assignment notwithstanding, most people give speeches because they feel drawn or otherwise moved to speak. In this sense, we can think of public speaking as a **calling**, as in we are called or motivated to speak into a given issue or concern. We hear of people being

The Dalai Lama is the political leader of Tibet believed to be reicarnated as a important Buddist deity who is to spend his life commited to benefitting humanity. We can compare this kind of "calling" to the type of "calling" a public speaker might feel to speak on a particular subject or about an important issue.

called to public or religious service; sometimes people describe this as listening to a higher power, and sometimes people describe this as delving deeply inward to acknowledge and pursue their own best qualities. Educator Parker Palmer (2001) describes a calling or vocation in this way: "Vocation does not come from a voice 'out there' calling me to become something I am not. It comes from a voice 'in here' calling me to be the person I was born to be" (para. 4). We find that as speakers, we experience calling more as a "calling out"; in other words, we feel challenged to respond to an issue about which we feel strongly. There is generally some kind of mission or purpose behind our impulse to speak, either because we feel personally implicated or because we care strongly about how a given issue affects others in our lives.

Aristotle gave us one of the most popular and well-circulated definitions of rhetoric—defining rhetoric as attempts to persuade. This marble panel shows Aristotle and Plato debating and is in the lower basement of the bell tower of Museo dell'Opera del Duomo in Florence, Italy.

Rhetoric Is a Means of Persuasion

Given the mission or purpose behind our impulse to speak it can be helpful to see public speaking as always already persuasive. In his authoritative collection *Rhetoric*, Aristotle gives us one of the most popular and widely circulated definitions of **rhetoric**: "Rhetoric may be defined as the faculty of observing in any given case the available means of persuasion" (Aristotle, *Rhetoric*, book I, chapter 2, para. 1). It may help to take this definition in steps, beginning with the word *rhetoric*. What does the word *rhetoric* mean to you? It is still quite common for people to use *rhetoric* as a dismissive word, a way of suggesting that a speaker isn't sharing much of substance. This has a lot to do with Plato's (n.d.) descriptions of rhetoric in relation to philosophy. Memorably, he described rhetoric as cookery, likening it to flattery, to something we do to manipulate a message. This concept will sound familiar to those of you who are interested in the ways that different organizations, from advertisers to media outlets to political campaigns, "spin" a given story.

Aristotle's definition asks us to think of rhetoric as attempts to persuade. Looking for these attempts to persuade us can help us be more discerning in how we develop and evaluate the communication around us. The phrase *any given case* suggests that anything might be persuasive, from the architecture of a building (for example, think how difficult it can be to find the exit on a casino floor) to someone's clothing (for example, think of how you use your

CHAPTER 3 | PUBLIC SPEAKING IS RESPONSIVE | 43

clothing to communicate to others who you are—and who you are not). Consider all the different ways people compete for your attention—from the sponsored links in your social media feed to the way your professor raises questions about current events. Being attentive to how others attempt to persuade you can help you make good decisions about the precious resource of your attention.

Consider all the different advertisements that compete for your attention—on billboards, on social media, on TV, etc. How do these advertisements affect you? Are you aware of the impact they have on you?

Persuasion Entails Appeals to Ethos, Logos, and Pathos

Public speaking as rhetoric is, at least to some degree, always persuasive. This is most obviously seen in a persuasive speech or a debate, but it is also true of informative speeches, speeches of self-introduction, toasts, roasts, and so on. Some kinds of public speaking are more intentionally or obviously persuasive than others, but it can still help us as listeners to be aware of the persuasive qualities of a given message so that we can critically engage it. Aristotle offers us three categories for persuasive efforts or appeals; these three **artistic proofs** are *ethos*, *pathos*, and *logos*. An artistic proof is persuasion that requires a speaker's craft and skill to be successful. Appeals to **ethos** rely on the authority of the speaker or source, establishing credibility and trustworthiness. Appeals to **pathos** rely on engaging the sympathies or emotions of the listeners. And appeals to **logos** rely on logic and reasoning to persuade.

"Speech is power—Speech is to persuade, to convert, to compel."

— Ralph Waldo Emerson

For example, if we take Aristotle's definition seriously, then we can take even something as routine as your performance as a student and consider how that is persuasive. No doubt you always want your teacher to believe you are a good student. Let's imagine a time when you are really feeling that you need an extension on an assignment. You might attempt to persuade your teacher that you are trustworthy and reliable by providing them with documentation of your trip to the emergency room. In further telling your story, you might also try to appeal to their emotions by describing the long wait time at the hospital or why you were there in the first place. You might also appeal to their sense of logic and reason by describing how, while you could prepare that assignment by the deadline, your understanding of the material and your performance on the assignment would be stronger if you could reestablish the fundamental conditions you need to learn well (e.g., a clear head, proper hydration and sleep, healed sinuses). You would follow a similar persuasive process if you are convincing an audience that you have a reasonable action they can take toward global climate justice, that you are knowledgeable about the U.S. civil rights movement, or are the fun former college roommate who is ready to lovingly tease the happy couple at the wedding reception.

Persuasion as Advocacy Means Speaking *With* Others

Here we would remind you that, while all public speaking can be productively understood as persuasion, persuasion is not as simple as trying to get what you want (though certainly many our efforts to persuade are just that). Public speaking is **advocacy**, an effort to speak on behalf of a position or cause such that others join you in that effort. Further, advocacy entails speaking alongside the people who may benefit or lose by your efforts, **speaking with** others rather than **speaking for** others. Rather than being self-serving, public speaking requires a thoughtful and intentional connection to others—the people whose minds and actions you're hoping to change and the people who are affected by those changed attitudes and behaviors.

> "We live by each other and for each other. Alone we can do so little; together we can do so much."
>
> —Helen Keller

This requires **reflexivity**—the ability to explore how you participate in both groups (the people you are hoping to change, and the people who may benefit from the change). Engaging in reflexivity challenges you to reflect and listen to others as to how you are or have been part of the problem and how you may be part of the solution(s). Given that our communication has the power to create and shape not only individuals but also relationships and cultures, it is crucial that we enter into public speaking occasions with an **ethic of care**.

Public Speaking as Advocacy Requires an Ethic of Care

Most people recognize that public speaking, like other professional endeavors, is or should be governed by an ethical code. Such ethics challenge us to make decisions that are consistent, trustworthy, and responsible. For example, an important part of ethical public speaking is making sure that you name and rely on trustworthy, credible sources; this way, you and your listeners know that they can be confident that their understanding and decision making is based on sound evidence. Similarly, listeners have an ethical responsibility to not just hear, but actually engage a speaker's ideas, exploring their meaning and possible impact. Taking seriously the belief that communication creates our realities—that our word choices shape our sense of past, present, and future actions—requires us to ground our decisions in care and regard for others.

The PGA's "Birdies for the Brave" program is the PGA tour's primary program for supporting military members and their families. In his speech, PGA Tour Commissioner Tim Finchem describes the PGA's commitment to an ethics of care.

EMPOWERING PUBLIC SPEAKING

Public speaking as advocacy requires a commitment to an **ethic of care**. By this we mean that our efforts at advocacy must be informed by our dialogue and relationship with the people who will be affected by our communication. In adopting the premise that we should care for others with our communication, we hope to emphasize the importance of engaging with others to learn more about them and ourselves. Unfortunately, a very real risk of classes in public speaking is that students don't always feel the consequences of their communication through required assignments and textbooks that move students step by step through a series of prescribed skills. For a variety of very good reasons, instructors place safeguards on communication in the classroom, from preapproving students' topics to carefully moderating students' feedback during question-and-answer or other discussion sessions. When students don't have the opportunity to make serious errors or face real controversy in public, they can feel like the class is a series of exercises rather than communication that changes people and processes. Further, it can be difficult to engage the multiple different audiences affected by a given argument inside the context of a particular public speaking class, especially if it comprises mostly "traditional" college or university students. It is all too common for student speakers to offer positions on or solutions to complex issues without having to share those ideas with the people most affected by their rhetoric. Care in this context means working to reach out to and better understand others who may hold vastly different understandings about an issue than your own.

Reflexivity Relates to an Ethic of Care

An ethic of care means engaging others in dialogue, especially if they see the world—or at least some important part of it—differently than you do. As American feminist and ethicist Carol Gilligan describes it, an ethic of care is "grounded in voice and relationships, in the importance of everyone having a voice, being listened to carefully (in their own right and on their own terms) and heard with respect" (Ethics of Care, 2011, para. 4). Too often, public speaking involves *speaking for* and *speaking to*, when ideally it would mean *speaking with*. Brazilian educator Paulo Freire (2005) can offer us some insight here. *Pedagogy of the Oppressed* as title of his book is especially significant. He did not title his book *Pedagogy for the Oppressed*—with that simple shift from *for* to *of*, Freire reminds us that we should be learning from and with others, especially people whom we hope to help with our communication. In order to engage in dialogue with others, we must first work carefully as speakers to be reflexive. Reflexivity, according to Freire, entails understanding how we both shape and are shaped by aspects of the world around us. We are implicated in the ideas we promote with others, and we are implicated in the ways those words help or harm others; these ideas shape us and shape the very issue we are working to better understand.

Reflexivity adds an important ethical dimension to our public speaking efforts. While credible speakers can, for example, carefully and correctly frame issues for their listeners, unless they engage in reflexivity, they are not otherwise obliged to try to experience that issue from the lived experience of the people who may profit or lose most by its exploration and resolution.

Public Speaking Demands Careful Attention to Power

Becoming more reflexive as speakers entails becoming more mindful of power in our lives. When we think of power, we might be inclined to think of gross abuses of it. Without question, oppression exists in our world; we should name it and fight it. However, the exercise of power is subtle, moving in and through individuals as well as institutions. Not every abuse of power is as clear as, say, genocide. Communication, while hopeful and uplifting as a means to develop **agency** and the sense that we can take meaningful action in our lives, can also create oppression and pain, from enabling anything from mass murder to subtle acts of everyday racism, sexism, heterosexism, ableism, and other forms of oppression.

Oppression Can Grow and Thrive Through Hegemony

Social theorist Antonio Gramsci (1971) offers us one way of understanding how oppression can grow and thrive in our most mundane communication through his concept of hegemony. **Hegemony** refers to how we grant others the power and privilege to shape our worldviews, attitudes, beliefs, expectations, and actions. This is, in a sense, a process of domination by consent; we consent to others' influence, even when that influence may be harmful to us. As examples, women participate in hegemony when they adopt the belief that only men can be effective as president, working-class people participate in hegemony when they vote to support economic policies that will service only the richest members of the least attainable tax brackets, and people with disabilities participate in hegemony when they feel as though it is unquestionably reasonable for Hollywood films to cast able-bodied actors as characters who have disabilities. It is essential to consider how every single one of us participates in hegemony, and to do so without wallowing in guilt or a desire to blame victims for accepting their (our) own oppression.

Michel Foucault, a French philosopher, can help us think about the complexities of power in useful ways. Of relevance here is his observation that power masks its own production. It is no wonder that the mechanisms by which we embrace, reject, and hold power over others are elusive; that slipperiness makes it easier for those with power to become still more powerful. One way that oppression comes to move in and through us is through the ways in which institutions (such as schools, churches, jails, and businesses) work to produce "**docile bodies**" (Foucault, 1977, p. 137). These institutions, by restricting how we attend to or call attention to our bodies through frequent and unreflective repetition, teach us to conform to their expectations. We learn to blend in, to minimize the differences in our thinking that emerge from our different bodies, and to comply with those in power. Our embodied differences—our races/ethnicities, our genders, our ranges of ability and so on—are **epistemic**. Something is epistemic when it has an effect on how we form knowledge. They are

> "By compassion, one can be brave."
>
> —Lao Tzu

48 | EMPOWERING PUBLIC SPEAKING

Restrictions on movement and touch in prisons are an obvious example of how institutions work to create docile bodies. However, our bodies are schooled and regulated in many, less obvious ways as well, in classrooms and cubicles.

meaningful because they provide us with different levels and types of access to learning about the world around us. Minimizing our differences usually serves those who are already in power, rendering their expectations and values the norm by which we measure all others. For example, many people strive to be "color blind," or what Ruth Frankenberg (1993), a scholar who studies race and the ways race is epistemic, calls being color evasive about race/ethnicity. Frankenberg finds that being color evasive has helped create a **mythical norm** (Lorde, 1984) where White cultural norms have shaped race relations in the United States. This is well illustrated in this often-repeated example (Kimmel, 2005): The White man who looks into a mirror sees only himself, the White woman sees that she is a woman, and the woman of color sees that she is both a racial/ethnic minority and a woman. Recognizing the mythical norm at work helps those of us working toward greater reflexivity acknowledge and seek to understand that those in power define cultural standards (of success, of beauty, and so on). Not having to confront one's differences is a form of privilege.

Hegemony Emerges From and Extends Unearned Privilege and Power

While some people engage in oppressive acts consciously, most people reproduce oppressive power relationships because they are unaware of their own unearned privilege. They never realize how their unspoken assumptions about culture shape and define others. **Unearned privilege** refers to those benefits someone receives simply because they match the mythical norm. In her elegant essay on White privilege and male privilege, Peggy McIntosh (1997) helps readers understand that the goal of reflexivity and attention to power is not to identify and

CHAPTER 3 | PUBLIC SPEAKING IS RESPONSIVE

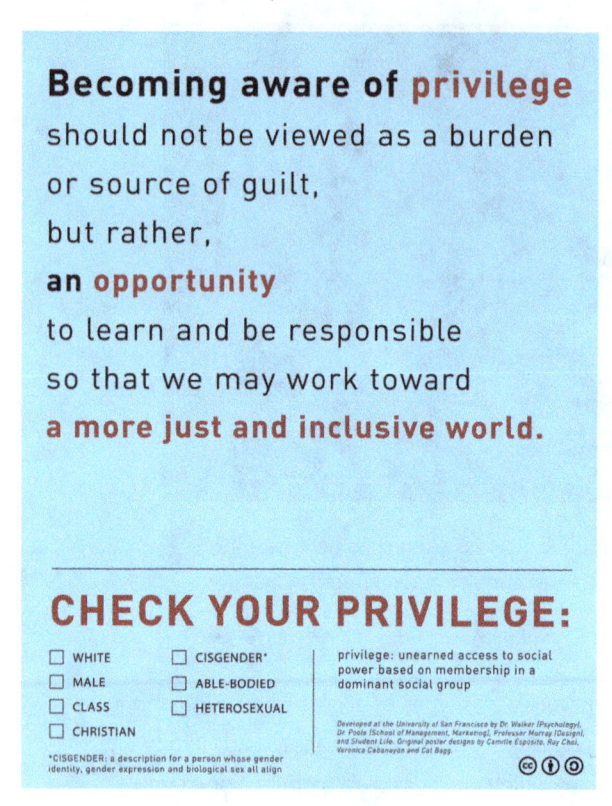

> **Becoming aware of privilege**
> should not be viewed as a burden or source of guilt,
> but rather,
> **an opportunity**
> to learn and be responsible so that we may work toward
> **a more just and inclusive world.**
>
> **CHECK YOUR PRIVILEGE:**
> ☐ WHITE   ☐ CISGENDER*
> ☐ MALE   ☐ ABLE-BODIED
> ☐ CLASS   ☐ HETEROSEXUAL
> ☐ CHRISTIAN
>
> privilege: unearned access to social power based on membership in a dominant social group
>
> *CISGENDER: a description for a person whose gender identity, gender expression and biological sex all align

> If you can use public bathrooms without stares, fear or anxiety, **you have cisgender privilege.**
>
> **CHECK YOUR PRIVILEGE:**
> ☐ WHITE   ☑ CISGENDER*
> ☐ MALE   ☐ ABLE-BODIED
> ☐ CLASS   ☐ HETEROSEXUAL
> ☐ CHRISTIAN

Check Your Privilege is a campus wide social marketing campaign at University of San Francisco that seeks to raise student, faculty, and staff awareness around social inequalities and privilege. The posters were designed to encourage individuals to think critically about privilege because often people are unaware of their own unearned privilege.

==punish== individual racists or sexists, but ==rather to recognize that all of us exist in an interlocking web of social systems==—such as the educational system or the judicial system—that unreflectively benefit the able, affluent, White, heterosexual, cisgender, Judeo-Christian, and male at the expense of people who do not fit this norm. We challenge you, as a reflexive public speaker and someone who wishes to advocate alongside and on behalf of causes that matter to you, to consider how you benefit by unearned privilege. That awareness will help you interrogate and challenge ideas so that you can better understand their consequences for others—both those who have power and those who are relatively disenfranchised.

Striving to be reflexive can help speakers better understand whether they are speaking *to* others, speaking *for* others, or speaking *with* or *alongside* others. Speaking *to* returns us to a sense of public speaking that is monologic, top-down, and characterized by transmission (remember Freire's description of teaching as banking?). Speaking *for* suggests that we are advocating on behalf of a group that is unable to speak. Before we assume that we should speak *for* someone else, we must first consider whether they are already speaking. Have we not been listening? Have they been speaking in settings where we do not belong or cannot (or should not) participate?

What consequences do they face for speaking in one setting versus another? And perhaps most importantly, what makes us feel we have the right or the ability to speak on behalf of others? Speaking *with* or *alongside* others implies a relationship of care and regard. It requires a willingness to share the consequences of speaking truths to power. To this end, there may be two different audiences for a given speech: (a) the people who directly encounter your communication and (b) the people who must live with the implications and outcomes of that communication.

Audience Analysis Is Part of an Ongoing Dialogue

In order to better understand the effects of your words on others, it is helpful to engage in some analysis of your audience and their backgrounds, values, and needs. Ideally this analysis will occur in the context of a relationship you have with the people with whom you hope to advocate. This can be challenging in some public speaking classrooms, where you will likely feel quite familiar with the people in the room and perhaps somewhat unknowledgeable about the people most directly affected by your ideas. Still, how will you know whether your efforts to move your listeners will be effective if you don't know what they will find compelling or powerful, disrespectful, or distancing? It's worth noting that even seemingly homogenous audiences are often more diverse than they would seem.

The process of **audience analysis** begins alongside—and sometimes even before—topic selection and continues with your reflection on whether your speech is or has been successful and for whom. It is part of a larger conversation about issues with others; remember Buber's (1970/1996) reminder that you are engaged with a "thou" and not an "it." Consider a less contrived setting than the public speaking classroom. You may find yourself invited to speak to a particular organization, assigned to provide a detailed presentation for your employer, or poised to present yourself in an interview with a prospective employer. Each of these audiences poses a different set of opportunities and challenges because each has different needs, goals, and expectations. Having insider knowledge about your audience (such as when you're already a member of the organization that has invited you to speak or when you've done some homework about what that new job assignment entails) is a real advantage. Never underestimate the value of speaking with informed others about the context or setting for your speech. Key members of an organization or community can help you understand the past history of a given issue, as well as the stakes involved in different kinds of interpretations or solutions related to it. Otherwise, it would help you to know more about your listeners' backgrounds, values, needs, and expectations so that you can shape your message accordingly.

Understand Audience Demographics

One way you can begin to engage in audience analysis is to make careful, provisional assumptions about your audience members based on their demographic characteristics. **Demographics** refers to statistical patterns we can identify in populations of people along different characteristics—for

Consider the two audiences in these pictures. Each of these audiences poses a different set of opportunities and challenges because each has different needs, goals, and expectations. If you were to speak to either one of these audiences it would be helpful to have insider knowledge about your audience. It would be useful to know about the context or setting for your speech and it would help you to know more about your listeners' backgrounds, values, needs, and expectations so that you can shape your message accordingly. Before you speak you should always analyze your potential audience and learn as much as you can.

example, age, ability, economic class, education level, ethnicity/race, geographic location, gender identity/expression, income, language of origin, military status, nationality, political affiliation, religion, or sexual orientation. Making educated guesses about your listeners' experiences, needs, and values based on demographic data can help you tailor how you approach a given message, as well as your examples, your sources, and your word choices.

It is important to remember that demographic inferences are just that—educated guesses; patterns, though helpful, don't always reflect the experiences of the individuals at the event where you're scheduled to speak. Consider the following statistic from the Pew Research Center's U.S. Religious Landscape Survey (2008): "Men are significantly more likely than women to claim no religious affiliation. Nearly one-in-five men say they have no formal religious affiliation, compared with roughly 13% women" (para. 15). This information might help inform your approach to a number of different topics and issues; however, it cannot answer a whole host of questions regarding the particular people in your audience, or whether and why they practice faith as they do. Demographic data can never be certain about complex issues and reasons.

It is also important to note that educated guesses will be affected, at least to some extent, by implicit biases. An **implicit bias** is an unreflective or unconscious belief or stereotype about a particular group of people. We are often unaware of our own implicit bias. As one small example: What does it mean if we refer to a father taking care of his children as "babysitting?" It is unlikely we would say the same of a mother, which is telling of our assumptions. Implicit bias figured prominently in the news cycle in 2018 when White employees at a Philadelphia Starbucks called the police to report that two Black men were "trespassing" in the coffee shop because they had used the restroom and not yet purchased any items. Police arrived and arrested the men, who were waiting for a third friend (this person arrived as the arrest was being made) and who had committed no crime. Starbucks later closed 8,000 stores for an afternoon for the purpose of attempting to educate 175,000 of its employees about racial bias, access, and

If you were to interview for a new job, you would want to continuously adapt to your audience throughout the meeting. You might shift your tone to better engage bored listeners or offer additional explanation when listeners seem confused. You would want to be able to tell quickly whether your listeners were open and engaged, hostile and defensive, bored and annoyed, or some combination of these. The more you understand your audience and can adapt to it, the better prepared you would be for the interview and the more likely you would be to get the job.

inclusion (Noguchi, 2018). Other instances of implicit bias are well documented in social media with the hashtag #LivingWhileBlack (Lockhart, 2018). Fortunately, it is possible to heighten our awareness of our own implicit biases and change our behavior (Tropp & Godsil, 2015). One way is to listen well to people who can help us understand how our unwarranted and unreflective assumptions may have powerful and painful consequences for others.

Consider an Audience's Hierarchy of Needs

A second way you can attempt to make sound inferences about your audience is to consider where your listeners fall along **Maslow's hierarchy of needs**. In his studies of human motivation, psychologist Abraham Maslow (1943) identified a series of human needs he set in hierarchical relationship to each other. The hierarchy consists of five levels. From the most basic or elemental human need to the most complex, they are physiological, security, belongingness, esteem, and self-actualization. Physiological needs are essential for our survival—for example, air, water, and food. Security needs reflect our desire to protect ourselves and the people we care about, and may include shelter, employment, and protection from danger. Belongingness needs reflect our desire to be loved, including a sense of connection and collective purpose. Esteem needs emerge from our desire to be highly regarded or respected. Finally, self-actualization needs reflect our desire to live our lives with purpose, including autonomy, agency, and creativity. Maslow argued that all people must first satisfy the needs at the base of the hierarchy before addressing higher order needs; however, like all representations of complex processes, you'll find that there are likely some exceptions to what the chart implies are rules.

While speaking, you will also engage in audience analysis by adapting in real time to the challenges and opportunities afforded by your audience, setting, and context for your speech. This adaptation requires a mindful awareness of how your listeners are encountering your ideas, which you can only really achieve if you have sufficiently prepared for the speech and can pay close attention to the world beyond your notes. Some adaptations will be easy to identify and implement, such as shifting your tone to better engage sleepy listeners returning from a long weekend or offering additional explanation when listeners seem confused. By scanning the room as you speak, you will be able to discern whether your listeners are open and engaged, hostile and defensive, bored and annoyed, or some combination of these. The more comfortable you can be with your purpose and specific goals for speaking, the more likely you will be to refine your responses to your audience in the moment.

"Here in Newtown, I Come to Offer the Love and Prayers of a Nation"

One of our challenges as speakers is to fight the urge to speak from the podium as if we are giving a monologue. While we may be speaking one to many, if the many fail to inform our goals, ideas, and approaches as speakers, then we risk doing more harm than good to them

President Obama's speech at the Newtown prayer vigil is a powerful example of understanding audience and using speech for advocacy.

and to the causes we care about. As we discussed in the previous chapter, successful public speaking as advocacy is dialogic and collaborative. Therefore, audience analysis is less a process of surveying your listeners—though that does occur—and more a process of learning with and about the people whose opinions and actions we seek to influence most directly. This is, in a sense, about establishing your right to speak, showing that you've engaged and learned from others in order to participate in a conversation that necessarily precedes you and ideally continues long after you've spoken.

When tragedy strikes, a world leader must speak. Yet their decisions as a speaker are never made in isolation; their voice exists as one among many in a conversation, however diffuse or formal. President Obama's speech at the Newtown prayer vigil for the victims of Sandy Hook was surely authored in advance and well prepared. However, he developed this speech in the context of many different interwoven concerns: the context of other mass shootings in the United States, the fear and pain felt across the United States, the age and vulnerability of many of the victims, his experiences as a parent of two daughters, the divisive debate on gun legislation, and his listeners' need for assurance that this would never again happen. His pain is palpable in the speech, and it reflects a genuine empathy for the victims and their families; his resolve is equally memorable when he states that he will use the power his office holds to prevent future senseless shootings. Though his speech was primarily a eulogy, he demands gun legislation. This speech, while inextricably tied to a particular moment in time, opened space for others to speak into these concerns. With his speech, the President advocates action with and on behalf of his listeners. In what ways will you become an advocate in your public speaking? And with whom will you speak?

Concepts

advocacy 41
agency 48
artistic proofs 45
audience analysis 42
calling 42
demographics 52
docile bodies 48
epistemic 48
ethic of care 46
ethos 45
hegemony 48
implicit bias 53
logos 45
Maslow's hierarchy of needs 54
mythical norm 49
pathos 45
rhetoric 43
speaking for 41
speaking with 41
unearned privilege 49

Toward Praxis

1. **Reflection:** Consider a time when someone advocated or spoke on your behalf. Did this person know you? What did they get right? Wrong? In what ways did this experience help you advocate for yourself? Where did/do you still struggle in advocating for your own needs? What would help?

2. **Discussion:** Who is disenfranchised in your community? How so? In what ways are those members of your community misunderstood or stereotyped? How has misinformation and misunderstanding affected opportunities for dialogue?

3. **Action:** Develop a plan to learn with and about a group that is different from your own background or upbringing. How can this become the foundation for a sustainable relationship that will continue to inform your understandings about issues that matter to you in your community? What steps can you take to be sure that the relationship you're pursuing is dialogic rather than primarily self-serving?

Discussion Questions

1. When have assumptions based on demographic data been wrong about you as an individual?

2. How are credibility and reflexivity linked? Must a credible speaker be a reflexive speaker?

3. What unearned privileges do you experience? How can that influence how you approach a given issue or argument?

CHAPTER

4

Public Speaking Is Specific to Time, Place, and Purpose

In this chapter, we will work together to:

- Identify and distinguish speaking occasions that shape the context and purpose of a public speech

- Identify and distinguish types of public speeches

- Define and shape a speech topic appropriate for the scope, context, and purpose of a given public speaking situation

- Create a thesis appropriate for the scope, context, and purpose of a given public speaking situation

> Out of respect for those grieving families, and until the facts are known, the NRA has refrained from comment. While some have tried to exploit tragedy for political gain, we have remained respectfully silent.
>
> Now, we must speak . . . for the safety of our nation's children. Because for all the noise and anger directed at us over the past week, no one—nobody—has addressed the most important, pressing and immediate question we face: How do we protect our children right now, starting today, in a way that we know works?
>
> (LaPierre, 2012)

On December 21, 2012, Wayne LaPierre, executive vice president of the National Rifle Association (NRA), addressed a group of reporters at a press conference in Washington, D.C. He spoke exactly 1 week after 20-year-old Adam Lanza, armed with a variety of semiautomatic weapons, killed 26 people—20 of them children between the ages of 5 and 10—at Sandy Hook Elementary School in Newtown, Connecticut.

Lanza's shooting of children at Sandy Hook Elementary School was a major national news story throughout the day of the event, and the event continued to have a significant media profile in the days afterward. One noteworthy and controversial response to the event came from then president Barack Obama, who called for the development of a "multifaceted approach to prevent mass shootings like the one in Newtown . . . and many other gun deaths that occur each year" (Shear, 2012, par. 6).

LaPierre spoke at the press conference 2 days after the president's call for such an approach. He represented his organization, the NRA, an organization that strongly opposes legislation that might curb ownership of firearms. The highly charged national focus on the tragedy at Sandy Hook Elementary School had clearly recognizable effects on LaPierre's speech. Three of those involve the time, place, and purpose of his speech, which are the topics of this chapter:

- the timing of his speech, 2 days after the president's call for action;

- the intended immediate audience for the speech, a group of reporters assembled in the nation's capital; and

- the speaker's explicitly stated purpose, which was to propose a "plan of action" that could enhance "the safety of our children."

In this chapter, we describe how public speeches are shaped by the social contexts that surround them and the purposes of the speakers. An effective speaker recognizes that they speak in an environment or setting much broader than their intimate circle. **Speaking contexts** include entire communities with diverse values, interests, histories, and areas of expertise. **Speaking occasions** are usually connected to the reason that people pay attention to a speech in the first place. These events are only sometimes within the speaker's control. The occasions or events then prompt effective speakers to consider how the context or speaking occasion can help them shape the speech in ways they *can* control. The speaker considers their **speaking purpose** to be the primary reason for the opportunity (whether by invitation, obligation, or choice) to speak to a group of listeners. The speaker also identifies the type of speech expected in this occasion, one that acknowledges the needs and values of the community in this time and place. The speaker then selects a general topic based on how the type of speech intersects with their own interests and expertise. Finally, the speaker begins to work with this general topic as a researcher; they assemble information and organize ideas. As they do this work, they shape and focus their topic so that it is appropriate for the opportunities and challenges posed by the speaking occasion. One important technique a speaker uses to judge whether their topic is appropriate to both audience and context is to develop a thesis statement that clearly establishes and argues their position in ways an audience will appreciate and remember.

Public Speakers Adapt to the Unique Circumstances of Speaking Occasions

A **speaking occasion** is the reason that attendees come together to witness someone speaking to a public group. Historically, such occasions were often linked to public events, such as celebrations or efforts to honor or memorialize a person or group; deliberations on important questions of public policy or law; or educational needs. Events like these usually gave speakers plenty of time to prepare in advance. However, current speaking occasions can be much more quickly convened; consider flash mobs that develop in response to social media messages. Current speaking occasions can also use technologies that change speakers' relationships to their audiences; consider televised speeches such as a presidential address and how different this occasion is from one that allows the speaker to watch and hear audience reactions in the same space.

A speaking occasion is rarely within a speaker's control, apart from the choice to create and deliver the speech itself. A speaking occasion includes a series of choices made by groups that precede and follow you as a speaker. As a result, you must always adapt to the opportunities and challenges afforded by a specific time, place, and location. Perhaps your political commitments lead you to take part in a demonstration in a public space, a demonstration in which you reach for a microphone to address fellow demonstrators and others nearby. Perhaps you are asked to deliver eulogizing remarks at a memorial service for a family member. Perhaps your public speaking instructor assigns you a speech and weighs your course grade according to your efforts. What unites each of these examples is that you did not direct the context that

A funeral is a speaking occasion where people come together to celebrate or recognize the life of someone who has passed away. At a funeral, the speaking occasion is rarely in a speaker's control, apart from the choice to create and deliver the eulogy itself and the eulogy usually must be carefully adapted to a specific time, place, and location.

gave rise to your speech. In this sense, even at its inception any public speech is always responsive to a community and a history that precedes it.

Speaking Occasions Are Defined by Their Relationship to Time

The longest standing academic effort to identify speaking occasions has come to us from Aristotle (1991). Aristotle links speaking occasions to the purpose of a speech. In centering his work on the purposes for making speeches, Aristotle broadly separated speaking occasions according to their relationship to time:

- **Forensic speeches** address events that have already occurred in the past. In this way, such speeches attempt to show causes for effects we are currently experiencing. Good examples of forensic speeches include attorney statements in courtrooms (which attempt to assign responsibility) and scientific speeches (which analyze events in the natural world). Bill Nye the "Science Guy" has given many well-known talks in mainstream media that explain how and why things work the ways they do—teaching his audience a bit about physics and chemistry as he does so. These are forensic speeches.

"... sometimes a scream is better than a thesis."

—Ralph Waldo Emerson

Bill Nye, the "Science Guy," is famous for his forensic speeches that explain how and why things work the ways they do.

Kevin Durant's speech when he won the NBA's Most Valuable Player award in May 2014 was an example of epideictic speech. In particular, his tribute to his mother as "the real MVP" and the person who kept him off the streets and helped him believe in himself highlighted his bond with his mother and family members.

- **Epideictic speeches** address events in the present. In this way, such speeches attempt to show how we currently stand in relation to one another in the community. Good examples of epideictic speeches include toasts at weddings (which highlight bonds of family and friendship) and award nomination and acceptance speeches (which establish

62 | EMPOWERING PUBLIC SPEAKING

The speeches politicans, like Bernie Sanders, give are examples of deliberative speeches because they call for policy change and anticipate a community's needs and solutions.

the worthiness of those receiving or presenting an award). Kevin Durant gave a widely acclaimed speech when he was presented with the NBA's Most Valuable Player award in May 2014. This is an epideictic speech, as are the speeches televised each year (and often discussed afterward) by winners in awards shows such as the Grammys, the CMA Awards, the Oscars, the Tony Awards, and the Golden Globes.

- **Deliberative speeches** address events that have not yet occurred. In this way, such speeches attempt to show effects in the future. Good examples of deliberative speeches include political speeches calling for policy changes (which anticipate specific community needs and propose solutions to those needs) and advocacy speeches (which urge listeners to take voluntary action to enhance their future lives or those of others). The speeches included in this textbook that were delivered by Emma González (discussed in Chapter 1) and Malala Yousafzai (Chapter 2), in addition to the one discussed in this chapter delivered by Wayne LaPierre, are each deliberative speeches.

Speaking Occasions Are Defined by Their Relationship to Community

Aristotle's classification system is only one approach to dealing with speaking occasions. We use it here to exemplify what we consider the most important aspects of the notion of a speaking occasion—such occasions will always be grounded in the speaker's relationship to a particular community at a particular time in a particular place. This is what makes efforts to define communication on social media like Twitter and Facebook as potential forms of public speech so challenging. Consider this question: Do online readers make up a genuine *public* community distinct from a community of intimates to which we control access, as many users carefully do for our own Facebook profiles or Instagram accounts? Do tweets, which can be retweeted easily and so might be closer to communication we can call a *public* speech, have any common features (in terms of time or place) that might suggest they operate within a particular community? These are challenging questions to resolve. For now, we choose to consider public speaking a form of communication in which a speaker implicitly (and often explicitly) begins speaking with a clear idea of *why* they are speaking and *to whom*.

Public Speakers Consider the Types and Purposes of Speeches in Each Speaking Occasion

Once you know why you are speaking and to whom, an important step in shaping your speech is to determine which type of speech is most appropriate. Since speeches have distinct purposes for distinct communities, as we explore above, these purposes and communities can help us understand speeches in another way. For example, how does one type of speech have important qualities in common with other speeches of that same type? How could these common qualities give an effective speaker a good starting point to determine how to approach an audience?

The most common distinction scholars make in discussing types of speeches is the distinction between an **informative speech** and a **persuasive speech**. An informative speech is one in which the speaker's primary purpose is to educate audience members about a topic. A persuasive speech is one in which the speaker's primary purpose is to convince audience members to take a particular action. This distinction matters so much because it involves a very important shift in the relationship between the speaker and the audience. As we will see, this relationship depends on time (present and future) and on different ways of sharing community. You may also be asked to deliver two other kinds of speeches: A **ceremonial speech** is one in which the speaker's primary purpose is to highlight for audience members the distinctive important elements of a special person or occasion. A **demonstration speech** is a specific type of informative speech in which the speaker's primary purpose is to allow audience members to develop the ability to accomplish a precise, narrowly defined task.

Informative Speeches Depend on a Present Community Relationship of Knowledge Levels

An informative speaker relates to audience members as an expert on a given topic relating to a group of relative novices. The speaker's *primary* orientation is to show how the speaker's

In a classroom, teachers often take on the role of informative speakers when they educate their audience about a topic. That role can change into one of persuaive speaker though, depending on the type of classroom and the goals of the teacher.

temporarily greater expertise creates a distinction from listeners—even if the speaker might have something in common with them. In this way, the informative speaker focuses attention on subject-specific *knowledge levels* that make them and the audience members who they *currently are* in the present. This is similar to (but not quite the same as) how a teacher relates to a group of students. This relationship is somewhat different than a teacher–student relationship because a public speaker has much less direct contact with learners than a teacher does. Speaking effectively as an informative speaker means packaging educational efforts within a very limited amount of time. Speaking effectively in this type of speech also means packaging ideas for audience members who are likely much less familiar to the speaker than a teacher would be with students. How, then, can an informative speaker make an effective connection to audience members? One way is that the speaker may have interests obviously in common with listeners as a result of their shared community, interests that the speaker highlights in the speech to establish trust. Alternatively, the speaker may take extra steps to specifically stimulate listeners' interests in learning about a new topic. Informative speakers in our everyday lives include docents at museums who inform patrons about art, artists, and historical items of interest; chefs using public platforms to teach people to cook; and emcees at car shows who are not interested in selling any cars (that would be a persuasive speech) but are instead describing interesting features of the cars.

> "Think thyself fit and worthy to speak . . . and let not the reproach, or report of some that may ensue upon it, ever deter thee. If it be right and honest to be spoken or done, undervalue not thyself so much, as to be discouraged from it."
>
> —Marcus Aurelius

CHAPTER 4 | PUBLIC SPEAKING IS SPECIFIC TO TIME, PLACE, AND PURPOSE

In a presidential political debate, the ultimate goal of the speakers is for the audience to take action. The presidential candidates each want audience members to vote for them as president at a future time. These speakers are not just educating their audience about their policy positions, but they are going a step further to empowering their audience to choose a president. Both the debates between Kennedy and Nixon and Clinton and Trump resulted in voters taking action at the polls.

Persuasive Speeches Depend on a Future Community Relationship of Possible Actions

In contrast, a persuasive speaker relates to an audience as a fellow changing, growing member of a community. The speaker's *primary* orientation is to ways their ideas about change and growth in the community make the speaker *similar to* their listeners, despite all the other ways they may be different from one another. An effective persuasive speaker focuses attention on *actions*; these actions will, if audience members take them, make them who they *should be* in the future. Persuasive speakers are common in our everyday lives; they include spokespeople and agents in sales and advertising situations. On-air reporters are sometimes considered informative speakers, but media studies scholars are increasingly attentive to the ways that such public speakers have carefully selected information and chosen language so that viewers and listeners have their understanding of news events shaped in certain ways.

We think this distinction between the two primary types of speeches, informative and persuasive, is interesting because most writers emphasize these types as stemming from a different purpose (primarily to inform; primarily to persuade). Remember that in this book, we are treating public speaking as an act of communication, something quite a bit like other acts we all have plenty of experience doing in conversations, writing, and so on. We instead suggest that a better reason to carefully distinguish between the informative speech type and the persuasive speech type is because they involve meaningfully different relationships to listeners, as we just described. If speakers know what type of speech they will deliver, they have sharpened their focus beyond occasion and purpose because they have begun to consider how they relate to their audience.

A speech offered at a retirement party is an example of a ceremonial speech. In these speeches, listeners reflect on what they know and feel about the person who is retiring. In addition, these speeches enourage listeners to show appreciation for the contribution the person retiring has made to an organization. Thus, these speeches have a way of both informing and persuading listeners.

Ceremonial Speeches Depend on a Past Community Relationship of Esteemed Values

Focusing on your relationship with your audience also helps us explain a third type of speech that writers commonly name: the ceremonial speech. Notice that when you are speaking in a ceremonial setting, like a wedding, a memorial service, an award ceremony, a retirement party, and so on, you are in some ways both informing and persuading listeners. In these speeches, you are encouraging listeners to reflect on what they know about a particular person or group of people, and sometimes adding to what they know. In addition, in ceremonial speeches you are encouraging listeners to take a specific action of appreciating someone, encouraging listeners to accept the truthfulness of what you say about that person or group of people.

Is a ceremonial speech a cross between informative and persuasive speech, then? One way to understand why ceremonial speeches merit their own special category is that these speeches involve a third kind of relationship between speaker and audience, rooted this time in the past. In ceremonial speeches, a speaker relates to the audience as a fellow member of a community that has already established—and lived by—a shared set of values. Ceremonies, and the speeches that happen within them, are usually ways of honoring the established successes of these past values—especially the successes of the person or group of people being honored.

To summarize, informative speeches depend on a present community relationship of knowledge levels; persuasive speeches depend on a future community relationship of possible actions; and ceremonial speeches depend on a past community relationship of esteemed values.

Demonstration Speech Involves a Changed Relationship

The fourth and final type of speech we discuss here is the demonstration speech. As you might expect, these speeches, in which the speaker helps audience members grasp the steps needed to accomplish a specific task, are quite a bit like informative speeches. In one way, they are also like persuasive speeches: Demonstration speeches always implicitly suggest that audience members *can* and *should* accomplish the task being demonstrated. These speeches, while similar to the other types of speeches we've discussed, differ because they involve another changed relationship. In the case of demonstration speech, the speaker's relationship to the audience is not grounded in time (past, present, or future common links) but to place. A demonstration speech is only successful in particular spaces in which the speaker can identify a task, with a set of required materials, that is meaningful and feasible to listeners. A speaker addressing an audience in a cold, northern climate would face serious challenges if they attempted to demonstrate how to recognize ripe garden tomatoes and pick them from the vine at just the right moment in their life cycle without tearing their skins. How could such a speaker succeed? If the community has access to technologies like small electric greenhouses and the

The difference between demonstration and informative speech is that demonstration speech always implicitly suggests that audience members can and should accomplish the task being demonstrated. Whether speakers are demonstrating cooking or science they all want listeners to be able to learn the skills they are demonstrating and put them to use in their everyday life.

speaker has access to advanced visual aids, perhaps the speaker will succeed. But notice that these conditions materially change what counts as a *place*. However, as we live in an increasingly connected society with enhanced access to technologies and materials across the earth, this fourth type of speech might collapse as a meaningful distinction. For now, we suggest that the speaker and their community's common relationship to a particular *place* makes the demonstration speech a relevant fourth type.

CHAPTER 4 | PUBLIC SPEAKING IS SPECIFIC TO TIME, PLACE, AND PURPOSE | 69

Public Speakers Choose Topics That Are Well Suited for Particular Occasions, Purposes, and Audiences

Once an effective speaker has considered the audience, occasion, and purpose that shape their speaking opportunity, they are prepared to develop an appropriate **topic**. A topic is, simply put, the main idea being discussed in a public speech. Developing a speaking topic requires three separate steps. Each step is motivated by a very different attitude toward the topic, but if you take these three steps seriously in the order we suggest, you can work successfully with speaking topics.

Undertake the Process of Brainstorming

The first step is to **brainstorm**. You may already be familiar with this term; maybe for you it suggests putting down a large number of ideas that are floating in your mind—ideas connected to one big, central idea. This type of idea generation is a good starting point for understanding what we mean by brainstorming. However, when you are developing a public speaking topic there is an important quality of this first step that will give you a strong foundation: Not only should you list ideas, you should also prepare your mind to generate ideas in the first place. This is not as easy as it may seem; we know that time is a precious resource that we have trained ourselves to conserve. We have to carefully conserve time not only when getting ready for a major speaking assignment but in doing most of what we do in our life. We have to get to and from school and work; we have to pick a checkout line at a store; we have to exchange messages with friends. Many of us live most moments of most days as if finding efficient paths through procedures is the best way to move. But when you need to brainstorm, the training you have given yourself to look for efficient paths is actually harmful; it restricts your chance to generate new ideas.

There are several reasons why efficiency and brainstorming do not work well together. Our minds use perceptions to organize our experience of the world around us—what we see, hear, smell, or intuit—all the input our minds take in. At any instant, there is far too much information for us to grasp without narrowing our intake of that information right when we take it in. We narrow our intake of information using a variety of perceptual tricks. We establish expectations for what we will experience, so that we focus most on those events that are most similar to what has happened before. We categorize information so that we focus not on raw, tiny bits of data but on larger, more manageable chunks of images and ideas that we think already relate to each other. We learn to trust our emotional triggers, so that we focus most on information that strongly appeals to us or, conversely, that strongly repels us. Our minds are usually a lot more efficient in processing information than we are in choosing checkout lines! But notice that these perceptual tricks involve a lot of prior assumptions about the world, assumptions about the future being mostly like the past. While this is useful for perceiving a profusion of overwhelming new information, it is less useful—even destructive—for generating fresh, previously unrecognized ideas. We have trained our minds so much to take paths of least resistance that we are often led not to our freshest inspirations but instead to our most predictable, worn-out ideas.

You can enhance your brainstorming and give yourself the chance to develop fresher ideas by putting aside, for a while, your perceptions about public speaking. Forget, for this first step, about everything you know about your future, still-to-be-selected speech topic other than the major factors we have discussed so far in this chapter: your audience, your occasion, and your purpose. Try not to focus on effective speeches you have previously delivered or attended; try not to make assumptions at this stage about your audience's interests or needs (though you should focus on your *relationship* to your audience); above all, try not to focus on detailed constraints associated with your speaking opportunity, like time lengths, grades, and so on.

Once you do what you can to clear your mind of prior perceptions about the "right" speaking topic, write down any ideas that come to mind as you reflect on your audience, occasion, and purpose. If you are struggling to identify ideas, answering questions like these can help generate ideas:

- What do you know about your audience? What do you *not* know about them?
- What are some specific things you have in common with your audience?
- What are some specific ways you differ from your audience?
- What are some areas in which you have experience or expertise?
- What are some areas in which you'd like to develop additional expertise?

Strive to list as many responses to these and other questions you create for yourself. The goal in this first step is to make lists of ideas that are as long as possible; list even those ideas that seem silly or off-target when they come to mind, because these ideas could help shape your speech later in the development process.

Undertake the Process of Topic Selection

The second step is to choose a topic from your list. An excellent procedure for choosing from an open-ended list of possible topics is to introduce at this stage some of the primary constraints connected to your speech. Again, answering a list of questions can help you make your choice:

- What is the speaking occasion? Is this a class assignment? An invited presentation? A moment of voluntary advocacy?

CHAPTER 4 | PUBLIC SPEAKING IS SPECIFIC TO TIME, PLACE, AND PURPOSE

- What is your primary purpose in speaking? Return to Aristotle's three types of speaking purposes that we explained earlier. Are you speaking primarily to suggest a specific action? Primarily to educate your audience? Primarily to honor a person or event? In a public speaking class, your teacher often limits your options in terms of purpose.

Undertake the Process of Narrowing a Topic

Once you choose a topic, you will need to *narrow* your topic so that you can shape it appropriately for the speaking context. The most important way to narrow a topic is to begin enhancing your knowledge about it. Start searching for compelling sources that educate you and/or that clarify and make concrete the knowledge you already have. Avoid the temptation to wait to start your research until you have narrowed your topic, for the same reasons you cleared your mind when brainstorming. When you wait to start research until you have narrowed the scope of your topic, you risk missing out on source material that could sharpen the focus of your speech in surprising ways, using material you might not have otherwise explored.

What do we mean by narrowing the **scope** of a speaking topic? Scope refers to both the breadth and depth of a topic: How many areas of a topic can you address in a single speech, given the context? In how much depth can you cover these areas, given the context? Notice that breadth and depth balance one another; the more areas you choose to cover, the less deeply you will treat them, and vice versa. Again, some questions can help you with effectively narrowing the scope of your topic; remember to enhance your knowledge on your chosen topic through research, before focusing on these questions:

- Where and when will you speak?
- Do you know what the physical environment will look and sound like? If so, what parts of it can support your speech? If not, what parts of your speech can you control no matter the environment?
- Do you know if you have a time limit?
- What does your audience currently know, in your estimation, about this topic?
- What areas of this topic will be of most interest to your audience, in your estimation?

Public Speakers Develop a Thesis Statement That Guides the Structure and Focus of Their Speech

Another vital tool that can help you narrow the scope of your topic appropriately for your speaking context is to develop a **thesis statement** for your speech as a whole. No matter what form you use to organize your speech, and no matter how you choose to document that form (see Chapter 6 for information on organizing your speech), you should create one single thesis statement for that speech. A thesis statement helps you as well as your audience. As you create and modify a thesis statement, you sharpen your focus and better understand *your own* ideas. Audience members need a thesis statement to help us organize what you say in your speech, and you will use other tools (e.g., evidence, repetition, presentational aids) to help with this at multiple points in your speech. However, you cannot make these reinforcements useful to your audience unless you the speaker first prepare an effective thesis statement to organize your own ideas. There are four key elements of an effective thesis statement that we will explore here:

- An effective thesis statement is precise.

- An effective thesis statement is unique.

- An effective thesis statement is direct.

- An effective thesis statement is argumentative, making an argument by showing *how* ideas are related to one another.

We will explore these four elements of an effective thesis statement by using examples from an informative speech in which you teach your classmates how to access scholarly references in your library's online database.

An Effective Thesis Statement Is Precise

Your thesis statement should be *precise* in identifying ideas. The statement should use noun phrases that are understandable (not based in special jargon). When your listeners hear a strong thesis statement they should be able to immediately recognize one or two primary ideas that define your speech. They should be able to distinguish these primary ideas from other similar ideas related to the same topic. They should understand what they are being asked to do with these ideas (e.g., learn something, accept the truthfulness of a claim, take an action). For example: An imprecise thesis statement for your library references speech might read, "A speech will be stronger if sources are found to back it up." A precise thesis statement might instead read, "Adding some scholarly sources contained in a library database can strengthen a person's speech."

An Effective Thesis Statement Is Unique

Your thesis statement should be *unique* because it should only offer ideas that relate to you, your audience, and your evidence. A good test for an effective thesis: If anyone else in your class could use the exact same thesis for this speaking assignment, then your thesis needs to

> "I believe that we learn by practice. Whether it means to learn to dance by practicing dancing or to learn to live by practicing living, the principles are the same. In each, it is the performance of a dedicated precise set of acts, physical or intellectual, from which comes shape of achievement, a sense of one's being, a satisfaction of spirit. One becomes, in some area, an athlete of God. Practice means to perform, over and over again in the face of all obstacles, some act of vision, of faith, of desire. Practice is a means of inviting the perfection desired."
>
> — Martha Graham

be tweaked a bit to differentiate your speech from any other. The noun phrases in it should include, whenever possible, local details of time and place relevant to your community. A common mistake that novice speakers (and writers) make is to create thesis statements that sound generalizable, believing that more generalizable claims belong in a thesis statement because they are easier for an audience to accept. But this is incorrect; indeed, it is backward. Your speech will have power when audience members understand why *you* are speaking to *them* in *this* context, and more generalizable—rather than local—ideas push against this goal of healthy, particular connection. For example: A general thesis statement for your library references speech might read, as noted above, "Adding some scholarly sources contained in a library database can strengthen a person's speech." A thesis statement unique to your speaking situation might read, instead, "Adding some scholarly sources contained in databases such as *Academic Search Premiere*, and others in our MLK Library, can strengthen your persuasive speech for the next round."

An Effective Thesis Statement Is Direct

Your thesis statement should be *direct* in offering only those ideas that are absolutely necessary for listeners to understand your speech. Those helpfully precise and unique noun phrases we have already explored should be subjects in your thesis statement, and they should be followed by strong action verbs that are not qualified or nuanced. Qualifications and nuances are important in public speaking. However, the thesis statement is not the time to acknowledge and examine these subtleties; they should develop during the body of the speech as you discuss evidence. In your thesis statement, you want to assure your audience as soon as possible that you are credible, and that your claims are well considered. You can enhance your speech by using direct, active verbs in your thesis statement because these active verbs help show that you are not bending the truth, omitting relevant evidence or offering fallacies as conclusions. You can also enhance your speech by using direct, active verbs in your thesis statement because most topics worth exploring in a public speech will have multiple intelligent perspectives associated with them, so you want to be clear about which of these is your focus. For example: An indirect thesis statement for your library references speech might read, as noted above, "Adding some scholarly sources contained in databases such as *Academic Search Premiere*, and others in our MLK Library, can strengthen your persuasive speech for the next round." A direct thesis statement, instead, might read, "You can strengthen your persuasive speech for the next round with scholarly sources contained in databases such as *Academic Search Premiere* and others in our MLK Library."

A Thesis Statement Is Argumentative

Your thesis statement should *make an argument* in just one (or at most, two) declarative sentences. This argument should be the core argument of your speech. Your thesis statement should show how its ideas are related to one another in one specific way that leads to the conclusion you want your audience to reach as they listen to your speech. In a persuasive speech, your assignment will often require you to call for an immediate action. But all types of speeches urge audience members to reach a conclusion (such as: "I can now make tamales myself"; "I agree that our former mayor deserves to be honored for her leadership during a distinctive time of civic crisis": "I now better understand the reasons some religious institutions are given tax-exempt status"). In an effective thesis statement, all ideas within the thesis statement (all the noun phrases) are linked together with strong action verbs that urge audiences to a single conclusion. For example: A thesis statement without an argument for your library references speech might read, as noted above, "You can strengthen your persuasive speech for the next round with scholarly sources contained in databases such as *Academic Search Premiere* and others in our MLK Library." A thesis statement that makes an argument might instead read, "The strongest persuasive speeches, like the one you'll give in the next round, include scholarly sources contained in databases such as *Academic Search Premiere* and others in our MLK Library."

Thesis Statement Development Helps You Focus on Important Questions

Working on your thesis statement in these ways can guide you in your development of the speech as a whole to ask a series of important questions: Which ideas in this speech do I make a strong claim about, and how can I best support that claim in a direct way? Which ideas in this speech are controversial or might foster disagreement from my audience, and how can I best defend my claims in a direct way that also acknowledges these differences? Remember that these are qualifications and nuances, and so, as discussed in point number three above, they are relevant within the body of the speech rather than the thesis statement itself. However, now you can recognize how your development of an effective thesis statement is helpful for *you* as you narrow your topic: An effective thesis statement helps you understand how to organize the work of creating the rest of the elements of your speech. As we have explored here, the thesis statement will evolve as you conduct research, sculpt evidence, and organize your claims. However, your thesis statement should evolve *with* your speech and serve as a framework, or scaffolding, for the speech. We suggest a scaffold as an analogy because your thesis statement should change in shape as a scaffold changes with a new building—moving to one side or another, growing taller or shorter, but always giving you an understanding, from start to finish, of where you are heading and why.

"They're *Our Kids*. They're *Our Responsibility*. And It's Not Just Our Duty to Protect Them— It's *Our Right* to Protect Them"

We have presented the concepts of speaking occasions, speaking purposes, types of speeches, and topic selection and development in this specific order, suggesting that they form a focusing process that can give you a strong foundation for speaking effectively within a particular context.

We make several choices in the first section of this chapter, on Wayne LaPierre's speech, that result from our ideas about *who* is reading this passage, *when* they are reading it, *why* we have been tasked (or have tasked ourselves) with writing it, and *how* we intend for audiences to read it. First, we chose a speech within a national policy discussion that we believe will still be recent enough to engage you, our readers, and may still be fresh in your minds even a few years after this book has been written. We also wanted to choose a topic that is explicitly tied by both President Obama and Wayne LaPierre to events that may still have powerful emotional resonance for you (we trust, for instance, that many of our readers will associate Sandy Hook Elementary School with a violent mass murder and an ensuing response from people in various leadership roles). Second, in describing historical facts we cite The New York Times rather than a different news source, because The New York Times has a long history of association with credible reporting of current events, a choice that reflects our sense of responsibility to write credibly within a scholarly setting. Third, in selecting which historical facts we include and which we omit as we characterize LaPierre's public speaking context, we remind readers that Adam Lanza committed these crimes using semiautomatic guns—choosing the adjective *semiautomatic* because we consider it important to the speaking context that the subsequent policy discussion often centered on the firing capacities of different types of guns and the resultant differences in guns' rapid killing power.

Note that our language choices in just this two-word phrase taken directly from information in a credible news source—*semiautomatic guns*—by themselves reveal quite a bit about the authors and our purpose. We could have chosen the adjective *assault* rather than *semiautomatic*, but we believe that doing so might have suggested to readers that we were trying to shade meaning too passionately in a pro–gun-control direction, muddying our efforts to frame the context, if we chose a word like *assault* that connotes intention rather than one like *semiautomatic* that connotes function. However, we also chose the word *gun* rather than *weapon* because we believe it parallels the word *semiautomatic* in being precisely descriptive (weapons include many objects other than guns) and also because we believe it more incisively points at the heart of the national policy debate (despite cartoons that lampoon the debate, no national leader has called for kitchen knives or baseball bats to be licensed, regulated, or banned).

There are two important ideas we hope you will recognize in examining how we frame the speech: First, our choices even in *writing* a single paragraph in this textbook, far from the national media spotlight, are shaped by considerations like these—the high profile of the Sandy Hook tragedy, the strongly held values about life and liberty that people bring to discussions of gun control legislation, and the sense of urgency and importance about these issues overall because they involve the life and death of children. How much more so, then, must these considerations be made for public speech in front of an assembled audience? A public speaker is *always* responsible for understanding the context in which they speak and the ways that context affects audience members and how they may hear the message. Second, our choices are also shaped by our particular values and purposes as scholarly authors and are not in any meaningful way objective, despite our citation of *The New York Times* and our reliance on a set of historical facts as framing context. When we write that we are not objective, we acknowledge that our contextualization of this speech is necessarily partial; it includes some ideas rather than all possible ideas, and it is shaped by our goals for this chapter and for the book.

LaPierre—like all speakers—must attend thoughtfully to the speaking occasion, to the purpose of his speech, and to the expectations and values of the community for whom he spoke. You can see his framing choices throughout the speech, including evoking for NRA members and supporters the right to bear arms in service of our responsibility to protect our children—a note that would resonate for his intended audience. You can support your own ability to speak effectively if you also consider time, place, and purpose; and if in doing so you use an evolving thesis statement as a support structure helping you guide your efforts.

Concepts

brainstorm 70
ceremonial speech 64
deliberative speeches 64
demonstration speech 64
epideictic speeches 62
forensic speeches 61
informative speech 64

persuasive speech 64
scope 72
speaking contexts 60
speaking occasion 60
speaking purpose 60
thesis statement 72
topic 70

Toward Praxis

1 **Reflection:** To what communities do you belong? Where are you invited to speak? Where are you expected to speak and by whom? Where and with whom do you have a responsibility to speak?

2 **Discussion:** What are the issues facing the communities to which you belong? Who talks about them, and where and how are they discussed? Who are the stakeholders in these issues? Are all voices present in the conversation? Why or why not?

3 **Action:** Set aside choosing a speaking topic that *seems* like a speaking topic. Instead, choose to speak into a conversation that is facing a community to which you belong and about whom you care. How can you help others develop nuanced insight into this issue? How can you invite other voices into the conversation?

Discussion Questions

1. Must a speech have a thesis statement in order to be effective?

2. How are all different types of speeches, at least to some extent, persuasive?

3. How are you and others affected by remaining silent on an issue? Must one always speak?

CHAPTER 5

Public Speaking Is Pedagogical

In this chapter, we will work together to:

- Explain how public speaking requires a commitment to agenda setting
- Explain how public speaking deepens others' understandings of complex phenomena
- Describe the qualities that audiences associate with knowledgeable, credible speakers
- Identify preparation and self-presentation techniques that establish speakers as knowledgeable and credible
- Identify strategies for effectively gaining and retaining the attention of a group of listeners in a public communication context

> Your honor,
>
> If it is all right, for the majority of this statement I would like to address the defendant directly.
>
> You don't know me, but you've been inside me, and that's why we're here today.
>
> Doe, excerpted in Beven, 2016

On June 2, 2016, "Emily Doe," a woman who survived a sexual assault in January 2015, delivered a victim impact statement during a hearing on the sentencing of her attacker. The statement was given in a Santa Clara County (California) court. The district attorney for this county described her impact statement as an "eloquent, powerful, and compelling piece of victim advocacy" (Bever, 2016, para. 5). Local and national news sources have identified her as "Emily Doe" to respect her wish to remain anonymous; we'll use that pseudonym here as well.[1] Doe's courtroom statement provides a compelling, socially significant example to explore with respect to the characteristics of informative speaking. A victim impact statement certainly has a persuasive purpose, given its role in advocating for justice according to the wishes of the victim(s) of a crime; yet the power of such a statement rests on its ability to educate audience members (judges, jurors, perpetrators, officers of the court, perhaps even courtroom attendees) about circumstances and situations on which their work depends. These circumstances and situations are, at the time of the public speech, outside the audience members' realm of knowledge. Furthermore, we suggest that in the specific context of a survivor of sexual assault speaking to others, the pedagogical dimensions of public speaking are highlighted, given the silence, shame, and vulnerability that can—and often does—erase survivors' stories from public discourse. Doe's courtroom statement provides an excellent case study of how speeches have links to complex audiences and how these audiences are changed by public discourse. This is why we title this chapter "Public Speaking Is Pedagogical." **Pedagogical** is an adjective indicating that something involves learning about the world and also connotes that, in the process of learning, changes our understanding of the world as a result of this new learning. This word reminds us that effective education is transformative.

In this chapter, we discuss the fact that a speaker who is successfully informing an audience is also changing that audience in the process. Audiences members change when informed; this fact complicates the notion of a merely **informative speech** without persuasion as its primary goal. We discuss how public speakers establish and maintain credibility with their audiences, especially when speaking with the primary purpose of informing their audience. We also explore strategies for establishing and maintaining audience members' attention while speaking.

---

[1] It's now common knowledge that Emily Doe is Chanel Miller (de León, 2019).

Public Speakers Set an Agenda for Audiences When They Speak

We choose the word **pedagogy** to describe what is happening when an effective public speaker educates an audience. In the simplest sense, a *pedagogical* act is any act that involves teaching and learning. Why not just write simpler words like *teaching* or *learning*? Consider this: If you wanted to give a piece of information to someone who does not already have it, you could send the information via text message, using carefully considered punctuation, abbreviations, emoji, and so on to make sure the message is well understood. A public speaker or teacher is in a similar situation when they decide how best to use their speaking time, words, body language, and visual aids to make sure the message or lesson is well understood. However, these choices are based on a decision-making level much more complex than the process of sending a text message. The term *pedagogical* helps get at this complexity.

We think this parallel between informative speaking and teaching, covered by the term *pedagogy*, is useful. We find that the parallel captures something of the commonsense view of teaching and of public speaking. But we also choose the term *pedagogical* to suggest that public speaking (much like teaching) is not only more complex than text messaging but also a qualitatively different action. When we speak in public settings, the focus of our audience is by definition on our ideas and our hopes for our speech. In this setting, we are not only sharing *information*, we are sharing *ourselves* and we are thereby staking a position in the community—whether that community is as small as a public speaking class or as large as all

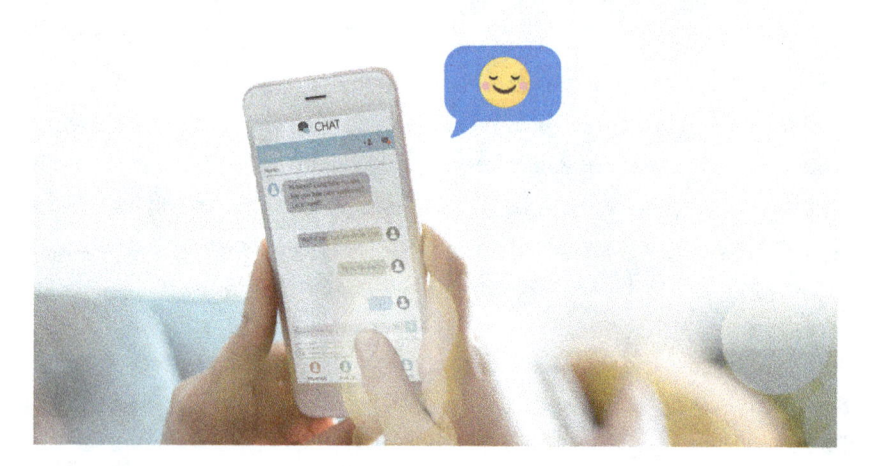

People send information via text message, with carefully considered punctuation, abbreviations, emojis, etc. to make sure the message is well understood. A public speaker, or a teacher, acts similiarly when they decide how best to use their speaking time, words, body language, and visual aids to make sure the message, or lesson, is well understood.

Internet users. That's how *pedagogy* suggests something more than *teaching*—a pedagogical act is one that communicates ideas as well as a specific relationship *to* those ideas, *among* the community, all at once.

Conceiving of public speaking as a pedagogical act means that whenever a person speaks to a group of listeners, the speaker is making use of listeners' time, attention, and other limited resources to offer assertions about the world. The public speaker's assertions help set an agenda for the community. These assertions encourage listeners to view the world in selective ways. After all, that's what **focused attention** means, selecting and privileging some points of focus rather than others. When we encourage listeners to view the world in selective ways, no matter what our explicit speaking purpose might be, we are implicitly suggesting that our listeners can and should *act* according to that view. In this chapter we explore the informative speech, a very clear-cut type of speech. In this type of speech, a speaker offers assertions about the world, of course, but the agenda-setting dimension of public speaking is less obvious or clear-cut in this type of speech compared to a persuasive speech or a ceremonial speech.

Here, we first consider how a person speaks most effectively when they embrace the pedagogical quality of the speaking opportunity. Second, we discuss how embracing a pedagogical mind-set can help a speaker prepare for the distinctive responsibility of addressing many others at once, and how this mind-set can help that speaker identify ways of establishing a credible relationship to those others. Finally, we address some strategies that a speaker can use for getting and keeping the attention of listeners. These strategies encourage listeners to willingly give some of their precious time and focus to the speech, and to its invitation to learn and to integrate what they learn into their lives.

Teaching an audience, in this sense, involves actively responding to an immediate speaking situation and framing oneself in particular relation to an audience. Emily Doe, in her courtroom statement, responds to the immediate situation and also focuses on her relationship with audience members. Her courtroom statement is both informative and persuasive (indeed, most public communication is). As we will show, she uses compelling strategies to mark the importance of her speech and her unique fitness to speak in this situation, to gain and retain her listeners' attention, and to ground each of her claims consistently in her relationship to her listeners, their shared values, and their shared community.

A Public Speaker's Role Relative to the Audience Shapes Their Efforts

Informative speaking occurs in settings in which your primary speaking purpose is to share your knowledge on a specific topic with your audience. You may find yourself speaking with such a purpose in several different kinds of common situations. For example, you may be a supervisor or trainer helping professionally develop a significantly sized group of colleagues in

This religious leader is an informative speaker in that he spends time teaching his audience about principles of the shared religion and brings the group together to understand their shared belief system.

a workplace setting; you may be sharing findings or results from your workplace with an assembled group of stakeholders, such as customers or press representatives. Or you may be engaged in spiritual practices in which you explicate scriptural passages or describe available resources for a community that shares your beliefs; you may be in a formal role as an educator in a learning environment; or you may be speaking to earn a grade in your public speaking class or another college class.

Each of these examples shares in common the idea that the audience assembles for one of two reasons related to who the speaker is. In some informative speaking situations, the audience assembles because the speaker has a designated role with respect to them (supervisor/trainer, organizational representative, teacher). Such a person helps make key decisions about how the community should spend its time and energy. In other such situations, the audience assembles because the speaker is one member within a community of broadly shared goals (a spiritual community, a classroom) who is temporally centered within that community. Many authors would suggest that the two defining qualities of an informative speech are what the speaker intends the speech to accomplish (to inform objectively, with neutrality regarding the material) and what the speaker should avoid (to persuade subjectively, with an agenda grounded in the material). Instead, we suggest something quite different: An informative speech typically derives its purpose from a certain kind of *relationship between speaker and audience*, namely one of mutually *shared resources* in which community members each have a stake in how resources are used.

Informative Speaking Is Shaped by a Speaker's Credibility With Their Audience

Consider again the two most common reasons you would be called to share information with a public audience. These reasons often hold true even if that public audience is more than simply those assembled face-to-face with you. You may have an information-sharing role formally designated to you because of your expertise or position, or you may temporarily adopt an information-sharing role because your audience includes many people who trust your ability to move the community forward toward its common goals.

When you have a formally designated role, you were almost certainly given this role because you have previously devoted effort within your own life to distinguishing yourself. You are someone worthy of this designated role within a private company or public institution. Organizations like these, in which you take up designated roles, involve the distribution of important resources such as time, space, human labor, machine labor, and money. Such organizations will keep you in this designated role only as long as you participate in wisely using and redistributing these same resources. Your choice of a speech topic in these contexts may be determined by someone other than you (such as in our training or teaching examples). However, even when you have an opportunity to develop and narrow your own topic, you will likely find your audience is most responsive to your messages, and is in the best position to learn from you, when members recognize that you are using these precious organizational resources in ways they consider appropriate. Their sense that this is true relates strongly to **credibility**, to their perception of your qualifications and character.

Informative Speaking is Shaped by a Speaker's Relationship and Understanding of Their Audience

Your purpose as an informative speaker, if you speak effectively, is grounded in your relationship to your audience, namely others who have made *choices* about their ongoing relationship to you. These choices shape your informative speech as you answer these questions in preparing to speak:

- What do audience members need to know, and why, within this context (the workplace, the classroom)?

- How much do audience members already know?

- How can you share knowledge in ways that your audience can recognize as meaningful within this organization?

- How can you share knowledge that your audience values enough to put effort into their own learning of it?

"Teaching is not a lost art, but the regard for it is a lost tradition"

—Jacques Barzun

In a classroom group situation you voluntarily take up a role as a fellow group member within a classroom. You are not in a position of designated authority or expertise, but you derive your opportunity to speak publicly entirely from your similarity with other group members. You can then shape your speech within the group by beginning with an understanding of your connections with them.

All of these questions demand that you develop your informative speech through returning, again and again, to how and why you and your audience all came together within this organization.

This remains true when you voluntarily take up a role such as that of a spiritual leader or as a fellow student within a classroom. After all, you are not in a position of designated authority or expertise, and therefore you derive your opportunity to speak publicly entirely from your similarity *with* other audience members (a fellow spiritual traveler; a fellow student). You can then shape your speech by beginning with an understanding of your connections with them. For example, effective informative speeches in your public speaking course might involve topics such as institutional processes that affect students on your campus; local histories or elements of local culture; aspects of your major area of study if your college groups students in public speaking according to shared majors; skills or areas of knowledge that students taking college courses often enjoy, such as ways to enjoy the outdoors, music, or other creative activities while in college; and so on. Within any of these informative topics, you can shape your speech appropriately because you know how *you* are involved in this resource-sharing community and what the stakes are for *you*, and you can therefore (with some careful reflection) easily gain more understanding of how and at what cost your listeners are involved as well.

Public Speakers Enhance Their Credibility Through Careful Preparation

Your relationship to the community helps you make sense of how best to use your time and direct your energy as you prepare to speak. As we note below, when you prepare to speak effectively, you are significantly establishing your credibility by ensuring that you will speak competently and with care for your audience, and as a result, your audience will positively assess your character. **Speaker preparation** refers to all of the ways you spend your time ensuring that you speak effectively—from researching evidence to choosing appropriate language to rehearsing with notes and visual aids.

First, consider your role in this community and how it has framed your current opportunity to speak. Have you been invited because of your unique expertise or experience? Have you been charged with a task by supervisors or clients (speaking for a grade in a class might fit this possible role)? Are you representing a group of people who expect you to reflect their values or interests in ways that honor them? Informative speeches, persuasive speeches, ceremonial speeches, and/or demonstration speeches could emerge from any one of these roles.

Preparation is an important part of establishing credibility by speaking with competence and regard for the audience.

CHAPTER 5 | PUBLIC SPEAKING IS PEDAGOGICAL | 87

Understand Your Role

As you prepare to speak, beginning with a clear understanding of your role can help you address such issues as:

1. Attire appropriate for the setting and the community's expectations of prepared speakers

2. Presentational aids with a **scope** that audience members can grasp immediately (e.g., a chart or graph with recognizable variables; an image with recognizable forms; a sound that listeners can parse into recognizable chunks like words or melodies on the first listen) and prepared in a style that meets the community's expectations

3. Language that the community can understand because the words used are well understood and commonly used or, in the case of technical vocabulary, are clearly defined in the speech

4. **Syntax** (e.g., the lengths of sentences; the arrangement of sentence elements like noun phrases, verb phrases, and modifying or qualifying phrases) that the community can track and use to understand why ideas are meaningful to them

5. A speech structure that suits the time expectations (speech length) and the level of depth necessary to convey only those ideas (and no other) relevant to the speech's purpose (speech scope)

These preparation ideas are most valuable to you as a speaker when you use them to guide your rehearsal process. For instance, there is not necessarily a "correct syntax" that you could use like a formula to guide you as you form sentences in rehearsal or when you deliver your speech. Such formulaic ways of speaking make spoken passages sound dull because your tone and face will reflect the fact that you are not forming the sentences in your mind as you speak them; you are merely reciting a formulaic series of ideas. Instead, our note about syntax and each of the five preparation points above should encourage you to reflect on how you are putting your ideas into sentences when you rehearse.

Understand the Importance of Syntax Structures

Do you tend to offer listeners several phrases before you use an active verb in a spoken sentence? Such syntactic structures can work well in academic writing or in casual conversations. But in public speaking contexts, audience members can organize your ideas better if an important noun phrase (usually the primary subject of the sentence) comes early in a sentence and if an active verb immediately follows that sentence. Here's an example of what we mean:

- A sentence with syntax less appropriate for a public speech: "Whenever tests were returned, especially with tests that counted for a high percentage of the grade, several of the same students, every time, because they wanted to ask about how the teacher assigned partial credit, would raise their hands."

- The same ideas in sentences with syntax more appropriate for a public speech: "The same group of students raised their hands every time the teacher returned tests. These students asked about how the teacher assigned partial credit on these tests, especially when the tests counted for a high percentage of the final grade."

While you don't want to minimize the complexity of ideas with your listeners, they will gain more from your speech if you are direct, concise, and evocative in your language. We recommend that when you rehearse, you work with a partner or record yourself then check each of the five preparation points above and explore if your choices of attire, presentational aids, language, syntax, and speech structure fit the needs of your audience.

Consider Speaker Credibility and Audience Learning Needs

We raise distinctive questions associated with speaker preparation for a second reason: In primarily informative settings, there is heightened attention on both a speaker's expertise and the audience's learning needs. Any speaker within any of the speech types (informative, persuasive, ceremonial, or demonstration) intends for their material to be "learned" by an audience in some sense. Ceremonial or persuasive speeches might narrow the scope of such learning to a small, pithy set of ideas that audience members can easily recall both in the moment of the speech and afterward. The process of narrowing focus in these two types of speeches requires speakers to prepare by understanding what their audience members currently know and what fresh ideas audience members will be able to easily recognize, comprehend, and/or recall. Similarly, a demonstration speech requires a public speaker to narrow their focus to what can be demonstrated immediately in the speaking environment. An informative speaker must also consider the speaking environment, but they can engage a wider or more complex range of fresh ideas compared to speakers offering one of the other three types of speeches.

When preparing to speak with informing as your primary focus, ask yourself how challenging your audience will find any material that might be new to them. Will you enhance their learning by breaking down a complex idea into multiple parts and show how the parts relate to one another as a whole? Will you need to define new terms? Will you more effectively communicate unfamiliar ideas with presentational aids? Answering questions like these requires you to consider both who makes up your audience and how you as the speaker relate to these audience members in terms of your expertise, your authority, and your goals in speaking—hence our suggestion that speaker preparation begins with a clear grasp of your role within a particular community.

Identify Audience Members' Learning Needs

Similarly, a strong sense of what you share in common with your audience will help you identify audience members' learning needs. Some guidelines apply across most speaking situations; these include the importance of variety and of reaching people across potentially distinct learning styles.

- **Variety:** Present ideas using more than one style of speaking, including varying your phrasing and your tone of voice. Offer presentational aids when possible.

- Distinct **learning styles:** Some audience members are most engaged by the spoken word. Others will understand your ideas best when they see visual representations of your ideas, such as printed words or images. Still others will learn best when you can help them move abstract ideas like words into a concrete form, like a three-dimensional object they can touch or a spatial relationship they can move within.

Other needs will be unique to the ways that your particular audience, your particular topic, and the time and place of your speech all intersect one another. One of your responsibilities as a speaker is to identify which unique learning needs apply to your speaking situation by reflecting on factors such as the age and experience of your audience; the social, cultural, economic and political factors relevant to your shared community; and the significance of

An audience is made up of members who have a variety of learning styles. When speakers use visual tools, like PowerPoint presentations, some audience members will better understand ideas the speaker is trying to get across. It is important for a speaker to understand their audience's learning needs to be an effective speaker.

EMPOWERING PUBLIC SPEAKING

recent treatment—whether accurate or inaccurate, whether comprehensive or partial—of your ideas in widely available mainstream media.

Enhance Speaking Effectiveness Through Competence, Character, and Care

Another vital way you can enhance your speaking effectiveness when preparing to speak is by exploring how you might best, given your shared community, highlight or strengthen your credibility. McCroskey and Teven (1999) describe three elements of credibility that affect learning in educational environments; we will use them here to discuss credibility in the parallel pedagogical context of public speaking. These three elements are competence, character, and care.

A speaker can establish **competence** while speaking by using several strategies; we explore three here.

1. **Oral citation:** Perhaps the most important strategy for a student speaker is using effective oral citation techniques in your speech. Using these techniques shows your audience that you have educated yourself carefully prior to attempting to educate them.

2. **Expertise:** A second strategy underscores your personal expertise. What do you already know that your audience members do not? How can you highlight your expertise through briefly explaining something precise you have done in the past? This need not be a strategy only for speakers with a great deal of experience on a given topic. For example, if you are speaking on a topic that you researched in response to a contemporary social problem, or on a subject that helped someone you know solve a problem, your connection to that topic helps underscore your personal credibility if you acknowledge that connection briefly in a few subtle phrases throughout your speech (such as "when I was searching for this answer").

3. **Precise language:** A third strategy for establishing your competence is to speak with precision—both in terms of language choice and in terms of scope. Linguistically, you can speak precisely by practicing how you say difficult words or phrases. This is an excellent way to use rehearsal time. In terms of scope, you can speak precisely by limiting your ideas and your examples to only those absolutely necessary for your speech. You will appear most competent when you avoid digressing or offering ideas that occur to you for the first time while you are speaking, and when you instead move directly and with intention from one key idea to a useful example or piece of evidence and then to the very next idea, as you prepared in advance. An added benefit of giving your speech a precise scope, only offering ideas that are absolutely necessary, is that you can then develop interesting or important ideas in greater depth. Depth signals competence very effectively in a public speaking situation. You can achieve this when you confine yourself to only to one or two signature ideas that make your speech powerful, and when you use these examples in a way that stimulates your audience's interest and does not confuse them.

San Francisco Mayor London Breed speaks at a "Families Belong Together" rally in San Francisco. By choosing to speak at this occasion and through the language she uses in her speech, she helps her audience positively assess her character as she demonstrates her understanding of the community's values.

A speaker can establish **character** while speaking by using a few carefully chosen phrases throughout the speech that consistently highlight their shared relationship to the audience and the wider community. When you speak about a topic you chose because it has an impact on your local environment, use a variety of words and phrases at a few key points in your speech to highlight this choice ("our neighborhood"; "technology we use every day"). Doing so will remind your audience that you share resources and needs in common with them and will thereby enhance your character as a speaker. Character for a public speaker is always rooted in values the speaker shares with the audience, and your audience will positively assess your character if you demonstrate your understanding of those values from start to finish—in how you dress, how you choose your words, and how well prepared you are to meet your audience's needs. In this way, character cannot be separated easily from the preparation dimensions we explored in the section above.

Closely linked to character is **care**. A speaker can establish a caring relationship to the audience while speaking by engaging whenever possible in taking perspective. How would you feel during your speech if you were an audience member, and what would you want the speaker to do for you? Being well prepared, using time well, and reflecting as much as you can the values you share with your audience are all ways of showing care. Interestingly, in contrast to the "shared community" emphasis we discussed above in connection to character, the most compelling demonstration of care a speaker can offer is to acknowledge—perhaps paradoxically—how the speaker and the audience might *differ*. What other value systems might shape some listeners' assessment of your ideas and might lead those assessments to be negative? How might a novice, inexpert, or (currently) uncaring audience member feel when trying to make sense of the fresh ideas you offer? Use words and phrases that attend to these possible differences ("I understand this can be hard to do at first"; "I ask you to try to imagine that this is true"). Structure your speech so that you can account for how your ideas may be novel, or even potentially unpleasant, to some audience members. If you are gracious and patient with audience members when you encourage them to agree, learn, and/or take action, then you have taken a crucial step toward encouraging agreement and preparing your community to accept change. Preparing your community to accept change—not just intellectually but emotionally—is itself a pedagogical act, one we urge all speakers to respect and take up with a sense of responsibility.

Public Speakers Practice Strategies to Attract and Retain Listeners' Attention

Encouraging listeners to turn their attention to you as fully as possible has always been a challenge for public speakers. Like all dimensions of public speaking, the challenges involved depend on the time, place, and purpose of your speech. Since speeches are dependent on

In a college classroom, students often have cell phones, tablets and/or laptops with them. The teacher (or speaker) in this classroom has to compete with these devices for students' attention. In this setting, teachers will need to use strategies to attract and retain listeners who might get distracted.

assumptions and perceptions grounded in the immediate context, attention-getting and attention-retaining challenges are also excellent opportunities to turn your speaking task into a critical, even transformative practice.

For instance, you are most likely reading this chapter because you were assigned to read it as part of an introductory college course in public speaking, a course in which you will also give several solo speeches for your classmates. These classmates probably have cell phones, tablets and/or laptops with them that compete for their attention, even in classrooms in which the instructor has tried to exclude these electronic devices from the scene. These same classmates may identify with you in a positive way. They may have empathy for you because they know they, too, will be giving speeches themselves in this same class. But their identification with you can have negative consequences: Your listeners may be thinking (especially if they speak on the same day as you do) about their own speeches instead of yours, or they may doubt their own knowledge and preparation and therefore approach your speech with doubts about yours. What can you do in this context to encourage your listeners to focus on your speech with positive anticipation and a genuine spirit of curiosity?

Change the Frame for Your Audience

One way to think about this question is to consider how to **change the focus** for your listeners. Changing your listeners' focus involves deliberately disrupting their sense that they know what you will say and do next. A sense that they will only get what they expect can dull audience members' attention and lead them to listen, look, and think less carefully. A very effective way to disrupt this "I know what's next" sense is to **change the frame** of the communication situation and to make that change obvious or explicit when it happens in your speech. A **frame** is a way we interpret messages, using an idea about what matters most to filter out some communication or treat it as less relevant than other communication. For example, suppose your public speaking instructor arrived for class on the first day dressed in professional attire, but when they opened their briefcase, they could not locate their notes or other materials, became frustrated and agitated, and left the room with red-rimmed eyes without first addressing the class. If just before this instructor arrived, a student in your class had leaned over and told you that this instructor is brand new to the campus and was teaching their very first public speaking class, how would you interpret what you saw? What if this same student, instead, had told you something else just before the instructor arrived: that the instructor, a neighborhood acquaintance of whom this student has some personal knowledge, has very recently had a close family member admitted to the hospital with a serious illness? Would this suggest a different set of interpretations? In this example, you can see how powerfully a frame can shift what we understand in a given situation. Frames can work backward (affecting what we remember) and forward (affecting what we expect), just as much as they can affect our interpretations of ongoing communication.

Now that you know what frames are, you can think of obviously or explicitly changing the frame as an overall strategy to guide your search for creative ways to gain your listeners' attention initially, and to effectively retain their attention later in your speech. You can also use changes to the interpretive frame as ways to heighten the taken-for-granted values in a given situation and call those into question, part of an ongoing critical practice as a speaker. Let's first discuss the initial attention-getting effort by using the concept of frames.

Use an Attention Getter

When you are scheduled to speak next, you might adopt a certain physical position or way of behaving that cues listeners to assume you will speak next—such as standing in front of an assembled audience, checking notes, beginning to control your breathing carefully. At this point, you have not yet redirected their attention in any meaningful way. You need more to draw them into the unique experience of listening to *your* speech rather than just *some* speech. Furthermore, simply checking for quiet mouths, forward-facing bodies, and eye contact cannot ensure that you have gotten their attention either—consider how often your professors make the mistake of equating those body language messages with learners' genuine attention! This opening "stage-taking" moment of your speech is the most important one of your entire speech in terms of encouraging your listeners to attend carefully to you. It is so important that we call the strategy you use in this moment a term all its own—an **attention getter**.

Following the logic of changing the frame, the most powerful way to gain our attention initially would be to change listeners' initial frame in some highly significant way. In your public speaking class, listeners likely expect, as an initial frame, that after taking your turn at the front of the classroom (perhaps behind a lectern) you will

1. begin speaking
2. in your own voice,
3. directly stating your own ideas while
4. looking at them as they look back at you.

Instead of accepting these expectations, how might you change this initial frame and thereby gain listeners' immediate attention? Here are some possibilities:

- **Ask a question** that complicates a key idea or theme in your speech.
- **Illustrate** a key idea or theme using a vivid example.
- **Dramatize** a key idea or theme.

- Use a **different communication mode** apart from your own speaking voice.

- Use **humor** related to a key idea or theme.

Ask a Question

Asking a question invites audience members to consider multiple possibilities. They might avoid listening if your speech involves only one set of certainties that you have settled in advance. When you instead invoke multiple possibilities at the outset of your speech, you create a context of ambiguity in which ideas are tentative and not yet resolved. This encourages listeners to pay attention by fostering their desire to resolve ambiguity and move toward resolution during the course of your speech. Anytime a speaker can send an unresolved message, listeners develop anticipation because we (usually) desire resolution as viewers, readers, and listeners.

The question you ask should be open-ended and genuine; that is, one with multiple possible realistic answers. If you are giving an informative speech about how to create grocery shopping routines that are nutritive and affordable, asking a question like "Would you like to extend your life by providing yourself with better nutrition?" is not an effective attention getter for two reasons: First, answers other than "yes" will seem ludicrous to nearly all listeners, giving the question a ring of falsehood that weakens your credibility right at the start and encouraging listeners to doubt your sincerity. Second, the answer "yes" is one of only two possible answers, given how the question is worded—and indeed quite obviously the much stronger of the two answers—so little ambiguity (and therefore little anticipation) results for your listeners. A better attention-getting question in this case might be "How do you organize your trips to, and around, grocery stores?" This question is open-ended and creates genuine ambiguity for listeners—consider how the introduction of your speech might then propose a few types of answers to that question that would ring true for various different groups of listeners. Also, when phrased this way the question can also become an anchor for additional questions later in the speech that could function as useful transitions, such as "How do grocery store display and marketing experts believe you respond to their messages in the store?" or "How can you organize your visits to grocery stores in ways that match your own dietary goals rather than being passively directed by what you see?"

Illustrate a Key Idea or Theme

You can change the "this is a public speech involving one person saying a lot of words" frame by using a variety of tools that can illustrate an idea right at the start of your speech as an attention-getting device. An illustration can be any form of communication that shows something rather than merely telling it in spoken words. An illustration need not be limited to a visual artifact like a photograph, drawing, or diagram (though these are three good examples of illustrations). You can illustrate an idea by sharing numerical evidence, such as **statistics** or other quantitative research that relates to an issue in your speech. If you choose to do this, be

Speakers can use humor in speaking situations to grab audience attention. Humor has great appeal as an attention-getter for many speakers because we associate our audience's laughter with affirmation of our role as speaker, and because humor itself is based on surprise—on changing the frame.

aware that listeners are sometimes wary of lot of numbers, especially if they are shared orally and therefore hard to keep in the mind. If you use statistical evidence as an attention getter, you should share very important numbers that are easy to understand (often, accompanying these with a chart or other visual image can help ensure this). You can also use an object as an illustration, an especially effective attention getter if you are giving an informative speech that demonstrates how to create or use the object or an informative speech that explores a theme closely associated with an object (such as the equipment used in a less-well-known sport). Remember that you are choosing an illustration because you intend to change the audience's frame, so your illustration should be visually interesting (drawing their eyes, heightening their curiosity) and easy to see.

Dramatize a Key Idea or Theme

One way that the authors of plays, screenplays, and novels strive to help their words show us ideas and themes, rather than just telling us about them, is to use drama. Drama involves human conflict, in which at least one person encounters other people whose needs or goals come into conflict with her own. The conflict need not be immediately resolved, and when you use drama as an attention getter, it should be deliberately left unresolved at first so that you create and sustain ambiguity for your listeners. An obvious example of a use of a dramatic attention getter would be to show audience members a scene from a film or television show; if you are fortunate enough to have willing classmates or friends, you could even use a dramatic attention getter involving a brief live performance (though time constraints can make this difficult for many classroom speaking assignments). Moreover, testimony from a person, such as a memorable quotation, is also a way of changing the frame to a dramatic one if you contextualize the quotation well, because you are putting those words in the body of another person besides yourself, highlighting that person's needs or goals in the process. An effective way to contextualize a quotation you use at the start of your speech is with a photograph of the person; another is to immediately follow the quotation with a brief (one- or two-sentence) discussion of what the quotation means. Either or both of these contextualization efforts are useful, as your goal is to gain your listeners' attention by shifting the frame to a dramatic conflict involving a person other than yourself.

Use a Different Communication Mode

Your listeners may well expect you to adopt the "public speaking voice" we have so often normalized in our society: calm rather than excited, serious rather than humorous, declarative (ending sentences with a slight drop in pitch on the final word or phrase) rather than interrogative (ending sentences with a slight increase in pitch on the final word or phrase). An attention getter has the advantage of creating a simple change in your vocal tone and pitch if you, for instance, ask a question. The **communication mode** is the manner or style in which you address others (for example, by sharing words in writing or orally; by using *we* language, *I* language, or *you* language when stating ideas; by using an angry or a silly voice). You can change the mode of your communication in other ways as well. The easiest example is changing your volume by shouting or whispering, though this has risks or obstacles depending on the setting and has very limited effectiveness (the more we shout, the less meaningful it becomes). You can change multiple qualities of your voice at once to create or mimic a speaking style other than your own (though see the section below on humor for challenges associated with this choice). You can sing a phrase. You can use a recording of your voice that you made in advance to change the mode as well. Again, the value of these choices is that they change the frame for listeners, fostering immediate attention because they contrast initial expectations.

Use Humor

Humor has great appeal as an attention getter for many speakers because we associate our audience's laughter with affirmation of our role as speaker, and because humor itself is based on surprise—on changing the frame. Consider one of our favorite jokes:

Two people walk into a bar.
The third one ducks.

This joke is an excellent example of changing the frame, from "entering a place where alcohol is served" to "while moving forward, striking one's body against a long, thin, hard object."

The joke also illustrates how humor involves rapidly setting up an expectation for listeners, then breaking that expectation in an unforeseen way, prompting laughter; a "bad" joke is one for which we can foresee the punch line from the outset.

Though it is easy to see why humor would be an effective way of changing the frame and simultaneously encouraging audience members to positively orient to you, there are a few challenges to consider: First, using humor requires precision and therefore practice. If you have not typically been an effective user of humor in your everyday life, you should rehearse your humorous attention getter with trusted friends or family first so that you develop comfort with your ideas. Second, some speakers are tempted to use humor in ways that are only indirectly—or very distantly—related to their key ideas or themes. Though the initial laughter from your audience is appealing, you should only use humor if it also directs your audience's attention to your topic (the joke quoted above, for instance, is likely not an effective attention getter even if you believe it is funny, because it is not related to any socially significant college-level speech topic). Third, some speakers are tempted to use humor that invokes stereotypes about people, cultures, or ideas—perhaps because such humor is mistakenly viewed as generalizable across groups of listeners. However, you should never use these forms of humor, for multiple reasons. Stereotype-based jokes dull listeners' empathy by promoting a view of human life that reduces a person to a type. Stereotyping actually happens commonly in communication and can be useful in reducing uncertainty in some situations, but it is an especially destructive form of humor in a public speaking situation. Stereotype-based jokes undermine your audience members' trust and thereby greatly weaken your credibility, because if you are willing to poke fun at *some* people on a public speaking stage, you are sending the message that you support—and indeed embrace—poking fun at *any people* in such a setting—including, of course, *any* audience member.

Public Speakers Reshape Their Frames and Their Expectations

We chose to describe the attention-getting strategies in this section as examples within the larger logic of **changing the frame**, instead of simply listing them as useful attention getters, for two reasons: First, if your ideas for attention getters flow from your efforts to change the frame for listeners in any one moment, you can use this same approach to generate ideas for transition sentences, and for ways to retain listeners' attention, throughout your speech. As you organize your speech into coherent groups of smaller ideas (see Chapter 6), you should consider changing the frame in some way to signal to your audience that they should attend carefully to a new main point, example, or argument. Transition sentences in an outline are one way to do this, but you will give yourself many more creative—and subtle—ideas for retaining attention if you brainstorm ways to bolster your transitions with changes to the listening frame.

> "The mind is not a vessel that needs filling, but wood that needs igniting—no more—and then it motivates one towards originality and instills the desire for truth. Suppose someone were to go and ask his neighbours for fire and find a substantial blaze there, and just stay there continually warming himself: that is no different from someone who goes to someone else to get some of his rationality, and fails to realize that he ought to ignite his innate flame, his own intellect."
>
> —Plutarch

Second, as a speaker the frames you consider as you prepare to speak can highlight for you any assumptions you may have about your audience, their communication values, and their expectations within the speaking situation. Once you begin to examine your own assumptions about how your audience is approaching your speech, you can recognize how your speech is always setting an agenda. Your speech sets an agenda in part by confirming some of your audience members' values and expectations about communication and about your topic (and your own assumptions about these), and also by extending or even challenging other values and expectations. In this way, planning a lively, mutually engaging relationship with the audience becomes a critical practice for public speakers. As we prepare to speak, our plans and our actions acknowledge the values underlying the situation and explore those values that may often go unexamined.

Emily Doe's victim impact statement, which opens this chapter, changes the frame. She changes the frame of discourse surrounding sexual predation and violence, both in her speaking choices, which serve to enhance the pedagogical intention of her words, and in her decision to publish the statement widely. Concerned citizens accessed Ms. Doe's impact statement online more than 6 million times in the 2 weeks following the sentencing of assailant Brock Turner to 6 months in county jail, leading directly to questions about Aaron Persky's credibility on the judge's bench (D'Angelo, 2016). She clearly was able to meaningfully engage her online listeners. On June 15, 2016, members of the U.S. Congress read Ms. Doe's statement aloud—the first time such a statement has ever been entered into the congressional record—challenging readers and listeners to acknowledge and address crimes of sexual violence on college campuses and beyond.

Public Speakers Advocate for Specific Transformations

We began this chapter with the claim that all public speeches are pedagogical. We consider this important because it emphasizes how effective speakers begin by attending to their relationships within a community and to their audience. It also emphasizes how speakers set an agenda while speaking and, in doing so, change their communities through the act of speaking. We contend that this is true even for primarily informative speeches, for the reasons outlined in this chapter. Let's take a closer look at Emily Doe's victim impact statement to discuss some of the pedagogical effects of her speech.

When offering her impact statement, Doe directly acknowledges her purpose and her multilayered, complex audience. She does so in the first two sentences of her speech by addressing the judge in the first sentence, signaling in that sentence that her attacker will be her addressee for "the majority of this statement," and then using a second-person mode of speaking in that second sentence with "you," "you" again, and "we" as language choices. The judge is the person in this context who authorizes her role and her opportunity to speak. In this way, he is parallel to the organizational and institutional forces always at work—from supervisors to colleagues to civic workers policing streets—who provide space and time for you to address an assembled audience. Doe is effective as an informative speaker because she attends, from start to finish, to the resources she shares with others in the community (for example, a safe public space in which each of us has the freedom to walk without fear; an assumption of common goodness even among strangers, as two strangers demonstrated when they helped her as they witnessed the assault) and how her role as an informative speaker depends on those resources.

Doe's Impact Statement Pays Attention to Audience

Doe's choice to address her attacker directly in the next sentence of her speech is an excellent example of the power of indexing your distinctive relationship to your audience when you speak. This is a complex speaking situation because a victim impact statement delivered in a public courtroom has multiple audiences: the judge (and potentially the jury in some other courtrooms) deciding on an appropriate sentence; the audience assembled in the courtroom who, given their attendance, likely have a strong personal connection to this case; and, as occurred in this case, the wider public who gain access to this statement through press coverage of the case. Doe's speech helps educate us about the experiences of a young woman enduring, surviving, and living beyond a sexual assault; it reflects her careful consideration of these multiple audiences and her relationship to them. The decision to speak in a mode that directly addresses a single audience member—her attacker—has profound implications for what we learn and how we learn from her experiences. It might be chilling and sorrowful for you to imagine the difficulty Doe faces in speaking directly to a person (Brock Turner) convicted of sexually violating her body while she was unconscious and vulnerable in a public place (behind a dumpster on a university campus); it is for us, the authors. Yet as we move forward with our discussion of this speech, consider how the choice to address Turner as "you" gives Doe the opportunity to inform him, and the additional audiences, about her experiences. Consider how her statement is precisely relevant to this speaker's roles within the community: daughter, sister, partygoer, girlfriend, stranger, survivor, advocate. Doe is effective as an informative speaker because everything she teaches us flows from those distinctive roles.

> "In transformative pedagogy [...] the goal includes generating knowledge but extends from the classroom to the community."
>
> — Joan Wink

Doe's Impact Statement Changes Frames

As Doe strives to educate her audience about the ways rape survivors are often further demeaned by subsequent narratives about the relative roles and status of women and men, she offers observations regarding press coverage. Her attacker, a university swimmer, was named and his athletic accomplishments noted in a news story about the assault, even though these accolades were arguably irrelevant to the sexual assault charges themselves. Doe says, "Throw in my mile time if that's what we're doing. I'm good at cooking, put that in there, I think the end is where you list your extra-curriculars to cancel out all the sickening things that've happened." This is an example of changing the frame for audience members both to help negotiate our focus and to better educate us. Her marked changing of the frame here—from a characterization of her response ("according to him [Turner] I liked it") to a list of swim times—helps sustain our careful attention to her enduring suffering beyond the assault itself. She indexes for us her role as a survivor whose life is taken up (often in inaccurate or demeaning ways) in news stories. This change of frame also helps her teach us about the potential impact of journalistic frameworks when those frameworks are yoked to sexist systems.

Doe's pedagogical work through much of this speech relies on the speaking strategy of juxtaposing two incongruous frames with one another. Another example is when she says, "The

In her impact statement, Doe changes the frame to help audience members stay intimately aware and present as she describes the suffering she experienced. Doe submitted language used in her impact statement to Stanford to be included on a plaque on campus marking the site of her attack. Unfortunately, Stanford and Doe were unable to agree upon language, and Doe disaffiliated herself with the proposed plaque.

night after it happened, he said he thought I liked it because I rubbed his back. A back rub. Never mentioned me voicing consent, never mentioned us speaking, a back rub." This device helps teach us what relevant consent to sexual activity means among two people.

Doe's Impact Statement Has Credibility and Expertise

An excellent illustration in Doe's statement of the way that informing and persuading an audience, in any public speaking situation, are always necessarily intertwined and inseparable is in this passage: "I was not only told that I was assaulted, I was told that because I couldn't remember, I technically could not prove it was unwanted. And that distorted me, damaged me, almost broke me." On an informative level, the evidentiary standards that shape criminal sexual assault cases, including those related to affirmative consent, memory, and burden of proof, are central to Doe's speech. She does not cite any criminal code or case law, and in this speaking context her claims have credibility grounded in her experience as the victim of a crime. Yet as she links in this passage what is technically true according to criminal probity standards to what is true for her as a speaker, citizen, and person ("distorted me, damaged me, almost broke me"), Doe also acknowledges that jurisprudential "proof" depends on *credible recall*. For this reason, she suggests that we must ask and answer questions about a survivor's ability to engage in both recall (after being intoxicated) and a credible testimony position. Doe reports that when she was required to maintain the posture of credible witness to her own assault, that posture in this case was at least "distorted" and "damaged," and "almost broken." She implies here that a grave injustice can result when the very factors strengthening testimony—precise recall of events and an assured posture of credibility—are themselves undermined by the crime of rape itself and especially by its aftermath as others narrate that crime for and with the survivor. Though few public speaking settings are as complex as this one, we suggest that untangling informative and persuasive purposes is not productive for parallel reasons: Issues such as credibility and expertise cannot be separated from the persuasive dimensions of a speaker's relationship to their audience.

"Assault Is Not an Accident"

Doe's courtroom statement demonstrates the positive effects of speaker preparation and the informative dimensions of public speaking (dimensions we have termed *pedagogical*). She acknowledges her purpose and audience directly. She allows her purpose and her beliefs about her audience to shape her choice of communication mode, her strategies for getting and maintaining audience attention, and her development of the frames of reference that she hopes will educate her audience. She is in a unique position to speak credibly on topics related to surviving sexual assault and preventing sexual assault. These effective choices, we find, make her victim impact statement much more far reaching in its value than the limited sphere of a courtroom. In short, she teaches us that sexual assault is never accidental.

Concepts

attention getter 95
care 92
change the focus 94
change the frame 94
character 92
communication mode 98
competence 91
credibility 85

focused attention 83
frame 94
informative speech 81
pedagogical 81
pedagogy 82
scope 88
speaker preparation 87
syntax 88

Toward Praxis

1. **Reflection:** Consider a time in which a speaker has attempted to educate you. In what ways was this speaker informative, and in what ways were they persuasive? How did this speaker's role in your life or in your community affect the way they approached educating you?

2. **Discussion:** What is the role of public speaking in sustaining and transforming culture? What is a speaker's responsibility to affirm cultural norms? What is a speaker's responsibility to critique and challenge culture norms? If we miss an opportunity to expose or challenge injustice, are we then complicit in violence?

3. **Action:** Practice discerning frames and options for changing them. You can do this by following a story in the media—what are the expectations surrounding communication in this situation? Who is served by those expectations? Who is harmed? How might a change in the frame alter the expectations of the people encountering that story? You can also explore frames in your relationships: Do you have a complicated relationship with someone? In what ways is that relationship sustained, for better and for worse, by the communication frame that surrounds it?

Discussion Questions

1 When have you felt heard by an audience? What conditions made that more or less likely? What steps did you take to share yourself?

2 In what ways is speaker preparation an ethical responsibility?

3 What would you say is the most important issue for people to better understand and address? How is that issue currently framed? Does that framing make it easier or harder for people to articulate their hopes and fears with respect to that issue?

Public Speaking Is Structured

In this chapter, we will work together to:

- Explore how the structure of public communication evolves from both the speaker's and the listeners' needs
- Use effective outlining techniques to structure your speech
- Identify different organizational strategies you can use to strengthen your message
- Identify elements of effective introductions, transitions, and conclusions

Earlier this year, I visited the Kara Tepe camp on the island of Lesbos, Greece. I sat with families in their 4×3 makeshift rooms. I walked with them along the grounds. The sun was out, but the air was heavy: full of hopelessness, exhaustion, and fear.

While I was there, I heard the same questions over and over again:

"Is this home?"

"Will we be sent back?"

"What do I tell my children?"

And, most of all, most urgently:

"Where do we go from here?"

These questions are being repeated 65 million times every day. In Latin America. Africa. Asia. Europe. And across the Middle East.

Global forced displacement has hit a record high. It is a record of tragic proportions. Millions of people have had the misfortune of being born in a place so wracked by violence, poverty, persecution, or insecurity that they had no choice but to leave.

To leave on foot . . . To leave by boat . . . To leave packed in trucks . . . not knowing what the next day would bring . . . much less where the future would lead.

Their question—"Where do we go from here?"—must be our question too.

(Queen Rania, 2016)

In her speech before the UN Summit for Refugees and Migrants, Queen Rania of Jordan draws in her listeners, organizing her thoughts to support her listeners' attention, engagement, and empathy. She immediately establishes her credibility as someone who strives to understand the experience of seeking refuge, inviting her listeners to do the same. She invites us to feel the fear and the hopelessness. She invites us to make refugees' questions our own: "Where do we go from here?" This sequence of steps demonstrates that Queen Rania has considered the ways that the ideas she wants to share are structured with respect to one another—which ideas should be shared first, which ones have greatest prominence, and so on. These elements of structure are the subject of this chapter.

Queen Rania, Selection from "Speech at UN Summit for Refugees and Migrants." Copyright © 2016 by Queen Rania Al-Abdullah.

Appropriate structure is essential to the success of communication, no matter whether we're talking about the written or spoken word. Yet all too often, we tend to think of structure quite rigidly, as a series of prescriptions about what must happen where, instead of as a necessary component of building meaning together with one's audience. For example, many students learn to write a five-paragraph essay at some point in school. Though there is logic to that structure—an introduction, supporting paragraphs, and a conclusion—there is nothing magical about the number five, and it certainly does not apply to every writing situation (as we usually learn when we have to write lengthier works). The same is true for our speech.

Our job as speakers is to provide enough emphasis and repetition to help our listeners remember and apply what we've discussed with them. While there are many fine recommendations to help you do that, there is no magic formula that will render universal success.

Our goal in this chapter is to help you understand and apply principles of effective organization to your public communication. An important part of this process involves recognizing that structure and organization emerge from a particular speaking context and from the needs of the speaker and their listeners. We will review common organizational patterns too—not because they are simple formulas or recipes to follow, but because they can help provide you with inspiration for meaningfully developing and arranging your ideas. This will mean exploring **outlining**, which is the process of organizing ideas so that they are precisely related to one another in terms of both appropriate sequence and level of importance. Appropriate sequence means which ideas come first, then next, and so on; level of importance means which ideas are most important, which ideas are smaller parts of more significant ideas. The process of outlining your ideas is essential to understanding and strengthening some of the more taken-for-granted and overlooked aspects of your communication. Finally, we will discuss ways you can make your speeches powerful by structuring your introductions, transitions, and conclusions.

Structure Emerges From the Speaker's and the Listeners' Needs

Structure, the effort to place ideas or objects in a meaningful order, is as essential to effective public communication as it is to other endeavors. Architects use blueprints to create safe, durable, and attractive buildings. Consultants or managers may use flow charts to develop and illustrate the movement of ideas or objects through an organization. Teachers develop lesson plans to clarify and better assess the outcomes of their lessons. In each of these cases, the person with creative force and drive must first identify their goals. For a public speech, you may have a specific goal in mind—and once your goal is named, you can set to work clarifying your rationale, identifying specific supporting examples and developing all the parts of the speech.

The goal of your speech guides the structure and organization of your communication, but your goal will always exist in relationship to your listeners' needs. For example, you may

Architects work with clients to identify their needs and goals when designing a house. Without the struture and vision architects bring to the design process, it would be hard to get a house started, let alone completed. Public speakers need to have a similar attention to structure and goals when preparing a speech.

want to persuade people to support an organization you've helped found, but to do that effectively, you will have to educate them on the issues at hand and how they are implicated in (how they contribute to or are affected by) those issues. This means that you must engage in audience analysis in order to determine the most effective structure for your speech. By thoughtfully analyzing your audience, you will be better able to sequence your examples and sources and shape your language in ways that a particular group of people will appreciate and take to heart.

People who engage in public speaking do so to effect change. In order to do this, they must first be memorable. Being memorable has a lot to do with saying and doing things as a speaker that are surprising to listeners. This might include unusual language choices, particularly vivid examples, or a passionate and engaging tone. However, being memorable also includes the important work of helping listeners retain or remember information from a speech. Helping someone retain or remember information involves crafting and carefully marking (through your words as well as your nonverbal delivery) the structural components of the speech.

Moreover, clear, memorable structure is undeniably helpful to you as a speaker. If you know your speech has stable, predictable elements (an introduction with three parts, a body with two main points—with one strength and one weakness each) then you will have an easier time sharing your message with your listeners. Knowing your talking points helps you speak *with* rather than *at* your listeners in a conversational, compelling way. Even in our YouTube era, most speeches are ephemeral—fleeting and inextricably tied to a particular moment in time. Speeches typically emerge from a unique and rapidly changing context. Because anything can change in a moment (imagine a speaker having to respond to a heckler or other distraction), structure helps keep both the speaker and their listeners focused. There's an old saying that

CHAPTER 6 | PUBLIC SPEAKING IS STRUCTURED

If you've ever been to see a comedian perform they probably utilized techniques that left you feeling a range of emotions. People who engage in public speaking need to be memorable, in order to effect change. Being memorable has a lot to do with saying and doing things as a speaker that are surprising to listeners. Sometimes comedians use engaging language, vivid examples, or do funny voices and imitations. What techniques might make someone memorable as a public speaker?

repetition is the mother of learning. In public speaking, repetition (in the form of structure, but perhaps also in the form of practice) helps you stay on point and helps your listeners understand and act accordingly.

Outlining Is a Helpful Means of Developing, Grouping, and Sequencing Your Main Ideas

Because outlining can help you develop, group, and sequence your main ideas, it is a helpful way to organize your speeches. By *developing*, we mean that outlining can help you flesh out what you mean to say so that you don't forget something important. By *grouping*, we mean that outlining can help you assemble your ideas so that your listener can better follow and remember them. By *sequencing*, we mean that outlining can help you put your ideas in the order that will most effectively respond to your listeners' needs, interests, and concerns. While we'll focus on outlining here and why we (and likely also your instructor) find it so valuable, it is important to know that there are also many other ways of developing and ordering your ideas (for example, free writing and concept mapping can help with brainstorming and demonstrating the links from one idea to another). If you have given outlining an earnest effort, and you still don't feel like it's the most effective means for you to organize your ideas, you still have other tools you can try.

Develop Your Speech

Though we could be wrong, we'd venture to guess that most people do not organically or automatically think in outline form—or, at least, not the sorts of outlines that contain Roman numerals and careful indentation. We usually learn how to outline in school, and this can be a frustrating exercise for some, especially if it's not obvious why outlining even matters. Perhaps the most valuable outcome of building an outline is that it helps you **develop** your speech. In other words, outlining can help you define early on what your speech should and should not include. Without outlining, speakers run the risk of repeating themselves or forgetting something important they'd hoped to say. Let's take, for example, a demonstration speech topic like "how to build a compost bin." How many steps are there in that process? Depending on how you develop the speech, there could be three steps or there could be 10 steps. Which step comes first? Second? Third? Listeners can only absorb a limited amount of information, even during a brief presentation, so speakers must clearly identify and order their main ideas. To help listeners retain information from their speeches, most public speakers strive to limit their speeches to addressing two to five main ideas. Further, because it serves as the spine of a speech, an outline helps the speaker remember to include important components, from attention-getting material to a final, memorable closing remark or **clincher**, and all the points in between.

Effective public speakers use outlines to help organize their speeches. Outlines can help you organize your thoughts, flesh out what you want to say, and make sure you haven't forgotten anything important. Outlines also help you group similar concepts together and help you decide on an order that will be most effective to get your message across.

Perhaps the most common formal outlines for public speeches are the full-sentence outline and the "keyword" or presentational outline. The first of these, the **full-sentence outline**, usually begins as a **working outline**, something you develop in stages and layers as you think through what you hope to accomplish with your speech. Part of what makes this outline formal will be the use of alphanumerically ordered complete sentences. (A **keyword outline**, in contrast, is as it sounds: a collection of key words and phrases that help you remember essential information and the logic that links it meaningfully to the listeners. That more skeletal outline helps you stay focused without being tempted to read word for word or otherwise compromise your delivery.) For example:

SPECIAL ELEMENT 6.1

Sample Keyword Outline

I. Main Point 1
   A. Supporting Point 1
      1. Evidence 1
      2. Evidence 2
   B. Supporting Point 2
      1. Evidence 1
      2. Evidence 2

Transition

II. Main Point 2
   A. Supporting Point 1
      1. Evidence 1
      2. Evidence 2
   B. Supporting Point 2
      1. Evidence 1
      2. Evidence 2

And so on . . . Remember, not every outline will look like this. Public speaking professors are very likely to have elements they recommend or require that deviate from this model. Moreover, your outline may have four main points or three instances of support for an idea instead of two. However, even this brief example helps illustrate that balance, creating a well-rounded and easy-to-follow structure that is desirable to formal oral communication. The more you can do to help your listeners track and remember information from your presentation, the more likely you will be to achieve your goals as a speaker.

Group Your Ideas

Outlining also helps speakers group their ideas, clarifying the connections between ideas. Outlines are distinct from lists or concept maps in that they can help you represent and clarify the coordination and subordination of ideas. In other words, you can use an outline to determine whether two or more ideas are equal in importance or whether one functions as a supporting point to the other(s). Further, by situating your ideas in relation to each other, you can also better evaluate whether you have comparable evidence (in amount and quality) to support each one.

Coordination refers to the process of developing ideas that are comparable and parallel, while **subordination** refers to the process of discerning which ideas are more significant to your argument than others. Using a consistent outlining format, with ideas coordinated with one another, can be helpful to you.

Coordination of ideas helps listeners remember information from your presentation by prioritizing the main points of the speech. Here are examples of stronger and weaker coordination from a persuasive speech about the need for a veteran student organization:

SPECIAL ELEMENT 6.2

Weaker:
I. Veterans may struggle with others' immaturity in the classroom.
II. There are many different kinds of student veterans.
III. Student organizations represent different types of students.
IV. Veterans need to be aware of campus support services.

Stronger:
I. Veterans face complex challenges we might not always notice or understand.
II. Veterans deserve a student organization that will increase awareness of their needs.

The first outline is weaker because the main points are not mutually exclusive or discrete. To say an idea is mutually exclusive means that it can stand on its own. Here there is overlap between the main ideas, which are uneven in importance and wording. The more you can group like with like (framing ideas as such for your listeners), the more you and your listeners will remember from your presentation.

Subordination also helps you develop ideas that are of approximately equal weight and importance. For example:

SPECIAL ELEMENT 6.3

Weaker:

I. Veterans face complex challenges we might not always notice or understand.
   A. They may struggle with trauma.
   B. They may struggle with their mental health.
   C. They may have lingering health problems.
   D. They may face social stigma and misunderstanding of their role.

Stronger:

I. Veterans face complex challenges we might not always notice or understand.
   A. Student veterans face social challenges.
      1. Other students may misunderstand a veteran's service.
      2. Other students may unknowingly frustrate a student veteran.
   B. Student veterans face health challenges.
      1. They may be recovering from visible injuries.
      2. They may be recovering from invisible injuries.

Again, the first outline is weaker because the supporting points are not mutually exclusive (they overlap), and they are not parallel in scope or importance. At this stage in the outlining process, the stronger outline identifies two specific types of challenges student veterans face (social and health). What can make outlining so special and so useful is the way engaging in it helps you focus on pattern recognition. Recognizing patterns—overlap of time and order, of importance or neglect—can help you strengthen your thinking and how you express those ideas with your listeners. This process of discovering (or building, depending on how you see it) the body of your speech can be an empowering process. It helps you take ownership not only of your ideas but of how you share them with others and the effect(s) you hope to have.

Order Your Ideas

Outlining can also help you **order** your ideas, putting them into sequences that you and your listeners will find logical or effective. There are common **organizational patterns** that can help you order your ideas in ways that are pleasing and useful to both you and your listeners. An organizational pattern is a guide for how to arrange your ideas. For example, you might choose to order your ideas **chronologically** (i.e., as they developed over time), **spatially** or geographically (i.e., by where they are located in space or on a map), or **sequentially** (i.e., as steps in a process). Because informative and persuasive speeches often involve many different perspectives, speakers may find it helpful to order their ideas along a **compare–contrast**, **cause–effect**, **advantage–disadvantage**, or **problem–solution** pattern. As their names suggest, these patterns help speakers shape the content of their speech into recognized, expected arrangements that help create a sense of interest and drama for the listener.

> "And this is why I like timetables, because they make sure you don't get lost in time."
>
> — Mark Haddon

A compare–contrast pattern sets two (usually; occasionally there are more than two) distinct ideas against one another, allowing the speaker to best illustrate and complicate each idea by showing which elements one idea has in common with the other and which elements make one idea meaningfully different from the other. A cause–effect pattern shows that one idea or set of ideas, usually ideas that have very strong evidence to support them or that are well-known to audience members, will necessarily and directly lead to an effect or series of effects (usually this series of effects are the key ideas in the speech, the ones newest to audience members). An advantage–disadvantage pattern is similar to a compare–contrast pattern in that two (or more) ideas are set against one another, but in this pattern all the comparisons and contrasts involve an assessment of what is worthy or useful about each idea in comparison or contrast to the next. Finally, a problem–solution pattern is similar in form to a cause–effect pattern, but in this pattern strong evidence is presented to frame a problem that must be solved in order for the community to be whole and successful.

Persuasive speakers will often choose a problem–solution speech pattern, but we'd like to suggest here another, slightly modified version of this speech pattern called **Monroe's motivated sequence (MMS)** (Monroe, 1943). This sequence, unlike a problem–solution pattern, challenges a speaker to more fully and explicitly meet the needs of their listeners. There are five steps to MMS: attention, need, satisfaction, visualization, and action. In the **attention** step, you draw the listeners in, helping them see the relevance of the speech to their lives. In the **need** step, you demonstrate to the listeners that they have a need that your speech can resolve (this is particularly important when listeners may not realize that they have the need you've identified). In the **satisfaction** step, you explain precisely how your proposal meets the listeners' needs (i.e., how you can solve their problem). The **visualization** step is perhaps the most important part of MMS and represents a departure from how many speakers approach a problem–solution speech. In the visualization step, you help your listeners imagine how their lives will be improved for adopting or harmed for not adopting your recommendations. Finally, in the **action** step, you challenge your listeners to take particular steps to make your solution a reality. Taken together, these steps form a sequence that is often effective in helping speakers craft convincing arguments.

Organizing your ideas begins from your thesis and goals for the speech and challenges you to develop balanced and well-supported main points. Outlining can help you develop your main points so that they are effective with your particular listeners. Those main points form the body of your speech, but your introduction, your transitions, and your conclusion form the spine. They guide your listeners into, through, and beyond your speech.

You Can Strengthen Your Introductions, Transitions, and Conclusions for a Powerful Speech

Because listeners will often only have one opportunity to hear your speech, it is important that you make the most of the opportunity. We have already considered how structuring your speech can help you better achieve your goals by making it easier for your listeners to track and remember information from your speech and also help you as the speaker. If you can easily remember the different elements of your speech, you will be more engaging and more credible as a speaker (you're also more likely to enjoy the opportunity to speak). The importance of organization extends to the role of introductions, transitions, and conclusions. These are the places in your speech where you're most likely to forecast or give transparent clues about the order and meaning of your ideas to your listeners. Moreover, these three elements of your speech are guided by structures of their own. Following these structures can help you make your introductions, transitions, and conclusions memorable and effective, for you and your listeners.

A Strong Introduction Establishes Your Relationship to the Topic and the Listener

A strong speech introduction does more than set you on the right path to sharing your ideas in a structured and compelling way—it also helps you establish your own relationship to the topic and cultivate a rapport with your listeners. Though chapters in public speaking textbooks run the very real risk of making the task of building a strong introduction seem formulaic, a good introduction is not only a creative art, it is particularly interpersonal. This makes sense if you think about other introductions you experience in your own life—for example, when you meet someone new. In those moments of introduction, you and the person you're meeting are engaged in **impression management**—efforts to shape your own and that other person's perception of who you are. No matter the context, a well-crafted introduction draws your listeners' interest, shows you are knowledgeable and trustworthy with respect to the ideas or issues at hand, implicates your listeners and shows how they are also affected or touched by the ideas or issues in your speech, and provides both you and your listeners with a structure to navigate the speech.

"In all chaos there is a cosmos, in all disorder a secret order"

— Carl Jung

EMPOWERING PUBLIC SPEAKING

When you meet someone new for the first time you usually want to make a good impression. Similarly, when you are beginning a speech you want to start your speech in a manner that is engaging and leaves listeners with a positive impression of you and what you intend to talk about.

A Strong Introduction Draws Your Listeners' Interest

Effective attention getters establish or reaffirm a connection between the speaker, the listeners, and the topic. To this end, it is important to remember that attention-getting material is usually more than a quick phrase, quotation, or joke—it is a sustained effort to align those three vectors. For example, an attention getter might be a story or extended example that opens a speech—one that the speaker revisits periodically throughout to create common ground with their listeners. It may help to think of the attention getter as dialogic, as an invitation to a conversation with (instead of at) the listeners. This might be a literal back-and-forth (where the speaker asks listeners open-ended questions that help guide and shape the speech), or it might be a metaphorical dialogue (where the speaker uses rhetorical questions that help open up spaces for the listeners to imagine or question).

A Strong Introduction Demonstrates You Are Knowledgeable and Trustworthy

It is important for speakers to establish themselves as credible very early on in the speech. This is, in the basest terms, a matter of showing that you've earned the right to speak to a given issue. As we've discussed earlier, your credibility may stem from your direct experience with a subject or from your own consultation of knowledgeable and trustworthy sources. You also establish your credibility when you engage your listeners directly and conversationally (instead of stiffly reading from your outline). Perhaps the most important resource you have—in some ways more valuable than money—is your attention. How you direct your attention and to whom has a lot to do with whether you think that source is worth your time and effort. If you

CHAPTER 6 | PUBLIC SPEAKING IS STRUCTURED | 117

Stories are often used in public speaking to capture the audience's attention. Expert public speakers know how to weave stories and examples into their speeches to create connection between the topic, speaker, and listeners.

are going to command the attention of a group of people, then you will need to help them understand that you are relevant and why your voice matters.

A Strong Introduction Shows Listeners How They Are Also Affected by the Ideas or Issues

In some ways, this observation goes hand in hand with the importance of establishing yourself as a credible speaker. Not only is it your responsibility as the speaker to clearly communication why you are someone whose ideas deserve your listeners' attention, you must also show your listeners that they affect or are in some way affected by the issue you're raising. In other words, in listening to you, your listeners need to understand that they are not only being courteous to you or doing you a favor, they are also serving their own interests and goals.

A Strong Introduction Provides You and Your Listeners With a Structural Forecast of the Speech

Many public speaking teachers like to clarify how structuring a speech works with the saying "tell me what you're going to tell me, tell me, and then tell me what you told me." While that may sound repetitive—in truth, it is repetitive—that repetition serves an important function: It helps the listener stay focused and attentive to your communication. Your introduction is where you begin to share your organizational structure to your listeners, often in the form of a **preview statement**. Your preview statement usually follows your thesis and indicates how you will support that thesis. This will often include enumeration (numbering your ideas for clarity—e.g., "first, I will show you X; second, I will establish that X leads to Y, and then finally I will show you how the two taken together lead us to Z"), and includes a structural overview of your main points.

EMPOWERING PUBLIC SPEAKING

Speakers who are able to stand in front of a large group of people and connect with the audience, rather than reading from notes, command listeners' attention. Think of the last time you saw someone give a speech. Did they look down the entire time and read notes, or did they look at the audience, make eye contact, and appear at ease?

A Strong Transition Meaningfully Links Ideas Together and to Your Thesis

Transitions are an essential component of forming a compelling argument. **Transitions** function as connective tissue that binds one idea or main point to the next. A speaker uses transitional statements not only to signal that they are moving from one idea to another but to show why that movement is logical and necessary to appreciating and acting on their ideas.

A Strong Transition Provides Order for Ideas

It is important for transitions to help listeners stay engaged, in large part by helping them follow the logic and order of the speech. To this end, transitions often include enumerators like *first*, *second*, and *third*.

A Strong Transition Identifies Causes and Their Effects

Transitions also establish the meaning that builds between ideas with phrases like "in order to better understand X, we must first discuss Y" or "in order to take action, you must first have a clear understanding of X."

A Strong Transition Gives Reasons for a Speaker's Claims

Finally, transitions help listeners discern and appreciate not only *that* they are moving from one topic to another but also *why they are doing so*. They are less a technical detail and more a meaningful connection between speaker and listeners—yet one more opportunity for the speaker to strengthen their case.

CHAPTER 6 | PUBLIC SPEAKING IS STRUCTURED

A Strong Conclusion Leaves a Lasting Impression and Inspires Your Listeners to Action

If a strong introduction is effective in part because it takes advantage of the **primacy effect** by making a memorable first impression, then a strong conclusion achieves a similar end by taking advantage of the **recency effect** by offering the listeners an idea or insight that will stay with them long after you've finished speaking. Just as the first 5 minutes and the final 5 minutes of a classroom lecture are often the most important to understanding the content of a lesson, the first thing and the last thing listeners hear will shape their perceptions of a given speech and whether it will continue to resonate for them long beyond the speaker's allotted time. A well-crafted conclusion provides a review of your main ideas, again implicates your listeners in the goal(s) for your speech, reminds them of the steps they should take next given what you've shared, and leaves listeners to reflect on a powerful closing statement or clincher.

A Strong Conclusion Provides a Review of Your Main Ideas

The conclusion is an opportunity to restate your case and remind your listeners of what they have learned in the course of your time together. A **review statement** revisits and underscores your earlier main points. Moreover, reviewing your main points helps create a sense of closure to the speech, that you are bringing your talk to a close.

A Strong Conclusion Shares the Goal(s) for Your Speech and Reminds Listeners of the Steps They Should Take Next

The conclusion is also your last chance—at least during this particular speaking encounter—to remind your listeners that now that they have learned this new information, they have an obligation to act responsibly on it. If you have succeeded in helping them understand the relevance of the topic to their lives, then this is the moment where you can help them take that first (or next) step. Ideally, by the end of the speech, your goal is no longer your own but is also appreciated by and shared with your listeners.

A Strong Conclusion Encourages Listeners to Reflect on a Powerful Closing Statement or Clincher

The last words you share in a speech are consequential. While you could conclude a speech with a simple "thank you," you would be missing an opportunity to leave your listeners with the palpable silence that stems from the moment when a difficult or powerful idea lingers in their minds. Ending on "that's it" or "that's all I have" suggests a lack of preparation and is yet another missed opportunity to make the most of your and your listeners' time and effort. What you say to evoke a sense of closure should revisit the ideas and language you introduced at the outset of your speech in your attention getter. This prepares the listeners for the ending of your speech and invites them to consider its implications for their lives.

> "The learning process is something you can incite, literally incite, like a riot"
> —Audre Lorde

In her speech about refugees, Queen Rania was able to credibly establish herself as someone who clearly cares about the plight of refugees around the globe. Her speech was structured in a way to grab listeners' attention and empower listeners to take action on behalf of refugees. She wanted the UN to understand the dire circumstances in which refugees find themselves so they would do something. When listening to well-organized speeches like hers it helps us to understand why it is important to take the time to focus on the structure of our speeches if we also want to inspire action.

"Let us remember . . . when displaced peoples ask, 'where do we go from here?', they are asking on behalf of us all."

Giving time and attention to the structural components of your speech is wise. Without an appropriately simple and logical structure, you compromise your speech goals—settling for the lesser outcome of a haphazard connection or ambiguous outcome. Including common and expected elements in your outlines can help you make your speeches more memorable and your impact as a speaker more lasting. Though it may seem paradoxical, transparent structure can free both speaker and listeners to engage and empathize.

The UN High Commissioner for Refugees (UNHCR) reports that in 2017 the number of people displaced by conflict and persecution worldwide had grown to over 68.5 million—approximately 1.5 times the population of California (UNHCR, 2018). As Queen Rania (2016) argues in her speech, the question she heard repeatedly from refugees in Greece is a question for us all: "Where do we go from here?" They are, as she puts it, "asking on behalf of us all." Given that conflict and injustice cannot be contained at the borders of nations, what role will we play in its resolution, or in the granting of safety and asylum to the people in greatest need? You may choose to speak on these issues or others, and doing so carries responsibility for you and your listeners.

CHAPTER 6 | PUBLIC SPEAKING IS STRUCTURED | 121

Concepts

advantage–disadvantage 115
cause–effect 115
chronologically 115
clincher 111
compare–contrast 115
coordination 113
full-sentence outline 112
impression management 116
keyword outline 112
Monroe's motivated sequence (MMS) 115
order 114
organizational patterns 114
outlining 108
preview statements 118
primacy effect 120
problem–solution 115
recency effect 120
review statement 120
sequentially 115
spatially 115
structure 108
subordination 113
transitions 119
working outline 112

Toward Praxis

1. **Reflection:** What were your first lessons about outlining and structure? How did these lessons shape your attitudes toward outlining and speech preparation? What first helped you appreciate the importance of adding planned structure to your spoken communication?

2. **Discussion:** Consider an issue you'd like to address within your community, however you choose to define it. How might different organizational patterns lead you to a stronger or weaker argument? What would you need to consider in order to build introductory and concluding material that effectively establishes a relationship between you, your listeners, and the issue you intend to address?

3. **Action:** Work with others who care about that community issue you'd like to address to organize and sequence action steps community members should follow. How many steps are in the process? Are they appropriately sequenced and simple without losing sight of the complexity of the issue? What factors would affect community members' willingness to embrace and act on these steps?

Discussion Questions

1 What would you say is the role of repetition in learning? Where is it harmful? Where is it helpful?

2 If your attention is a finite resource, how do you spend it? What helps you decide how and to whom you pay attention? How might this vary from one context to another, from the classroom to the office to the dinner table? What do you do when you feel like you've misspent that attention on someone or something that didn't deserve it?

3 Reflect on some powerful uses of language, whether in the public sphere or your own personal and professional life. Who said what to whom and why? What made these moments so memorable? What was it about the speaker's language use that caused what they said to stay with you for so long?

Chapter 7

Public Speaking Is Informed

In this chapter, we will work together to:

- Define academic integrity and explore how to embody it
- Identify strengths and limitations of different types of supporting material
- Develop strategies for locating and rigorously evaluating research and evidence
- Competently cite source information in both oral and written communication

Mr. President, near the beginning of the document that made us free, our Declaration of Independence, Thomas Jefferson wrote: "We hold these truths to be self-evident . . ." So, from our very beginnings, our freedom has been predicated on truth. The founders were visionary in this regard, understanding well that good faith and shared facts between the governed and the government would be the very basis of this ongoing idea of America.

As the distinguished former member of this body, Daniel Patrick Moynihan of New York, famously said: "Everyone is entitled to his own opinion, but not to his own facts." During the past year, I am alarmed to say that Senator Moynihan's proposition has likely been tested more severely than at any time in our history.

It is for that reason that I rise today, to talk about the truth, and its relationship to democracy. For without truth, and a principled fidelity to truth and to shared facts, Mr. President, our democracy will not last.

2017 was a year which saw the truth—objective, empirical, evidence-based truth—more battered and abused than any other in the history of our country, at the hands of the most powerful figure in our government. It was a year which saw the White House enshrine "alternative facts" into the American lexicon, as justification for what used to be known simply as good old-fashioned falsehoods. It was the year in which an unrelenting daily assault on the constitutionally-protected free press was launched by that same White House, an assault that is as unprecedented as it is unwarranted. "The enemy of the people," was what the president of the United States called the free press in 2017.

(C-SPAN, 2018)

Perhaps emboldened by his decision to not seek reelection, Republican senator from Arizona Jeff Flake addressed his colleagues in Congress with a scathing indictment of President Trump. Situated within the context of eroding respect for and outright violence against journalists worldwide (the so-called fourth estate), Flake entreats his colleagues—and his president—to appreciate and engage the invaluable role of truth, and the role of people who will speak truth to power, in a functioning democracy. In his speech, Flake includes source material, juxtaposing his claims about the president against similar actions undertaken by dictators and autocrats in flouting research and evidence marshalled by journalists. If communication constitutes us, our communities, and our government, then how are we forever altered or damaged by consuming misinformation and outright lies?

In this chapter, we will consider an explicitly ethical dimension of public speaking—the role of the speaker as credible and their responsibility to render into creation worlds of understanding and action that are truthful and keenly aware of consequence. Effective and empowering public speaking is informed; it is grounded in and emerges from investigation (whether scholarly or journalistic) that is comprehensive, multidimensional, and meaningful. As a public speaker, it is important for you to share your own experience, but additionally to situate your insights from that experience in a context of dialogue that includes others who may not see or live as you do. This will mean consulting and then citing or naming your sources as appropriate.

Speakers Participate in Ongoing Conversations That Precede and Follow Them

In a letter of support to author and political activist Helen Keller after she was accused of plagiarism, writer Mark Twain observed:

> The kernel, the soul—let us go further and say the substance, the bulk, the actual and valuable material of *all* human utterances—is plagiarism. For substantially all ideas are second-hand, consciously and unconsciously drawn from a million outside sources. . . . When a great orator makes a great speech, you are listening to ten centuries and ten thousand men—but we call it *his* speech, and really some exceedingly small portion of it *is* his. But not enough to signify. (Twain, 1917, p. 731)

As was often the case in his writing, Twain identified a frustrating and meaningful paradox: There are no original ideas, but the ideas are—at least in some small way—transformed with each speaker. While it is tempting to use this paradox as a reason to charge forward and claim all ideas as your own, there is an important insight we may heed here: Knowledge is collaboration, a dialogue that precedes us and will continue long after we have stopped speaking. Though our ideas may not be entirely original, we can and should reveal our own original trajectories through knowledge in hopes they further the conversation and invite new participants. Recognizing ourselves as participants in these conversations—as speakers and as listeners—may be challenging, but it is important.

Think about everything that competes for your attention: people in your world (whether friends, partners, teachers, or employers); politicians and other government entities and agencies; companies that want you to purchase their product. If you were to take an inventory of all the attempts people make to strike your attention and persuade you to take some action, you would likely discover that your attention is one of your most valuable assets.

So how do you determine where to dedicate your attention? In a world of finite resources, even the best multitasker has to be selective. Sometimes we choose to attend to something if it is startling or novel, and sometimes we attend to something because we know it matters to us. As any bored student on a bright sunny day knows, even a captive audience can choose to give their attention to something or someone else.

To that end, there are better and worse, more and less meaningful, targets for our attention. Here it might help to make an analogy to nutrition. People concerned with a healthy diet usually eschew empty calories (such as sugary drinks) that have little or no nutritional benefit. Instead they opt for nutrient-dense foods (whole fruits, nuts, cruciferous vegetables), knowing that these will help them grow and heal, achieve performance goals, and so on. If we have a limited amount of time in our days (and we all do!), we can choose to fill it with empty, vacuous content, or we can choose something more deeply engaging and meaningful.

As an 11-year old, Helen Keller was accused of plagiarism when she wrote a short story that was similar to one she had read. Mark Twain, in writing to her, communicated the idea that there are no original ideas, but the ideas are, at least in some small way, transformed with each writer. We can relate this to public speaking in that speakers participate in on-going conversations that precede and follow them.

Similar to the idea that we should eat nutritious food to add value to life and enrich our diet, public speakers should speak on something that adds to their listeners' lives, in particular, topics and arguments that add to their audience's understandings of the world.

CHAPTER 7 | PUBLIC SPEAKING IS INFORMED

We hope you'll agree that this idea of adding value is an important consideration for public speaking too. Rather than stand up to speak on something that adds little to your listeners' lives, we hope you'll choose to explore topics and arguments that lend depth and nuance to their understandings of the world. The purpose of this chapter is to support you in these efforts by helping you practice academic integrity.

Speakers Must Practice Academic Integrity

As you'll recall from our earlier exploration of ethos, integrity connotes trust and character. **Academic integrity** refers to one's efforts as a learner to engage in ethical research, from data collection and analysis to how they share their insights with others aloud or in print. One's behavior is informed by the desire to exhibit sound character and good judgment (the Hippocratic oath, "first do no harm," springs to mind here). In this way, integrity characterizes a process that begins with a question and extends through revision and extension of the answers to that question. As professor, activist, and cultural critic bell hooks observes in her treatment of critical thinking:

> Integrity is present when there is congruence or agreement between what we think, say and do. The root meaning of the word has to do with wholeness. In *The Six Pillars of Self Esteem, writer and psychotherapist* Nathaniel Branden defines the term: "Integrity is the integration of ideals, conviction, standards, beliefs—and behavior. When our behavior is congruent with our professed values, we have integrity." (hooks, 2010, p. 32)

The idea that academic integrity is a *practice* is significant: A speaker isn't simply possessed of academic integrity, but rather they enact academic integrity when they research their topic, cite their sources, and engage their audience. You are what you do. The practice of academic integrity helps strengthen a speaker's credibility, so it is worth exploring how to do it consistently and well.

You can help establish yourself as credible by living your life in a principled way. This entails "walking the walk," or acting and behaving in ways that are consistent with your espoused values. You can help listeners appreciate this by describing your own past experiences, as well as moving through the world in ways that are consistent with your values. For example, when you ask for an assignment extension, it helps your credibility and strengthens your argument if you routinely follow through on your promises. In other words, if you have not already established trust with your instructor (or your listeners), then you can do so by exhibiting ethical conduct such as fulfilling your promises or sharing care and regard for both the content and process of your communication.

It may help to think of your role in this way: When you became a student at your college or university, this institution made a commitment to you (and when you attend a public college or

Students who want to get an extension on an assignment from a professor are more likely to get one if they have already established credibility with their professor. You can establish this trust by fulfilling promises and communicating effectively.

university, to citizens of the state) to teach you not only the content of a particular discipline or field but also the process of scholarship, of building truths within that discipline or field. To do this, you became an apprentice, learning how to learn. Indeed, as you navigate your career path you will likely find that the value of your time in school was not in learning specific content, but rather in learning how to engage in practices of investigation and application. Ideally rather than being a student who sits in passive reception of an instructor's pearls of wisdom, you are becoming a *learner*, someone who participates in the process of understanding and shaping the world.

The Speaker Has a Responsibility to Find and Critically Source Material

You can work to establish yourself as credible by showing that you are knowledgeable about your topic, about the conversation that has preceded you. You achieve this by choosing topics with which you are already experienced and by educating yourself—through investigation of news accounts, published research, surveys and polls, interviews, and observation. Remember that audience members cannot know what's in your mind or your heart unless you share it with them; sharing the steps you've taken to become knowledgeable helps your listeners take you seriously.

Supporting materials include the information and ideas that we call on to develop our own arguments. In a public speech, for the reasons described in the above section, such materials rely on information reported, created, and/or developed by people other than the speaker,

It is imporant for a public speaker to use supporting material to build credibility when speaking. In this picture a speaker is using a graph to support what he is saying.

and speaking with academic integrity requires acknowledging the work of these others. The process of acknowledging others' work is known as **citation**, and the original materials you use to locate others' work are known as **sources**.

It may help to remember that, until you are a credentialed or otherwise acknowledged expert on your chosen topic, you will need to build your credibility by referencing sources carefully and accurately. For example, consider whether you would respect the advice of a person in your life who recommended medical treatments to you. Would you take their advice if they were not a medical doctor? If you might, and if the person is not a medical doctor, what could they say that would help you take their advice more seriously and not dismiss it? You might be inclined to accept their advice if they spoke from personal experience as a patient, or if they gave you trusted source material to read shared facts or expert writing. Your audience is in a similar situation when you are a public speaker, and this is true regardless of your credentials. Even medical doctors, when they speak publically, must develop credibility through building arguments based on sources and not just on their medical licenses, because the relationship that can develop between a doctor and a patient is a very different communication context than the one a speaker develops with their audience (as we discuss in Chapter 2). That's not to say that you aren't capable of giving a speech that responsibly frames an issue for listeners and is worthy of their attention. It is to say, however, that if you plan to speak with integrity you must do so by researching then citing sources and not just relying on your own ideas or opinions. We discuss citation in the next section.

Understand Different Types of Sources

Generally speaking, there are four different types of sources: empirical, testimonial, anecdotal, and narrative. **Empirical evidence** often comes in the form of statistics, definitions of terms, or concrete descriptions of people, places, objects, and ideas. Empirical evidence focuses on providing and interpreting broad predictive patterns in events, beliefs, and/or behaviors. Further, this type of data emphasizes facts (information that can be verified), such as dates, policy decisions, and so forth. **Testimonial evidence** involves sharing someone's experience with or perspective on an issue. Just as a juror may be called to provide their testimony in a court case, testimony in a speech functions to lend insight from people with positions on that topic. There are three different types of testimony: lay, prestige, and expert. **Lay testimony** reflects the perspective of the average person who is affected by the issue at hand. For example, to better explain the issue of why faculty members might choose to go on strike, you might include information from an interview with faculty members about how they are affected by a lack of cost-of-living salary increases. **Prestige testimony** refers to the sort of commentary a celebrity might provide on an issue. As a speaker, you might choose to share how a celebrity feels about a given issue, even if they don't have direct experience with it or expertise on it. **Expert testimony** is as it sounds: Someone knowledgeable and credible shares their understanding and experience of the issue at hand. Sometimes speakers choose to share **anecdotal evidence** from their own or others' experience. This is essentially a brief example that humanizes or lends a personal connection to something that may be complex. **Descriptive/narrative evidence** refers to examples that are extended and detailed. Such examples help a speaker fully describe how a given topic or phenomenon affects someone's life. This kind of evidence is sometimes interwoven throughout the entirety of the speech, from attention getter to clincher and all points in between.

Testimonial evidence involves sharing someone's experience with or perspective on an issue. Testimony in a court case is similar to testimony in a speech in that both a juror and a public speaker give insight from their knowledge and expertise on a topic.

CHAPTER 7 | PUBLIC SPEAKING IS INFORMED

Speakers and listeners can evaluate their approach to sharing forms of evidence by considering these two questions:

1. Is this evidence appropriately compelling given the ideas of my speech?
2. Is this evidence distinctly different in kind from other evidence I will offer my audience?

A temptation for speakers in introductory courses is to locate sources as quickly and efficiently as possible, typically using web browsers in conjunction with search engines. But if you keep in mind the purpose for including sources as support for your speech, you will recognize the importance of asking each of these two questions about each source you plan to share. If you choose to share material from a source because you found it efficiently, but it is not compelling enough to help significantly strengthen your claims and/or shape your audience members' thinking, then you should find a more compelling source. Sharing sources that merely reinforce what audience members already assume or that redundantly echo the impact of your other sources weakens your speaking credibility, rather than strengthening it, because such sources suggest to your audience that your argument is not interesting or robust. A good approach to developing sources for your speech is to use the list of different types of evidence provided above, deliberately selecting a range of types rather than repeatedly identifying the same type of evidence.

Evaluate the Quality of Sources

As you search for sources that can provide compelling evidence for your speech, you will need to evaluate the **quality of sources** in several related respects. A source is of high quality, and useful as a location to provide compelling evidence for your speech, when it is published by a reputable source that shares—transparently and consistently—with its readers the way the information came to be published. For example, suppose you are a big fan of a local pro sports team and very interested in the outcome of today's game, but you are busy and unable to watch the game live. If a friend who you know is also a fan texts you with an update on the score, you probably trust that the score they share is accurate; that person is a high-quality source for that information. But if another friend who could not even reliably name the teams involved tries to remember the score when last they saw it and reports it to you in a casual conversation, with a hesitant tone of voice and searching their mind for the numbers and names involved, you would likely have doubts, check the actual score on the *ESPN* website, and so on; that person is a low-quality source for that information, even if they are otherwise a reliable and honest person. Your audience engages in something like the skepticism you might have about the accurate score, on a more indirect level, each time you offer supporting evidence in your speech and link that

"It is the responsibility of intellectuals to speak the truth and to expose lies."

— Noam Chomsky

evidence to a source. Your credibility with audience members depends strongly on cues you give them as a speaker that suggest the sources for your evidence are of high quality.

Characteristics of sources. Consider the characteristics of sources that might provide evidence for your speech. Ideas are shared in a range of different forms related to their different scope and timeliness; these include books that are intended to be more or less permanent sources of information; newspapers and magazines intended to provide timely but sophisticated information on current issues to a wide range of readers; scholarly journals intended to establish new research findings of interest to readers in particular academic disciplines; and web-based forms such as blogs, vlogs, and information-sharing sites intended to provide wide-ranging access to many different kinds of ideas—some sophisticated and others casual—very quickly.

Researching sources. Notice that as a researcher hunting for sources, you will likely use software that looks and works very much like a web browser to find sources in every one of these forms. Libraries housing collections of books and scholarly journals (as well as other periodicals) are typically digitally catalogued in that library's database and accessed through an interface structured very much like a search engine. The newspapers, magazines, and other periodicals you regularly read are likely available online and often accessed through a web browser. Blogs, vlogs, and information-sharing sites are also typically accessed through a web browser. As a result of this consistent set of experiences of accessing information that you

Through computer databases you can find a wide variety of sources when you are researching for a speech. Libraries have a variety of books and scholarly journals (as well as other periodicals) digitally catalogued. Also, newspapers, magazines, and other periodicals are usually available online. Other places to look are blogs, vlogs, and information-sharing sites. While it is easy to find information, it is important to learn to distinguish which are credible resources.

CHAPTER 7 | PUBLIC SPEAKING IS INFORMED | 133

> "Did you ever read my words, or did you merely finger through them for quotations which you thought might valuably support an already conceived idea concerning some old and distorted connection between us?"
>
> — *Audre Lorde*

likely have as an end user, you might find it hard to distinguish among different forms of information at a first glance. It can be especially hard, when using a search engine such as Google, to distinguish in your results list among articles first published in a scholarly journal, articles first published in a mainstream periodical, and articles first published on a website created and maintained by an organization or individual user. However, even though it's difficult, it's very important for you to make such distinctions for each source you consider for evidence in your speech in order to prepare for audience members who have the kind of indirect skepticism we noted above.

Reliable strategies to evaluate sources. You should actually cultivate this skepticism in your audience through how you include evidence and cite sources, encouraging them as you speak to critically evaluate your evidence along with you. A study by *the Pew Research Center* helps us explain why. This study found that in the task of distinguishing fact from opinion in news statements—a task that is of great importance given the current political climate rife with accusations of "fake news" and "echo chambers" of isolating political debate—younger Americans do significantly better than older ones (Gottfried & Grieco, 2018). You will speak with the greatest credibility not only when you critically evaluate evidence first but when you show respect to your audience by inviting them to think critically about the quality of each of your sources.

There are some reliable strategies you can use to evaluate the quality of sources that you might use for evidence. If the source for your evidence is an article in a scholarly journal, it will normally have been reviewed by experts in an academic discipline before being published. Library databases often have check boxes you can use to search for only these kinds of sources in your results, and that's an important tool because sources in this form are of very high quality. Sources in book form are also considered of high quality if they are published by academic publishers such as a university press for similar reasons, and you can locate the name of the publisher on the back of the title page. Books published by more mainstream presses meant for wide-ranging audiences can be of high quality if they include information that is precisely grounded in a narrow subject, such as a person's biography, a historical period, or a specialized topic area; these sources can be especially valuable for testimonial or descriptive evidence.

An increasingly useful starting point when you are struggling to find ways to gather high-quality sources on your topic in your initial brainstorming stage is **Google Scholar**. This is a specialized search engine that can point you to a range of scholarly sources about topics of broad scope. You can often use less narrow search terms than you need to use in your school library's databases. Google Scholar can generate results with just a few key terms that fit your overall topic idea. Results from Google Scholar are best used as starting points; a few interesting hits for sources in Google Scholar searches can then lead you to better, more precisely defined

Google Scholar

Articles ◯ Case law

New! 2019 Scholar Metrics Released

Stand on the shoulders of giants

Google Scholar is a great place to start when you begin gathering sources. It is a specialized search engine that directs you to a range of scholarly sources about topics of broad scope.

search terms in your school library's databases and/or to the names of respected researchers of interest to you.

An important principle that should guide your evaluation of sources is that more recently published information is of higher quality than older information in most cases. The reason for this is that research published more recently can build on the knowledge gained through prior studies and incorporate additional, or more nuanced, findings. Mainstream periodicals such as newspapers or magazines can also be useful for all types of evidence when it is important that the evidence is timely; you might find these sources especially helpful when speaking on a topic related to current public issues. However, your effort to use timely evidence requires you to take great care in determining the original source of the information. Increasingly, many sources of information that are easily found through search engines like Google have made an effort to have names and formats that closely resemble long-established journalism institutions like newspapers or reputable news magazines. The trouble is that such sources frequently present information that hasn't been developed through careful journalistic practices such as multilayered fact checking, corroboration of testimony, and review of original documents. Also, such sources (such as Breitbart, InfoWars, Occupy Democrats, or ThinkProgress) frequently exist to advocate political positions, functioning like propaganda rather than like impartial sources of factual information.

What can you do, then, to make sure a periodical source is of high quality? The first step is deliberately seeking information from established news sources whenever possible, privileging those above other sources in your search even if this takes you more time. Newspapers such as *The New York Times, The Washington Post,* and *The Wall Street Journal* are reputable sources for information on national and international topics, as are magazines such as *Time, U.S. News & World Report,* and *Newsweek*. Your local community newspaper would be a high-quality

Image of a newspaper stand showing a variety of periodicals

source for information of interest to the region. If you find potentially useful evidence in another form, such as a website, the most important question to ask is: Who creates and maintains the material on this website? Organizations such as government agencies maintain websites and often provide high-quality empirical data about their constituency. Nonprofit organizations might provide high-quality evidence closely related to their mission; the same is true of medical organizations. You should **contextualize**, meaning you provide context or meaningful background and interpretations for these sources when you provide evidence from them, as we discuss below. Private organizations also maintain websites, but these are considered of lesser quality because their primary purpose is usually to enhance the online exposure of the organization rather than to inform, so choose evidence from these sites only when it is unavailable elsewhere and then contextualize the source for your audience. You should also carefully contextualize the source whenever you use information from an individual user's website, which should be rare. Contextualizing a source often entails briefly acknowledging, when you cite that source orally, the name and purpose of the organization that maintains the website as well as the reason you consider the evidence to be of high quality despite it having come from such a source. You do not need to do this oral contextualizing with highly reputable periodicals like the high-quality sources we named above or with peer-reviewed scholarly sources, which is why you should only use evidence from the websites of nongovernmental organizations and individuals when it is absolutely unavoidable.

In summary, our key recommendations for speakers and listeners is that you evaluate the quality of the sources that supply supporting evidence by asking these three questions:

1. Is the information appropriate in scope (i.e., is it as relevant as possible)?
2. Is the information as current as possible?
3. Is the information published by a reputable source?

Speakers Have a Responsibility to Share Their Source Material

The quality of the sources you use for evidence is only meaningful to audience members if you use appropriate citation practices when speaking; if you do not do so, all of your hard work in carefully evaluating your sources will have no impact. Providing accurate and sufficient information about sources is therefore vital to your credibility. Part of how you show your character to your listeners is by treating your source material very carefully, attending to even the smallest details. When your work includes errors in citation, listeners may call into question the care and regard you brought to the speech overall.

You should cite each source at least four times: aloud to your listeners while speaking, in the text of your speech outline, in the references or works cited page of your outline, and on any visual aid that uses information from that source. This repetition of citations provides your listeners with multiple opportunities to note and evaluate your source material, allowing them the chance to consult that source themselves if they want to do so.

Keep in mind what we shared above: Speakers participate in ongoing conversations about ideas and experiences that precede and follow them. When you use others' ideas, you must provide a citation that acknowledges others' work, no matter how you share the ideas—through a **direct quote** or through **paraphrasing**. Quoting directly is as it sounds—sharing a source's language word for word, contained in quotation marks. This is distinct from the practice of paraphrasing, which entails a restatement or summary of a source's ideas in your own words.

How you cite sources depends on the community who will engage your work. In your public speaking class, for instance, your instructor will probably require everyone in the class to use a specific citation format contained in a special academic format known as a **style guide**. Two common style guides that contain specific rules for citation are **APA**, which stands for the American Psychological Association, and **MLA**, which stands for the Modern Language Association. Style guides are designed primarily for written work, and you should follow the citation rules for written work in your required style guide when citing sources in your speech outline, in the references or works cited page of your outline, and on visual aids.

Citing a source aloud while speaking is a bit different than doing so in writing, however. In an oral citation, you only want to give listeners the precise range of information necessary for them to make some sense, quickly and without distraction, of the specific source and of its quality. In most cases, this means offering them only one or two key pieces of information: the name of a person and/or the name of a source. Whether you provide one of these pieces of information, the other piece, or both depends on the evidence itself. If you are providing a direct quote, always state the name of the person whose words you are quoting to acknowledge their words. Always state the name of the person if you are providing testimonial evidence,

> "No one has a monopoly on the truth, but the whole premise of our democracy is that truth and justice must win out. And the role of a trained journalist is to get as close to the truth as is humanly possible. Make no mistake: We are being tested. Without a vibrant, fearless free press, our great American experiment may fail."
>
> —Dan Rather & Elliot Kirschner

because the strength of such evidence depends on who is offering the evidence; in this way, testimonial evidence is parallel to a direct quote even when you are paraphrasing. It is sometimes helpful, when orally citing the name of the author(s), to also name the source if the source is highly credible (such as a scholarly journal or an established and widely reputable periodical). Conversely, you should always provide the name of the source itself when offering empirical or descriptive evidence, because such evidence gains its strength from its truth value rather than through its link to a particular person or group. When offering empirical or descriptive evidence, you do not need to offer the name of the author(s) unless the ideas themselves are very closely associated with a specific person or group of people. You should avoid providing page numbers, article or book titles, and dates in oral citations unless the date itself is important, such as when you are making an argument in your speech about a historical event or about the significance of very recent findings.

Try your best to vary your phrasing when offering oral citations, so that your audience does not begin to find these monotonous and start ignoring them as your speech progresses. Here are some examples of effective ways to phrase oral citations:

> "According to Moore, raccoons are most closely related to bears."

> "The journal *Science* names genetic testing as the most reliable current procedure for determining relatedness among different animal species."

> "'Many visitors to our natural history museum are surprised when I tell them raccoons are most closely related to bears,' Moore recalled."

Speakers Help Create Reality as They Share Information

One final dimension of the process of critically evaluating the quality of a source is considering its bias. First, it's important for us to address this term *bias*, which is often construed as a bad thing because it sounds parallel to *prejudice* or *harmful discrimination*. **Bias** simply means distortion of reality in communication based on one's assumptions or beliefs. But we cocreate reality through our communication—from that standpoint, all communication reflects a bias of some sort because all communication involves human beings' imperfect efforts to negotiate meaning together. All sources of evidence, then, reflect bias. Attempting to identify and cite only sources that are unbiased would be an impossible goal.

What we suggest, then, is that you try instead to acknowledge as directly as possible the ways that your sources reflect certain kinds of biases, and strive to provide as wide a range of sources as you can. Especially when using sources such as news organizations, citing only the same source (for instance, *The New York Times*) repeatedly for a range of evidence can weaken your credibility because it suggests that you are unable to critically evaluate potential biases in that newspaper's claims. Consider the included chart that attempts to place many mainstream news sources on a spectrum from "most left wing" to "most right wing" but is itself the source of controversy over its assumptions, as noted by linguist, philosopher, and social critic Noam Chomsky (2018): https://www.reddit.com/r/chomsky/comments/7yk4vw/2018_media_bias_chart_still_wildly_off_source.

This chart itself should not be taken as factual but instead as a visual reflection of what we recommend you do to manage bias in your identification of sources: First, recognize that each source you use will distort reality in a unique way based on its history, scope, and values; second, account for this as directly as you can in your speech while striving to provide a range of sources for your audience.

"No Longer Can We Compound Attacks on Truth With Our Silent Acquiescence"

Senator Flake marshals a broad array of evidence in support of his challenge to the president and to us all: It is dangerous to pretend that we live in a world where this is no truth and no fact. While it is true that truths may collide or contradict, it is still incumbent on us all to insist on the best available information, on a diversity of perspectives that can guide us to humanizing and empowering action.

In his remarks, Flake cites *1984* author George Orwell to call our attention to the consequences of respecting truth and those who seek it and speak it: "The further a society drifts from the truth, the more it will hate those who speak it." We have seen this play out on a global state as journalists and intellectuals are exiled and murdered for refusing to remain silent (see for example, the troubling and painfully necessary Internet presence for the Committee to Protect Journalists, n.d., which notes that over 850 journalists have been murdered worldwide since 1992, or the Scholars at Risk Network, which strives to protect the human rights of more than 300 intellectuals and academics worldwide each year). As a speaker and listener—in classrooms and beyond—you must refuse to acquiesce. Ask the difficult questions, insist on attention to detail, demand fulfilled promises—and fulfill them yourself.

Concepts

academic integrity 128
anecdotal evidence 131
APA 137
bias 138
citation 130
contextualize 136
descriptive/narrative evidence 131
direct quote 137
empirical evidence 130
expert testimony 131
Google Scholar 134
lay testimony 131
MLA 137
paraphrasing 137
prestige testimony 131
quality of sources 132
sources 130
style guide 137
supporting materials 129
testimonial evidence 131

Toward Praxis

1. **Reflection:** What approaches do you use to evaluate the reliability of information when you encounter and read news stories online?

2. **Discussion:** What have you heard about the bias of specific media outlets? How many of the outlets named on the media bias chart above have been a part of your direct experience? How many have you never experienced directly but heard something about? How many were new to you when you first reviewed the chart?

3. **Action:** Spend a week gathering information on current events from sources that are outside the range of the sources you normally use on the media bias chart above. For instance, if you usually watch MSNBC talk shows or check CNN's website, spend a week watching Fox News talk shows or reading *The Wall Street Journal* every day. How is reality constructed differently for you as an audience member over this week? What specific perceptions about reality that are different from your own appear embedded in the discourse that you encountered over this week?

Discussion Questions

1 What forms of evidence do you find being used to persuade you in your everyday life? In your other classes? As a consumer? As a community member? How effective are these forms of evidence in persuading you, and why?

2 How do content creators, when attempting to compete for our attention online, use strategies to persuade us to take their information as true or accurate? What phrases do you notice that are common to headlines used to draw attention to online articles? What visual imagery do these content creators consistently use? Why are such strategies considered effective (which they must be, given the resources used on them)?

3 How have you observed your teachers using evidence in teaching over the course of your life as a student? In what ways have your teachers modeled strong, credible use of evidence for you? In which ways might your teachers have improved their work in this area?

CHAPTER 8

Public Speaking Is Performance

In this chapter, we will work together to:

- Describe unique opportunities and challenges in oral/aural public communication contexts

- Identify distinct modes of public speaking and explain how these affect preparation and rehearsal

- Define concepts related to embodied performance in public communication contexts, including vocal and physical choices

- Use effective strategies to prepare and rehearse public speeches

> Currently, NASA's Mars science exploration budget is being decimated, we are not going back to the Moon, and plans for astronauts to visit Mars are delayed until the 2030s—on funding not yet allocated, overseen by a congress and president to be named later.
>
> During the late 1950s through the early 1970s, every few weeks an article, cover story, or headline would extol the "city of tomorrow," the "home of tomorrow," the "transportation of tomorrow." Despite such optimism, that period was one of the gloomiest in U.S. history, with a level of unrest not seen since the Civil War. The Cold War threatened total annihilation, a hot war killed a hundred servicemen each week, the civil rights movement played out in daily confrontations, and multiple assassinations and urban riots poisoned the landscape.
>
> The only people doing much dreaming back then were scientists, engineers, and technologists. Their visions of tomorrow derive from their formal training as discoverers. And what inspired them was America's bold and visible investment on the space frontier.
>
> (Tyson, 2012)

On March 7, 2012, Dr. Neil deGrasse Tyson, director of the Hayden Planetarium at the American Museum of Natural History, testified before the U.S. Senate's Committee on Commerce, Science, and Transportation in Washington, D.C. The committee had convened a hearing on the priorities and plans for the National Aeronautics and Space Administration (NASA), and Tyson offered his remarks in the wake of a budget proposal by President Barack Obama. This budget proposal called for cuts to NASA's budget that would especially curtail robotic exploration within our solar system (Chang, 2012).

Given the importance of his purpose—requesting funding for a scientific organization from a very powerful decision-making body—Tyson had to plan carefully to ensure his speech would have maximum impact. He had to make strong choices in terms of how he would use voice and his body, and in order to develop those choices he had to prepare carefully in advance. Delivery and preparation are the primary topics of this chapter.

You would be in good company if, when you think about giving a speech, you feel tremendous pressure to get your words *just right*. This pressure leads many of us to want to script our speeches, to write them word by word, in hopes that we can deliver the perfect language to change our listeners' minds. But how we deliver those words is crucial. **Delivery** refers to how we perform or enact our public communication—that is, *how* we share our message with our listeners. Successful delivery involves balancing our verbal communication with our nonverbal communication. When we focus on the words that make up our message, we are focused on **verbal communication**. **Nonverbal communication** refers to those elements of public communication that go beyond the words of a message. Nonverbal communication is embodied, encompassing your voice, your facial expressions, your gestures and movements, and even your use of time and space.

We will explore how the concepts in this chapter help us understand what is special about communicating with a public audience primarily through *speaking* with them and expecting them to *listen*—as distinct from writing for them, creating something for them to view, and so on.

Compelling Speakers Perform Their Speeches and Create Social Reality

In this chapter, it may help to think about delivery as performance. Tyson's speech is an excellent illustration of how compelling speakers perform their speeches. When we use the word **performance** to describe how a public speaker says and does certain things in certain ways for certain reasons, we are relying on a rich tradition in communication studies, performance studies, that explores communication as creative and embodied. In particular, the Tyson speech we use as an example in this chapter demonstrates some key characteristics of compelling speakers.

Compelling speakers "perform" their speeches. Their delivery (how they share their messages with their audience) involves balancing non-verbal and verbal communication.

EMPOWERING PUBLIC SPEAKING

Speakers Participate With Their Audiences in Creating and Maintaining Social Reality

- Compelling speakers understand the rules of the speaking situation. In this case, Tyson shows that he understands what's expected of him in the context of testifying before Congress.

- Compelling speakers are exceptionally well prepared. In his testimony, Tyson shows how prepared he is to speak in terms of his knowledge of his purpose and the time requirements.

- Compelling speakers understand that live performance requires both exacting preparation and an openness to improvise. This particular presentation shows Tyson balancing the act of saying what he wrote in his carefully prepared manuscript with that of speaking conversationally and choosing his words as fit the occasion.

- Compelling speakers must adapt as they speak, all the while remembering the reason they are speaking. In his testimony, even though Tyson changes some language, he always considers of the scope and focus of his entire message so that he can be faithful to that scope and focus within the limited frame of "congressional testimony."

- Compelling speakers use their bodies in ways that are natural to them, but also appropriate for the speaking situation. Tyson is dynamic, to be sure, but in ways that are appropriate for his body in the context of a particular speaking occasion.

One type of communication that performance studies scholars find quite interesting is traditional aesthetic performance. This might include plays written to be performed by actors onstage, solo or group presentations of poems and stories that students deliver in competitions, oral folk tales that parents and other elders tell younger people in their cultures to pass on traditions, and so on. When we think of how a person acts when on stage or when reading a story to a gathered audience, we often think that they act by choosing to imitate or pretend. Such a performer might display sadness in their facial expressions, for instance, or change the pitch and volume of their speech to show how a new person in a dialogue is responding to a previous speaker. As audience members who are no longer children, we understand that the person in these situations is not really the character who has been saddened by an experience in the story, and not really becoming a new person when a different character speaks. That's why we might tend, without more careful reflection, to use words like *imitate* or *pretend* to describe this kind of acting. We might come to think of *acting* as synonymous with faking an emotion or a way of speaking.

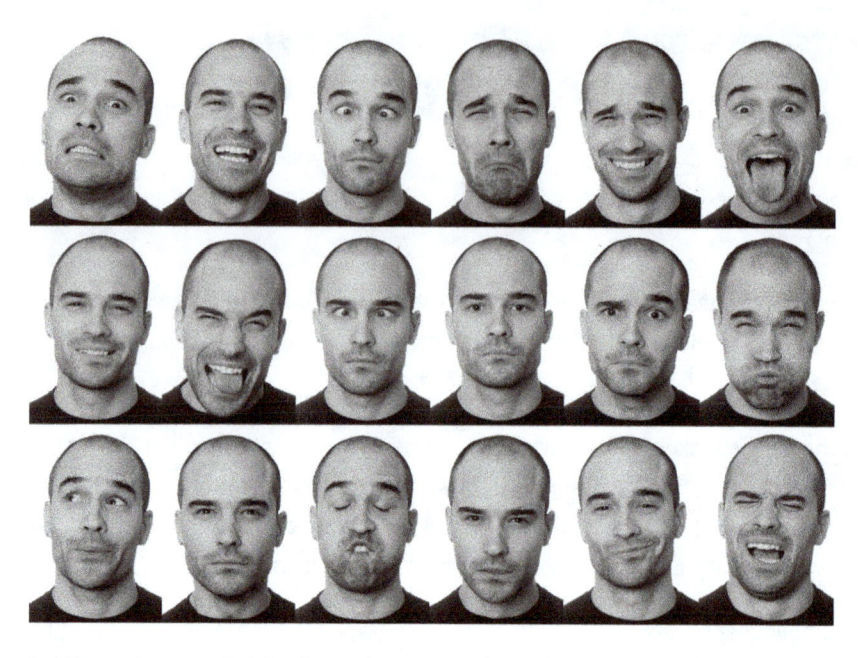

Public speakers use their bodies and voices, similar to the way actors do, to create a relationship with their audience.

Yet performance studies scholars help us understand that it is misleading and inaccurate to easily equate *acting* with *faking* (Turner, 1982). Instead, they suggest we think of *acting* in aesthetic performances as more complicated than just *faking* by thinking carefully about another sense of what we do when we create performances for others to witness: We can understand performers as making up things, creating characters and stories with our voices and bodies. Making up things is creative, and through performance, we can create or make new social worlds. When we make any choice with any part of our bodies to communicate with our audience, we are making and remaking our relationship with that audience, and our relationship with the world, by acting in certain moments for certain reasons.

Speakers Need to Be Intentional in How They Create Social Reality

That our performances make (rather than represent or portray) social reality is significant for a nuanced understanding of delivery. Consider this: The story we tell would be quite different—the feelings our story gives us and our audience would be different, the clarity of who is involved in the story and what each person wants or needs would be different, the sense we all have of *what matters most* and *why it matters* and *for whom it matters* would all be quite different—if we chose different facial expressions or different tones of voice. In this sense, our performance choices directly make and remake the social world of our stories, our arguments, and our messages.

Because every aspect of a speaker's communication will contribute to the creation of the social reality they share with their listeners, it is essential for speakers to exercise meaningful, intentional choice with respect to both their verbal and nonverbal communication. If you make a face, or make a new sound, when communicating a character in an aesthetic performance, you don't simply do this at random. Instead, you try your best to rely on your knowledge and experience of similar emotions, or similar people, when choosing to act as you do. Notice also that these choices have to be repeated and sustained over a period of time: Making a sad-appearing face or making a distinctive character voice might be effective the very first time, but the story quickly becomes dull or lifeless again if the performer does not sustain their commitment to their vocal and physical choices across the entire story. The more consistently and precisely a performer maintains their choices from start to finish, the more genuine the storytelling feels for the audience.

With this more nuanced understanding of acting in mind, we can improve our performance as public speakers by becoming more conscious of how we create our realities with our listeners in how we use our bodies. It will help for us to explore how public speaking is a distinct form of communication, one that is **ephemeral**. An idea or process that only exists for a very short time frame is ephemeral; the term especially connotes that the core elements of the idea or process are closely linked to the brief time frame in which it exists. Public speaking, like staged performances, is often ephemeral, which is to say that it does not exist *across* time, but rather *in* time. In other words, ephemeral moments are fleeting. Unlike an essay or other form of written communication, which you can read and reread, a speech in a public setting often responds to a specific moment in time, after which its impact is often lost or diminished.

Public Speaking Is a Distinct Form of Communication

Public speaking is a distinctive form of communication that has its own distinctive opportunities. For instance, as a speaker, you can reach a large audience of people at once, some of whom may be strangers to you. This may be significant for your efforts to effect social change, organize people along their shared interests and values, or coordinate complex processes that affect many people. However, public speaking also has distinctive challenges. For instance, it may be difficult for you to develop a meaningful sense of which values, experiences, and perspectives your audience may or may not share in common with one another (or in common with you). Public speaking is similar to other forms of communication (such as a conversation with your partner or a team meeting at your workplace) in that it depends on shared meanings and is typically purpose driven and therefore rarely impartial or neutral. So what makes public speaking unique, and how does speaking well depend on understanding this uniqueness?

In politics, public speaking helps create a community around a particular candidate by bringing people who are sometimes strangers or those who before the speech were only partially committed, together as one group.

What Characterizes a Type of Communication as Public Speaking?

Historically, public speaking was the only way a communicator could share messages with large groups of people all at once. Public speaking in these contexts was especially important for simultaneously sharing ideas in a particular community, and that large-scale simultaneous sharing of ideas was important in two notable ways: First, the ideas did not need to be passed on slowly and laboriously in person, through one-on-one conversations or other means. Second, the sharing of ideas itself became an act of creating a particular community by literally bringing people—sometimes strangers or those who before the speech were only partially committed—together as one group.

Think of stereotypical images of leaders in stories we tell about classical and medieval times, as often depicted in films like *300* or plays like *Macbeth*: These leaders share vital ideas and in doing so, they create and/or sustain communities. They often stand on high ground or structures built to elevate them, with their intended audiences gathered around them in concentric formations of human bodies making rings—sometimes in semicircles like we see in theatres, and other times in full circle like we see in arenas. An easy explanation for these ways of organizing large groups of bodies for a public speech is that the elevated ground and the circular audience positions give us the best chance for *each* person in the audience to hear and see the speaker. But notice that these ways of organizing also make and remake social relationships at the same time. We use phrases like *elevated status* to describe not just people who physically stand on higher ground but people who are deemed more important than others in a given context. We use words like *central* to describe not just people and ideas that are geometrically within a circle but people and ideas that are seen as more important than others in a given context. In these ways, our acts as communicators can be said to make and remake the social world, and not only when we tell fictional stories.

Various forms of technology have allowed us to create much more rapid and wide-ranging ways of sharing messages with large groups of people all at once. We can now share the written word, images, and sounds almost immediately with anyone in the world who has access to the Internet. With these technologies of shared communication available, do we still engage in a distinctive act that we can describe as public speaking? Is it valid to consider a speaker sharing ideas through a podcast or a YouTube video a public speaker?

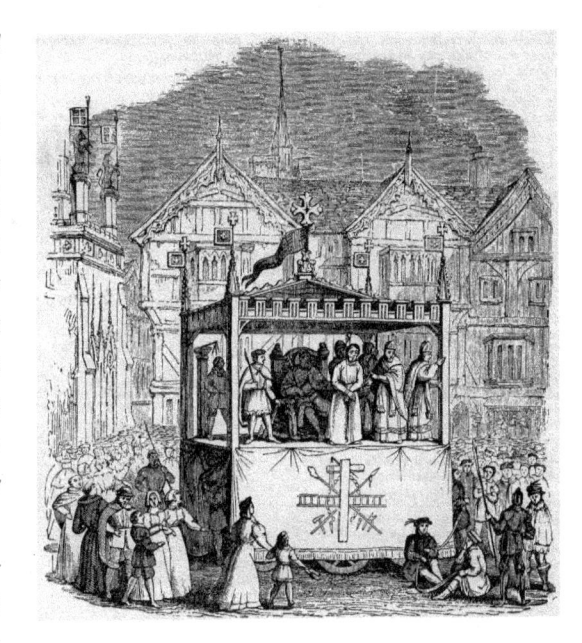

In medieval times, speakers often stood on high ground or structures built to elevate them, with their intended audiences gathered around them in semicircles. This elevated ground and the circular audience positions gave everyone in the audience the best chance to hear, and see, the speaker.

Media convergence makes questions like these increasingly difficult to answer in a definitive way. Video recordings of speakers who have obviously carefully prepared to speak, conducted relevant research, analyzed their potential audience, and made conscious delivery choices can be shared online—sometimes anonymously with the general public (such as on bulletin boards and forums), sometimes with only a limited group of potential audience members (such as on social media or by subscription services), and sometimes in creative combinations of these various communities. So what are we left with? Are we are still left with something we can call public speaking?

Here we suggest that public speaking may be characterized primarily by three distinctive elements that make it unlike any other form of communication: (a) Public speakers use their voices and bodies in particular moments; (b) speakers define qualities they believe their primary audience members share, though these audience members may be otherwise limitless in number or distance; and (c) by choosing this moment to speak and by defining common qualities among their audience members, speakers engage the audience as a bounded community that would otherwise be unbounded except for the terms and focus of their speech.

Would you consider (Goldie Hawn, Monica Lewinsky, Edward Snowden) a public speaker when they gave a TED talk to a live in-person audience and a global internet audience? The definition of public speaking changes as we navigate how it in today's technology centered world.

Public speaking could therefore happen across any physical distance in space as long as speakers take advantage of technologies that would reduce that distance. Public speaking could happen at any point in time as long as we recognize that the speaker's choices, once they begin to speak, establish a unique relationship to a community and shape that community going forward. Public speaking could therefore occur virtually, so long as the speaker's voice and body remain.

Analyze the "Public" Tyson Was Addressing

In his speech before the Senate Committee on Commerce, Science, and Transportation, Tyson spoke in person into a microphone while being recorded on camera, looking into a camera positioned between him and the senators whose judgment about science and technology he hoped to help shape. Certainly, Tyson would have known that his remarks were being recorded. He likely would have known that the Hayden Planetarium website (given that he oversees this institution) would eventually document his testimony with a link to the video recording. Thus, we might say that his speech was for more than one public. He may well have shaped his speech in part for a congressional audience; in part for intellectuals in the United States such as fellow scientists, NASA leaders, and/or patrons of the American Museum of Natural History; and in part for the general American voter. Yet wouldn't we agree that the *primary* audience shaping both why and how he spoke was the committee itself? After all, if he were most focused on how

Consider the audience of this Senate Committee hearing. Kirstjen Nielsen is testifying before the Senate Judiciary Committee. Her audience is the committee members, the American people watching, as well as anyone who will watch/read/listen to the hearing after the fact.

fellow intellectuals understood his claims—even leaving aside for now his use of language and his choice of speaking mode—we can assume that he would choose a more prominent, lofty occasion on which to speak rather than speaking at a midday weekday hearing within a series of other testimonies. In addition, if American voters were his primary audience, he likely would have chosen an on-camera set without the visible presence in the background of other people engaged in other activities and/or looking off camera toward the senators.

Public Speaking Is Situated Oral/Aural Communication

Tyson's focus on the way his voice would be received by his audience points to an expectation in public speaking that we often take for granted, but that is important: Speaking in this form happens primarily (but not always, given the range of physical abilities speakers may have) through oral and aural uses of our body. **Oral communication** is communication with the mouth, while **aural communication** is communication we perceive through our ears. This may seem obvious, but the primarily oral/aural nature of public speaking (and other forms of communication) has a couple of interesting consequences—we tend to place special value on this type of communication, and we are more able to recognize how it is meaningful only when it is situated in a particular time and place.

This speech happened in the context of Tyson testifying as a witness in a hearing. Senators, similar to investigators, attorneys, and judges, choose to interview a witness like Tyson face-to-face because they place special value on messages that live in a speaker's body—messages that affect a speaker's focus, breath, muscle tension, and so on. Very often audiences consider these more trustworthy, more truthful than messages removed from the body. This may change in the future as communication evolves, but speech created using a speaker's own body (and amplified or aided by technology) remains, for now, speech that we give greater credibility to, especially when truthfulness matters.

Of course, not all public speakers have as much control over their speaking opportunities as Tyson, an expert invited by senators for an uncommon speaking occasion. But if we consider how oral/aural communication like a testimony is situated in a particular context that gives the speech meaning, we can see how in a different situation Tyson would have created a speech that addressed these audiences in a different way, both verbally and nonverbally. Note that verbally, he begins by simply referring to NASA's age and his own as "the same" rather than giving any explanatory information or specific year. He also refers to his speech as testimony in his second sentence, immediately confirming his role with respect to the specific invitation to appear before a purpose-driven committee. Note that, nonverbally, he is in a suit and remains seated, shifting his eye contact between occasional glances at his notes and sustained looks at the faces of the senators, his chin tilting his face upward, given the senators' elevated status at seats on risers in the front of the room. These verbal and nonverbal choices create and sustain a particular relationship between speaker and audience. We can describe this relationship as a knowledgeable specialist, Tyson, speaking from greater authority than his audience in his area of expertise. The greater legislative authority Tyson's audience has allows that audience to determine whether to fund projects the speaker considers important. The meanings that flow from the speaker's choices are shaped by how the speech is situated in a particular time and place.

In the context of an imbalance of power, with a knowledgeable specialist speaking to a financial influence, Tyson's choice to emphasize the equal status he and his audience share as Americans of a certain age is noteworthy. Through it, he finds what we might call a common point of departure in both time and place, one that he hopes will allow him to bring his audience to a common point of return, mutually embraced values, by the end of his speech. However, had he given this speech when he was markedly younger than a typical U.S. senator, as many scientists have historically been when they achieve public prominence, the speech would have needed to stress a differently shared point of departure. The same is true if he had given this speech when he was markedly older than a typical U.S. senator, or if he had been born and raised in another country before achieving his position with the Hayden Planetarium.

Public Speech Relies on Timeliness

Each public speech thus stakes its power on **timeliness**. This means that its power is anchored by the particular moment the speech originates and by how the speaker and audience share a particular relationship as community members at that moment. Even speeches that are not deliberative, that are not directed toward shaping policy or calling for action must begin with the anchor of a particular community at a particular moment to be effective. Think of two different kinds of **epideictic** speeches: (a) **demonstration speeches,** which depend on levels of expertise that can—and do—change over time; and (b) **speeches of celebration,** such as a toast or a graduation speech, which must be timed so that the community a speaker invokes is coming together at a particular moment. Think also of **forensic speeches,** which only take the form they do if the outcomes of past actions (like those discussed in courtrooms) have already occurred. Note how each of these speeches would be different depending on how *long ago* in the past they occurred—witness testimony, for instance, loses its power after too much time has elapsed, while scientific findings take time to test and accept.

Performance Speech Is Ephemeral

The unique role of time in public speaking, as a key factor shaping how a speaker relates to their audience, is closely related to the oral/aural aspect of public speaking, in a way framed by another key concept from performance studies: Performances are **ephemeral**. This means that unlike printed words or broadcast images, public speeches—and other speech acts made by the human body—do not endure but instead fade over time. This quality of decay is due to how sound works. Unlike **visual messages** or **tactile messages**, which can endure over time in our bodies in the same form, because of how our bodies receive them (light in the eye, physical deformations on the skin), **sonic messages**—messages that vibrate "empty" air molecules—cannot endure for long without being constantly reinitiated (think, for instance, of a child exerting energy, continuing screaming to annoy a parent). So we can recognize, in this dependence on the body acting to energize air, one reason that we place such importance on oral/aural communication: When we communicate with one another using speaking and listening, we can often quite literally feel the energy, the movement of air, and the work being done in our mouths and in our ears.

Of course, we can record speeches using electronic equipment and thus archive them, but the speech is not the "same" speech once we have done so. The speech by Tyson is already different in power, as we write this chapter, than it was when he delivered it. The budget decisions he hoped to influence have been made, and the themes he uses to organize his speech—robotic exploration on Mars, the 2008 congressional bailout of major banks—are already changing in cultural relevance a few years later, and they will continue to do so rapidly. We cannot simply retrieve an archived speech and have the speech maintain its force, because the community the speaker invoked has changed too much. The timeliness so important to effective speaking also means that no speech can be delivered the same way more than once without having a quite different impact.

Public Speaking May Emerge From Different Modes of Delivery

In this section, we discuss four distinct modes of delivery, including what makes each a useful mode depending on your goals or your assignment. These modes include:

- Extemporaneous speaking
- Speaking while fully memorized
- Speaking from a manuscript
- Impromptu speaking

Above, we mention that many of Tyson's important speaking choices, the choices that make the speech distinctive, result from his role as an invited expert witness offering testimony at a Senate committee hearing. Though he refers to a manuscript, he is such an effective speaker that he speaks as if he is choosing most of his words *as* he speaks, moment by moment. This is highly effective when offering testimony because audiences are much more likely to trust what you say when you speak in this way. Speaking from a base of knowledge with a precise plan for your speech, while also sounding to your audience as if you are choosing most words as you speak is a mode known as **extemporaneous speaking**. In this mode, a speaker carefully prepares in advance to speak about a topic, typically developing a brief set of notes or a speaker's outline. Then the speaker works from occasional references to the notes or outline as they deliver the speech, focusing on the audience and choosing most words in the moment rather than precisely choosing each word in advance.

Consider what it means to be invited to testify before a congressional committee, a committee with the power to influence budget decisions affecting public resources that are dear to your heart. First, you must speak in a way that reflects the depth of your knowledge, given that this depth of knowledge prompted the invitation. Second, you must also show in your delivery that you are not merely a

There are many modes of public speaking delivery. Using a teleprompter is similar to reading from a manuscript, but because of the way it is used it can come across more naturally than reading word for word. When public speakers use teleprompters they seem to be looking at the audience and speaking extemporaneously.

disinterested expert but that you care deeply about the impact of your words and the decisions the committee will make. Finally, you must be extremely sensitive to how formally or informally you speak, balancing two competing pressures. On the one hand, you cannot take up too much of the committee's time, because even if the committee did not specify a time limit, you cannot exhaust their focus and attention without harming your cause. On the other hand, you also must make some kind of personal connection with the committee members so that they feel addressed as individuals rather than just as government functionaries.

Extemporaneous Speaking Is Prepared and Practiced

Extemporaneous speaking is the most common mode of delivery precisely because it enables effective speakers to navigate goals like those described in the paragraph above. For this form of speaking, you need to know your ideas and your material well, but you also need to engage your audience directly. Also, you need to choose most of your words in the moment of speaking, talking through the material in a conversational or even interactive way, rather than reading to your listeners. The following questions may help you better prepare for extemporaneous speaking:

- Where will you position yourself in relation to your audience? Will you be at the front of an auditorium or lecture hall, both of which often include a raised platform putting you on a significantly higher vertical level than your audience? If not, will you be at the front of a classroom or other space without any change in vertical level?

- Will you be allowed to move at all, either side to side or in the direction of your audience, or will you be required to speak from one position only?

- Will you be able to consult paper or electronic notes, or are you required to use only note cards?

- What sort of notes should you develop? If for a class assignment, must you develop a keyword or speaker's outline in addition to a full-sentence outline?

Once you have clear answers to these questions, what do your answers mean to you as an extemporaneous speaker? The key to speaking effectively in the extemporaneous mode is to find a balance between two goals: You will have key points, citations, ideas, and exact phrases that you believe you *must* offer your audience in order for them to understand your speech. You will also have audience members who will respond most positively if you make eye contact with them; speak in a natural, conversational style; and choose most of your words as you speak. Note cards and keyword or speaker's outlines are useful resources that can help you find this balance if you prepare them well in advance. On your note cards or speaker's outline you should consider including the following items:

- Key points (main points as well as any supporting points you want to make sure you remember to say in a specific order)

- Any citations you plan to offer, worded in ways appropriate for an aural/oral setting (see Chapter 7), printing these so they are easy to read at a glance (such as in a large font or in large handwritten letters)

- Any ideas of your own that are vital to your speech in terms of their order or wording, such as attention getters, signposts, transitions that show how points are related to one another, and a conclusion

- Words that must be spoken precisely in order to be useful, such as exact quotes from sources, difficult vocabulary, or unfamiliar ideas

If you have these items prepared and you rehearse with these materials, you can balance your two goals of saying what you want to say and speaking to the audience in a conversational way that connects directly with them.

Time Is Important in Extemporaneous Speaking

An important aspect of the balancing act in extemporaneous speaking relates, again, to time. We argue that a very helpful way to make sense of the different speaking modes involves thinking about how to manage time when you have the opportunity to speak in public. This can

Teachers are good example of extemporaneous public speakers because they often speak from a base of knowledge, with a precise plan for their speech, while also sounding to their students as if they are choosing words as they speak.

also help you figure out how to choose among the speaking modes discussed in this section whenever you are not obligated by the context to choose just one. An effective extemporaneous speaker wants to have a strong sense of how much time it takes to offer an audience each main point, to cite a complicated source, to describe an example, and so on. You will want this strong sense even (and perhaps especially) when you will not be explicitly graded for your management of time, because effective speaking involves responding in the moment to an audience's interest, attention span, fatigue level, and so on—and these vary greatly with each speaking context, often in ways you cannot predict in advance.

You can speak effectively even when audience responses vary if you enhance your felt sense of how long it takes to share each key element of your speech. An extemporaneous speaker, balancing the need to speak precisely on a prepared topic with the need to connect as much as possible with an audience, does so by balancing the need to *take time* to carefully say what they hope to say with the need to *give time* to an audience to share together the common experience of the speaking moment. Reflect on your most positive experiences with classroom teachers: Isn't it true that these teachers, too, have an excellent sense of how to balance *taking time* with *giving time*? Less effective teachers, in our experience, teach less effectively by either too tightly controlling each moment of learning according to their own vision, or too loosely, by allowing time to slip away without respecting the importance of the shared learning community and the students within it.

There Are Benefits and Drawbacks to Fully Memorized Speeches and Speaking From a Manuscript

Note cards and keyword or speaker's outlines are the most common materials extemporaneous speakers use to guide them when speaking, because these materials encourage speakers to look only briefly at them and therefore to attend more directly to their audience. You may notice, however, that Tyson uses what appears to be a more detailed set of notes on the papers in front of him. You can also read a transcript of his prepared remarks—which could be delivered, if he had chosen to do so, exactly as they are written in this transcript. Had Tyson chosen to deliver this written speech in the exact form you find it in the transcript, one way he could have done so is to offer a **fully memorized speech**. Doing so would require him to prepare with the goal of full memorization in mind, making memorization his primary focus in rehearsal. An advantage of a fully memorized speech is that you have a very high level of control over time—much more than an extemporaneous speaker—because you have timed in advance (in rehearsal after rehearsal) how long your speech takes. However, audiences quickly tire during fully memorized speeches because we can recognize when the speaker is not choosing their words as they speak. We often feel less directly connected to the speaker. We may even begin to wonder whether the speaker would care if we were their audience or if any similarly sized audience would do just as well, given that the words are memorized in advance. A fully memorized speech, then, is a speech that is most appropriate when your audience (and often someone in power, who controls resources) grants you a certain amount of speaking time in advance. Perhaps you are a spokesperson for an organization addressing stakeholders, or an official representative addressing the public about an issue of public concern; these are possible opportunities for a fully memorized mode of speaking. For most speaking occasions, however, a fully memorized speech brings more challenges than advantages. It is all too easy for a nervous speaker to forget some element of a memorized speech, which can derail the entire message if they cannot recover. Moreover, when a speaker memorizes their speech without a natural rate of speaking and tone of voice, then the speech may seem robotic or monotonous. If you choose to memorize any portions of your speech, we recommend focusing on the material you use to gain your listeners' attention, as well as whatever you say to leave them pondering your message.

A speaking mode closely related to the fully memorized speech is **speaking from a manuscript**. When you speak from a manuscript, you have written your entire speech word for word, but rather than trying to memorize it in rehearsal, as you would with a fully memorized speech, you use your rehearsal time to deliver the speech as written, doing this often enough that you can eventually speak while only occasionally referring to the manuscript. Speakers using this mode will usually prepare their typed, printed manuscript with notes that help guide them: They may use highlighters to indicate passages that are difficult to say and must be read

People who use prepared statements often do this so they can have control over the message they are presenting and the time it will take. This type of speech is often used by those who have power. One of the downsides to this type of speech is that often the audience feel disconnected from the speaker. This is often the type of speech to use for press briefings.

158 | EMPOWERING PUBLIC SPEAKING

from the page, or time markings in the margins to make sure as they speak that the elapsed time during their speech matches the elapsed time they practiced in rehearsal.

Tyson's speech is an effective example of a manuscript style of delivery. The speech is carefully structured, as you can see if you compare the manuscript's opening and closing words with the speech Tyson delivered. Though he opens with about 42 seconds of new ideas not in the manuscript, he delivers his epigraph word for word, an epigraph that sets up his central theme of how imagination and vision fuel practical innovation. This theme then guides each of his main points and examples. Though he changes some wording throughout the speech, Tyson integrates ideas related to contemporary federal funding at the same point near the end of his speech that he did in the manuscript—which is necessary because he closes his speech word for word, just as he prepared to close it with the clincher "How much would you pay for the universe?" The speaker integrated first at the appropriate point in his speech, examples that moved from themes about "dreaming" to practical technological innovations that flowed from those themes, *then* described these innovations as the result of a national vision about space exploration and competition, *then* returned to the question of funding for NASA with which he began. This precise sequence allowed the clincher to work effectively. The speech's impact depends on this carefully shaped arc of themes and logical relationships; it takes time to develop this arc. Yet Tyson maintains a strong connection with his audience. So we can see that a manuscript-based speaker can succeed in gaining much of the power that a fully memorized speaker has in terms of taking audience time, while also marshaling the extemporaneous speaker's power to give an audience time to connect, share experiences, and explore the speaker's ideas.

Impromptu Speaking Helps Novice Speakers Improve Public Speaking

How might a novice speaker begin to build the kind of experience that allows Tyson to speak effectively in this way? One excellent strategy is to find opportunities to practice the fourth and final mode of speaking we discuss here: **impromptu speaking**. In this mode, a speaker does not develop a speech prior to the speaking context; they receive a topic (often one not of their own choosing) only once they are within the speaking context. You can recognize why impromptu speaking can so significantly help a novice speaker develop experience if you consider again the two time-based factors we discuss above—the need to take time from your audience and to give them time to share with you.

Remember that the fully memorized speech, in many ways the exact opposite of an impromptu speech, involves taking an often predetermined amount of time from an audience that often wants to hear you in particular. The impromptu speech might then be usefully described as the opposite in terms of taking and giving time: You have not prepared in advance and have no special expertise to share, nor has an audience gathered just for you to share

A toast at a wedding is an example of an impromptu speech. In an impromptu speech your audience expects you to honor the speaking opportunity by being yourself, by speaking as articulately as you can in your own voice, and by using your body in ways you find comfortable.

something you know, have learned, or find meaningful. In this sense, you can take *no time* from your audience in any respectful way. However, the contexts in which impromptu speeches happen—frequently, classrooms or competitions involving students, but occasionally celebrations or unplanned events—are very much organized around giving time to one another. Impromptu speeches happen, in other words, in contexts and communities that form specifically to share experiences, to grow together, or honor a common moment together.

In this sense, impromptu speaking involves giving time to one another. Your audience expects you to honor the speaking opportunity by being yourself, speaking as articulately as you can in your own voice, and using your body in ways you find comfortable. You benefit from this experience as a speaker, because the more you speak in public contexts the more confidence you will build and—especially—the greater control you have over the passage of time while you speak. Impromptu speeches are an excellent way to develop a felt sense, like the senses you develop while learning to drive or learning to cook, of how time moves forward as you speak. Having an accurate embodied sense of time while speaking is one of the most useful strengths an effective public speaker can have. However, it's not quite as simple as saying whatever you want in your impromptu speaking opportunities—keep in mind that these are grounded in you and your audience *giving time* to one another, so you should use these opportunities to become more and more attentive to how people respond to you, your ideas, and your choices. It may help to think of your in-class communication as impromptu speaking. When you work to formulate a question or respond to your instructor's question, you are engaging in a spontaneous and collaborative effort to organize and share your ideas.

Don't Let Public Speaking Anxiety Stop You From Your Best Delivery

Because public speaking is ephemeral in the ways we describe above, when we compare it to other forms of public communication like writing or recording, we find that public speaking depends to a much greater degree on how you perform in the moment of the speech itself. Understanding these stakes can make public speaking situations and preparing for them stressful.

It is very common for speakers to experience **public speaking anxiety**, which is a discomfort associated with speaking before a large group of people. Scholars who study this anxiety across contexts suggest that the kind of apprehension or fear many of us experience about public speaking is unique to those contexts. We may feel confident as speakers and listeners in face to face or group settings, but not as much as public speakers. Some scholars also suggest that changing these apprehensive feelings, even with practice or by using special techniques, is quite difficult—in other words, they suggest that such apprehensive feelings are not simply the result of being a novice speaker or of being unprepared.

Public performances, such as the aesthetic performance or a job interview or a speech in a public setting, share a heightened focus on our voices and bodies. We recognize in these contexts that all eyes and ears are on us and that the stakes are therefore different because we

It is very common for speakers to experience public speaking anxiety, which is a discomfort associated with speaking before a large group of people.

may become unusually conscious of our voices and bodies—and we may expect that others are unusually conscious of our voices and bodies as well. Furthermore, the ways that people recognize communication apprehension, and the ways that people reflect such apprehension in their performances, will vary significantly from culture to culture and even from context to context. From this standpoint, speaking anxiety is not necessarily a single problem to be conquered; instead it is a set of perceptions that each speaker can use as a resource to help shape their speech. Each speaker—and each speech—will differ, and our responses to each new speaking context change us and change our audiences. Experiencing anxiety can then become a resource that helps motivate us to productively strengthen our attention to how we perform and how we prepare to perform.

The Speaker's Voice and Body Are Important Elements of Delivery

The voice is perhaps the most prominent resource most speakers use when speaking in public. Four important concepts you can use to consider how your voice engages your words in a public setting are articulation, rate, pitch, and dynamics. If you take time in both your rehearsals and in your speeches to attend to these four aspects of your voice, you can enhance your effectiveness as a speaker.

> "We must know what we think and speak out, even at the risk of unpopularity. In the final analysis, a democratic government represents the sum total of the courage and the integrity of its individuals. It cannot be better than they are. . . . In the long run there is no more exhilarating experience than to determine one's position, state it bravely and then act boldly."
>
> — Eleanor Roosevelt

Articulation refers to the ways you use your mouth and breath to form and project each sound with your voice. Each of us has a unique voice in terms of its sound quality (this is how we can recognize very quickly, or long remember even after the person is gone, the voice of someone close to us). Yet when we learn our first language, we learn a much more narrow range of ways to use our mouth and our breath; these ways vary from person to person, but not nearly as much as the sound quality of our voices vary. We use our mouths and our breath in very similar ways because we learn to do so in order to be understood by listeners who share that language.

Effective speakers work to clearly form each vowel sound by rounding out their lips fully and not changing their lip position until the vowel sound is completed. Often, for vowel sounds, *completing the vowel sound* means pushing air through the open lips. When we learn to speak we also learn shortcuts to avoid getting short of breath when we say vowel sounds that are close together or that are packaged with certain unusual consonant sounds, but generally you can feel air move through your lips when you make a complete vowel sound. Rounding out your vowels and breathing through them can help you ensure that you are clearly understood even when speaking to a room with a large audience or when you use a microphone to speak. Doing so can be especially helpful when your speech uses complex vocabulary or words that are unfamiliar to you.

Rate refers to how quickly these vowel sounds pass through your mouth as you move from syllable to syllable, from word to word, and from phrase to phrase. Each of us makes choices, in everyday conversation, that make our ordinary speaking voice unique; we also make distinctive choices to move across vowel sounds to communicate emotions—more rapidly when we are excited or frightened, for instance, or more slowly when we have doubts or when we are being sarcastic. These changes in rate can have quite different meanings from culture to culture, even within the same language community. Effective speakers work to become aware of the rate at which they are speaking and of how changes to that rate of speech might be understood by listeners.

Pitch refers to the frequency of the oscillating sound waves that your listeners hear in your voice; we refer to pitches with a higher frequency of sound waves as *high-pitched* and those with a lower frequency as *low-pitched*. Cultural variations exist, again even within the same language community, but nearly all cultures hear variations in pitch—following a higher pitched sound with a lower pitched one, or a lower one with a higher—as meaningful in some way. A very common example of how we hear pitch changes as meaningful relates to age: Most young people experience a drop in the overall average pitch of their voices as they age through adolescence, and as a result, many communities associate higher pitches with lightheartedness and lower pitches with seriousness. Effective speakers work to vary their pitch, like everyday speakers, in ways that signal their ongoing interest in their own ideas. Because pitch variation nearly always conveys curiosity about one's own words—changes in pitch become a way of responding to the flow of ideas as those ideas change over time as we speak. One of the most common qualities of "dull" speaking voices, those that leave audiences feeling bored and restless, is that there is very little variation in overall pitch.

Dynamics refers to the volume of your voice when you speak. As with rate and pitch, what matters for a public speaker is not the absolute volume, as speakers' ordinary average volume varies, but instead changes to volume. In ordinary speech, speakers often use a combination of variations to rate, pitch, and dynamics to communicate a wide range of expressive qualities; we learn to use these combinations early in our lives in our languages of origin and often take them for granted. Effective speakers work to become attuned to these variations across all three of these elements of the voice so that they can avoid taking them for granted, instead making choices about them to shape their speaking performances.

Your goal, as you work to treat articulation, rate, pitch, and dynamics as choices rather than just "how you speak," is not to become a stiffer, less natural speaker. Instead, you should use your rehearsal process (see the section below) to note what choices you find yourself making as you speak without your audience present. How articulate are you the first or second time you deliver a portion of your speech when rehearsing it? How do you use variations in

> "Rationality is what we do to organize the world, to make it possible to predict. Art is the rehearsal for the inapplicability and failure of that process."
>
> — Brian Eno

rate, pitch, and dynamics to express your attitude toward your ideas? As you become more experienced in noticing your use of these four vocal elements, you can identify ways to enhance or repeat those you believe are meaningful to you or potentially to your audience.

Tyson Effectively Uses His Voice to Communicate

In the sample speech, Tyson offers several excellent examples in which he uses variation in his rate, pitch, and dynamics to communicate with his audience. Two we find especially exemplary: First, at around 2:39 in the videotape of his testimony, Tyson uses a pitch variation with which you are likely very familiar: As he asks the question "What inspired them?," he raises his pitch on the vowel in the word "them," a way we often signal a questioning tone in English. He also slows the rate of his speech across this speech, creating slightly more distance between the "ed" sound in "inspired" and the word "them" than he uses between the word "what" and the first part of the word "inspired." He then follows his question with a command that describes how his audience can learn the answer: "Ask them!" His pitch across these two words is much more consistent, without the variation we heard in the previous question, which is one important way of marking the shift from the uncertain rise and fall of the feeling of being puzzled (in a question) to the confident stability of the feeling of knowing the right answer (in a command). He also raises his volume on "Ask them!" as way of reinforcing his certainty and of emphasizing the command-like phrasing of the sentence.

Another good example of Tyson using vocal variety effectively is near 3:45, when he describes "the iconic Unisphere which donned three rings." As he does so he slows the rate of speech quite significantly, highlighting the importance of the moment for him—a moment that appears to trigger a pleasant memory. Complementing this change in rate is a slight lowering of volume on this phrase and the sound of a chuckle (not a word but a vocalization, something we do with the throat, mouth, and breath) as a smile crosses his face. Try listening to this moment in the video without looking at the picture—can you *hear* Tyson smile? Though facial expressions are not vocal, smiles and other facial expressions are often audible in the ways we use our voice when we make them. If you attend to this in everyday conversation, you will notice how often this is true.

The Speaker's Body May Meaningfully Complement Their Message

As with the voice, the body is an important resource most public speakers use to shape meaning. Consider the moments of Tyson's speech that we describe in the last section: He accompanies his command that senators "ask them!" with a gesture of a pointing finger as his hand sweeps through the air. His smile, again, when saying "donned three rings" is a use of his body.

Gestures (ways that we move our hands and arms to create meaning) and **facial expressions** (ways we use the muscles in our faces to create meaning) are two of the most important aspects of a speaker's use of the body in public speaking. A third is **gross bodily movement**, which means how we use the larger part of our body—our shoulders, hips, and legs—to create larger movements that change our relationship to the space around us.

One reason these uses of the body are so important involves ideas we describe in the above section in exploring Tyson's vocal choices: Movements in the face especially, but in the body as well, change the shape and size of our breath column as we move the chest, neck, mouth, and jaw—all parts of our bodies that affect how air flows and thereby affect our voices. A second reason these are so important is that they indicate, as much as our vocal variety, our own commitment to our words and to the immediate speaking context. Just as audiences can hear in a lack of vocal variety, a speaker's loss of interest in the speaking moment, they can also see a speaker's loss of interest when they are not engaging with the body.

> "Procrastinate now; don't put it off"
>
> —Ellen DeGeneres

Tyson Effectively Uses His Body to Communicate

Again, we turn to two examples in the Tyson speech to show how he uses his body to communicate his engagement with his audience and his ideas. As he says "the landscape was poisoned" near 2:18, he offers a broad sweep of his open hands, which are turned downward. This sweep physically suggests a horizontal span, and he completes the gesture with a downward stroke that indicates the negative feeling he hopes to evoke by choosing the word *poisoned*. Just afterward, near 2:22, as he describes "the American crown" he again offers a horizontally aligned gesture; this time, though, there is less space between his hands, suggesting a smaller image than a landscape, and he completes the gestures by rounding the edges of the horizontal line and then drawing them downward as if to sculpt the sides of the crown.

Tyson's choices in his voice and body are significant because they arise in ways that he finds comfortable, ways that reflect his interests and imagination and curiosity about his own ideas. He speaks as if he were telling a story to a friend, using his voice and body to bring his words to life through directly engaging his listeners with shifting modes of address (questioning, commanding, describing), shifting emphases, and shifting "sketches in the air" that move through his hands and body. Your own speaking style and use of your voice and your body will differ from his, but if you gain a similar level of command of your physical resources—whatever those are for you—you can speak effectively.

Rehearsal Is an Essential Element of a Speaker's Success

Rehearsal, the time a speaker spends intentionally performing and reperforming their communication, is essential to impactful public speaking. We are fond of the term *rehearsal* because it reminds us of a theatrical performance, where actors practice for long hours to transform themselves—through their vocal and physical resources—into memorable characters. That said, if you find the idea of rehearsal intimidating, it may help to engage in some **reframing**. When we reframe an idea or experience, we choose a new metaphor to help us find aspects of that idea or experience we find powerful, meaningful, or relevant. Here it may help to reframe rehearsal as practice, which may bring to mind hours spent lifting weights at the gym or on the field. If you can link rehearsing your speech to another activity you enjoy, you will be more likely to spend plenty of time practicing until you are both confident and competent.

As a general rule, it is important to rehearse or practice your speech in ways that involve your body. If you only practice your speech by sitting in your room, referring to your notecards, you will not be prepared for how you will bring that speech to life with your listeners with eye contact, gestures, and movements. Where possible, try to practice your speech with the conditions you'll have when you formally present. If you will be at the front of a large lecture hall, you would be wise to practice a few times in that same setting. If you will be sharing slides or other presentational media as you speak, you should practice with those aids so that they

This business executive is practicing his speech for an upcoming board meeting in a conference room. Rehersal is a good time to practice gestures, movements, eye contact, and to get used to any any presentational aids.

166 | EMPOWERING PUBLIC SPEAKING

feel natural to you if you're feeling at all anxious. Everyone's body is unique, but one way any speaker can recognize and draw strength from their bodies as they rehearse (as well as when they speak) is to focus on their breathing.

It's a common misconception that the purpose of rehearsal is to become calm—for example, breathing deeply and evenly as an antidote to anxiety. However, recent research suggests that perhaps the most helpful step speakers can take is to tell themselves that they are excited about speaking (Brooks, 2014). Trying to become calm when you're nervous can make you even more anxious (especially if you feel frustrated that you can't control how you're feeling), but if you can see yourself as excited, then all that energy can become productive—an anticipation that helps you speak in ways that are dynamic and powerful. If nothing else, when you're excited about the opportunity to speak, to share your ideas and to make a difference, then you will be more inclined to spend time with your ideas, in consideration of your audience, in making the most of the opportunity.

"How Much Would You Pay for the Universe?"

Maybe you'll never be invited to offer your insights before a Senate committee, but it will always remain the case that when you care about your message and its effects in the world, the stakes of communication are high. When your communication matters—and it very often does—attention to both structure and spontaneity is essential. Feeling so confident as to be conversational requires rehearsal—practicing with your whole body (including your voice) so that you feel like the best, most natural version of yourself when you speak.

Concepts

- articulation 162
- aural communication 151
- delivery 144
- dynamics 163
- ephemeral 147
- epideictic 153
- extemporaneous speaking 154
- facial expressions 165
- fully memorized speech 157
- gestures 165
- gross bodily movement 165
- impromptu speaking 159
- nonverbal communication 144
- oral communication 151
- performance 144
- pitch 163
- public speaking anxiety 161
- rate 163
- reframing 166
- rehearsal 166
- sonic messages 153
- speaking from a manuscript 158
- tactile messages 153
- timeliness 152
- verbal communication 144
- visual messages 153

Toward Praxis

1. **Reflection:** What frame(s) do you bring to public speaking? In what ways are these helpful?

2. **Discussion:** What are the qualities and behaviors you associate with confidence? How are these influenced by cultural assumptions about race/ethnicity, gender, sexuality, ability, or other aspects of identity?

3. **Action:** Find occasions to practice the talking points from your next speech. Make sure you speak with people who will be most affected by the ideas you intend to share. What manner and tone do these listeners expect you to take? How do your voice and your body change as you practice articulating and modifying this position?

Discussion Questions

1. How is public speaking like (and unlike) theatrical performance?

2. It may help to reframe rehearsal as practice. What other kinds of reframing do you find helpful in your life?

3. If public speaking—like performance—is making and not faking, what does it (what do you) make?

CHAPTER 9

Public Speaking Is Impassioned

In this chapter, we will work together to:

- Identify and distinguish between connotative and denotative meaning used in public speeches

- Define rhetorical tropes and use them in public speeches

- Use precise language choices in public speaking that directly include a wide range of audience members in appropriate ways

- Explore how communication in public speeches constructs particular social realities

> This is now a national moment of grief, a national moment of pain, and searching for a solution, and you've heard in so many places, people of all backgrounds, utter the same basic phrase. They've said "Black Lives Matter." And they said it because it had to be said. It's a phrase that should never have to be said—it should be self-evident. But our history, sadly, requires us to say that Black Lives Matter. Because, as I said the other day, we're not just dealing with a problem in 2014, we're not dealing with years of racism leading up to it, or decades of racism—we are dealing with centuries of racism that have brought us to this day. That is how profound the crisis is. And that is how fundamental the task at hand is, to turn from that history and to make a change that is profound and lasting.
>
> (de Blasio, 2014)

On December 3, 2014, New York City mayor Bill de Blasio spoke at a press conference immediately following the grand jury decision not to criminally indict New York City police officer Daniel Pantaleo in the killing of city resident Eric Garner (Keneally & Margolin, 2014). Garner died in July 2014 as a result of injuries sustained in a chokehold Pantaleo used while he and other officers attempted to subdue Garner in a street arrest. Garner's death had provoked a series of demonstrations, decrying the actions of police and the deaths of African American men as instances of racist police brutality, in both New York City and nationwide.

In the aftermath of this speech, additional demonstrations resulted from the announcement of the grand jury decision. The mayor himself became a central figure in the controversy. The day after this press conference, Mayor de Blasio indicated his intention to make changes to the city's police department, and this claim, combined with the speech we examine in this chapter, made de Blasio a public target of criticism for those defending the actions of the police. Most notably, many police officers and firefighters turned their backs as the mayor spoke at the public funerals of two police officers who were shot and killed 17 days after this speech, and several personnel attending the funeral were vocally critical of de Blasio by name (Greenfield, 2014).

In this chapter, we explore de Blasio's speech using concepts related to a speaker's tone and a speaker's use of language and style. We consider how the highly charged, emotional context of his speech—in the wake of public demonstrations and daily media coverage of the story, with a long-anticipated grand jury decision still very fresh for citizens—makes it easy to see how meaning is contested and negotiated through public communication. This speaker acts in this context as an elected supervising official who, according to the city's political system, speaks as a representative of the entire citizenry. Yet he also adopts the stance of an individual citizen in his speech. Specifically, he underscores that he is the

The Eric Garner grand jury case verdict was controversial and led to demonstrations and protests. Posters like this one were created by protesters to capture their impassioned feelings about the "Black Lives Matter" movement.

Mayor de Blasio became a public target of criticism for those defending the actions of the police in the aftermath of the Eric Garner grand jury decision. Most notably, many police officers and firefighters turned their backs as the mayor spoke at the public funerals of two police officers who were shot and killed seventeen days after this speech.

concerned parent of a multiracial teenage son is often perceived as African American. We consider in this chapter how de Blasio uses language in this speech in ways that are responsive to the situation and to his audience.

Public Speakers Actively Construct Social Realities When They Speak

Everyday speakers commonly think of their communication as a way of labeling ideas, then organizing these labels to share ideas with others. We develop names for what's around us when we are very young, for objects like *toy* or living things like *kitty* or people like *Mama*. But when we are very young, we also develop more complex ways of using communication, like the concept of *mine* that so many toddlers use to negotiate their power over what's around them, thereby often irritating other people. As young people develop language, they move through the process of recognizing their own limits and appreciating the independence of other living things, from plants to animals to other people. These more complex concepts indicate that communication, from very early in our lives, can best be understood as a constant human activity like breathing or having sensory perceptions. From this perspective, communication is not a single set of behaviors we choose to take up or leave aside, like a way of using a tool or playing a game. Communication is a constant activity that affects us in every way at every moment, parallel to being awake or alert.

We hope that as you read this book you are considering the power of a different model of communication, one that moves beyond a so-called stacks of labels model to what scholars call a **social constructionist model** of communication. A social constructionist model, despite its complex name, captures a simple idea: Communication is much more complicated than one person choosing a message that they want to send and then sending it through a channel to a group of intended receivers. There are many reasons for suggesting that communication is much more complicated than this simplified definition; some such reasons we have already explored in this book include:

- Histories, cultures, and social expectations link our messages to other people and constrain our communication even when we are first forming ideas, not merely when we decide to send them;

- Dynamic contexts involve people engaging in many mental and physical activities at once, with messages thus circulating in partial ways rather than being fully formed and undisrupted by their channels; and

- Differences in power and privilege shape communication in ways communicators themselves often cannot easily recognize or change.

The man in this photo is speaking animatedly at a rally about Veterans Affairs medical centers being closed nationwide. He might be hoping through his actions and words that he will draw attention to the issues he is presenting and that he will be able to enact change through his words.

Each of these reasons distinctively affects public speaking. One of the effects of communication's complexity on public speaking is that the words a speaker chooses have great importance for the speaker and the audience. This great importance lies not only in the simple sense of words sending messages through speech but also in the more complicated sense of words creating and sustaining a particular social reality, specific to place, time, and many other factors, that the speaker shares with the audience.

We therefore suggest that a speaker who carefully considers language and its many nuances and meaning-making dimensions can speak with tremendous power. Language can function as a valuable resource that gives a speaker who lacks other more obvious resources—money, time, social status, access to sanctioned public channels—the power to actively shape relationships to others and the world.

In this sense, we describe public speaking as *impassioned*. We make this claim in part because *passion* denotes a strong feeling, and a central goal of this chapter is to help you make language choices that are lively and rich with feeling ranging beyond the direct, literal, dry meanings of words—choices that will help you fully engage your audience's attention, interest, and commitment. But *passion* also has a theological origin associated with a messianic figure's suffering—an act linked to transformation of the body, the spirit, and the wider community. **Impassioned public speaking**, then, is not only speaking with strong feeling, with attention to the felt sense of your words and their impact, but also speaking with transformative power, with the capacity to enact change through words.

EMPOWERING PUBLIC SPEAKING

Public Speakers Frame the Speaking Situation Through Their Use of Language

Words have power because they do work. They do the kind of direct, literal work we count on them to do, for example, when you ask an instructor for an extension on an assignment and hope that instructor understands that you mean a later the deadline for a specific assignment. Yet words do more indirect, associative work as well. Your instructor might be willing to grant you the extension because you choose that particular word, a word that implies a small modification of something that already exists. In the case of an extension, the thing that already exists and that you want extended might be your in-progress effort to finish the assignment. Alternately, the thing that you want extended might be the instructor's plan to evaluate your learning at this point in the semester. In both of those mind-sets, a request for an extension might be reasonable. The word *extension* is, for that reason, what we would consider an effective **rhetorical frame** for your request. A rhetorical frame is the way a speaker focuses their words in relationship to a given time, place, set of values, and immediate needs. Any single speaker, in any single speech act, cannot expect their ideas to have equivalent meaning at all times, in all places, for all audience members regardless of shared values, and for all situations regardless of how urgent or low-key the immediate needs might be. To be effective, a speaker must always choose a narrow, more precise subset of these contexts in order for their words to have impact for audience members. The word *extension,* in our example about an assignment request, frames reality—the situation—in ways your audience might find convincing or appealing.

Understand the Rhetorical Frame

Let's explore this idea of a rhetorical frame a bit more fully. Consider some other ways you might make the same request, using different language than *extension*, that might demonstrate less effective rhetorical frames. You might get a less favorable response to your request if instead of asking for an "extension" you ask the instructor to "change the due date," because some instructors who pride themselves on being consistent might associate *change* with a poor teaching decision. You also might get a less favorable response if you asked the instructor to "give you extra time," because some instructors might associate *extra time* with a precious resource difficult to give away easily. You also might get a less favorable response if you asked the instructor to "excuse the lateness" of your assignment, because describing the assignment as *late* suggests something negative about the assignment, while asking to be *excused* could associate your previous behavior with inappropriate actions.

Most students who decide how to ask an instructor for an assignment extension do not necessarily think carefully through all of these options; instead they act on instinct and experience when choosing words, even in important situations. Isn't this what you do? When we operate on instinct and experience, we are relying on our felt sense of meaning—we choose

Words have power. How might your professor respond if you asked them if you could turn in your assignment "late"? How might they respond instead if you just asked for an "extension" on your assignment? What might the difference in words mean to them?

words that *feel* right, that *feel* like they get across our ideas and that put those ideas in a favorable light. So we are more than just robots, first scanning our mental file of word definitions for the correct labels, then scanning our memory for the correct sentence construction rules. Instead, we are human beings who engage the world through words that have both precise, logical meanings and radiant, affective meanings.

Know the Differences Between Denotative and Connotative Meaning

For scholars, the precise, logical meanings of words that involve correct definitions and correct grammar are examples of **denotative meaning**. Denotative meaning is the literal meaning of a word or phrase. This type of meaning can easily be accessed in a dictionary or checked by reference to a grammar textbook. Therefore, denotative meaning is always important because through denotation with words, we create and sustain with our audience a common understanding of the world and our place in it. Without denotative meaning, we could not make sense of one another's ideas; some scholars argue that we could not in this case even make sense of our own ideas—a scary thought!

For scholars, the radiant, affective meanings of words that involve associations and memories are examples of **connotative meaning**. Connotative meaning is the cloud of ideas suggested by a word or phrase. This cloud of ideas cannot be understood by reference to definitions and rules but only by a shared set of experiences and/or knowledge. Therefore, connotative meaning is always important because through connotation with words, we create and sustain with our audience a common understanding of our shared lives and how far that sharing extends. Without connotative meaning, we could not act on the instinct and experience we described in the example above, talking with your instructor about a deadline. We would be like robots treating each interaction without regard for our own or others' feelings—a scary thought!

Whenever we speak, our words have both denotative and connotative meanings; these two types of meaning are conveyed in all words and phrases each time we communicate. The radiant, affective meanings of words are not merely "added" to denotation as if they were decorations. The clouds of association that words produce are always in play because listeners cannot discard or dismiss their experiences and sets of knowledge during interaction; these experiences invariably influence meaning making. The influence of connotative meanings cannot always be easily pinned down; your instructor in the example above, for instance, may not even realize how the difference between a request for an "extension" and a request to "excuse the lateness" of an assignment make her feel differently inclined to agree to the request. Meaning shifts; contrary to the fixed notion of meaning conveyed by denotation, connotation is dynamic and changing. The connotative meanings of words remind us that meaning itself is negotiated actively in communication.

Language Is Poetic

As we discuss in the section above, the associations that shape connotative meaning making are often hidden to us even as we choose our words as speakers or hear words as listeners. One reason for this is that we often act as communicators by emphasizing efficiency in our negotiation of meaning. Being direct and precise can help us save time, avoid conflict, and enhance mutual understanding; all of these are benefits to communicating efficiently and minimizing associative implicit uses of our words. Public speakers, who are always negotiating the precious shared resources of time and attention with their audiences (see Chapter 8), can find it especially compelling to err on the side of being precise and direct.

As we also discuss in the section above, however, a speaker can actually conserve time and enhance listeners' commitment to their ideas when they choose words deliberately—because of the words' associations, because of the words' wide-ranging suggestiveness, and because of the words' connection to audience members' experiences and sets of knowledge. Using language consciously in this way, to gain power through nonliteral meanings, can be an effective decision for a public speaker. Executing this can be difficult, though, because these **poetic** uses of language—uses that attend to the *feeling* of words in addition to their literal meaning—takes practice and care. In this section, we describe several important approaches to poetic language that, if you work with them, can significantly enhance your power as a public speaker.

Use Rhetorical Tropes

When we choose words or arrange words with the explicit goal of creating meanings for our audience that range beyond denotative meanings, we are using **rhetorical tropes** or **rhetorical schemes**. A rhetorical trope involves substituting one word or phrase for another to freshly illuminate an idea. A rhetorical scheme involves arranging words in unusual patterns to create surprise and draw attention to a relationship among ideas.

Four of the most important rhetorical tropes are metaphor, simile, metonymy, and synecdoche. One such trope we commonly use in everyday communication is **metaphor**. We use metaphor when we substitute one word or phrase for another in order to highlight the quality or character of an idea, even though our substitute word or phrase does not fit the literal meaning of the idea. "This classroom is an oven today" is an example of a metaphor. Obviously, the classroom is not literally an oven, but you might choose this metaphor, substituting *oven*" for *very hot enclosed space*, to highlight the extreme and persistent quality of the heat inside the classroom today. A special type of metaphor is a **simile**, in which you link your two ideas in the substitution by using the word *like* or the word *as*. If you said, "this classroom is like an oven today" or "this classroom's hot as an oven today," you would be using a simile. We have a distinct word for this type of metaphor because there is a bit more separation implied in the substitution: notice that "this classroom is like an oven" is a less extreme claim than "this classroom is an oven," so in this respect a simile is slightly more literal, and slightly less intensely poetic, than a metaphor.

Using the phrase "the White House" to refer to the Office of the President of the United States is an example of metonymy.

EMPOWERING PUBLIC SPEAKING

Two other nonliteral substitutions of word or phrases that are closely related to the rhetorical trope of metaphor, but that also have distinct names, are **metonymy** and **synecdoche**. Each of these directly involves an association, engaging the audience's existing knowledge of an important idea so that the speaker can emphasize what she considers most worthy of focus within that idea—and this strong reliance on shared experience is why these two rhetorical tropes have a special name. We use metonymy when we substitute a widely known quality or characteristic of something for the literal name of the thing itself. A common example of metonymy is using a building in which a government office resides to refer to that office itself—such as using *the White House* to refer to the Office of the President of the United States or referring to an item of food on a menu as *the dish*. Synecdoche is the substitution of one single part of something in place of the literal name of the whole thing itself. Common examples would be referring to a professional mercenary as a *hired gun* or to an automobile as *my wheels*.

Synecdoche is the substitution of one single part of something in place of the literal name of the whole thing itself. For example, the word "police" can be used to represent only one or a few police officers.

The final rhetorical trope we consider here is **personification**. Personification involves using words that attribute human qualities (movement, thought, intention, feeling) to nonhuman objects. Like metaphor, this trope is common in everyday speech, and you are likely familiar with this way of speaking through common examples such as "my car's not going to put up with that" or "fortune smiled upon me." What's significant about personification, and about rhetorical tropes generally, is that through poetic language we can sustain our audience's imagination and speak in public in a fresh, interesting manner that encourages reflection, feeling, and excitement.

Use Word Patterns in Rhetorical Schemes

Several rhetorical schemes involve the patterning of words rather than substitution to shape meaning in evocative ways. **Syllepsis** is using more than one different object for the same single verb; doing so often subtly shifts the meaning of the verb, creating surprise for listeners and encouraging them to carefully consider the shadings of meaning carried by the verb. Suppose you introduced yourself to someone like this: "I like to play basketball, and the saxophone, and

> "The limits of my language means the limits of my world."
>
> —Ludwig Wittgenstein

poker, and sometimes student." This would be a way of suggesting that being a student involves choosing certain behaviors, behaviors you might practice more carefully at one time or place than another; it is a way of suggesting that "student" is not a permanent part of your identity. You would have accomplished this using syllepsis. Notice that the meaning of the verb *play* shifts as it is linked to its final object, *student*.

Another way speakers can pattern words to create emphasis, in this case an emphasis on opposition, is **antithesis**. Antithesis closely positions two opposing ideas to frame how their opposition includes more than just their definitional distinction but additional elements as well. Suppose you introduced yourself to someone like this: "I play poker like it's fun, but I play blackjack like it's serious." The meaning here is more precise than simply opposing something that is "fun" with something that is "serious"; your audience understands this introduction better if they recognize that you expect to win when you play blackjack, something you likely do with greater concentration than when you play poker, and that despite their apparent similarity as wager-based card games you think of one quite differently than another in your own life. Antithesis thus uses patterned words to show that oppositions entail more contrasts than their obvious, literal contrast with one another. In this way, antithesis—like syllepsis, the other rhetorical scheme discussed here—works very much like rhetorical tropes work, by carefully and thoughtfully choosing and arranging words so that they carry much more complex meaning than their direct, denotative definitions.

Language Is Nuanced

Speakers who strive to keep their relationship with their audience lively and immediate speak most effectively. In addition to using poetic language, a speaker can enhance their relationship to listeners by carefully considering the nuances of language. Nuance is a dimension of language that can be easy to forget because one important role of language is to bond us together, across bodies and even across communities. Yet language's ability to bring people together, perhaps paradoxically, depends on its ability to differentiate. Language differentiates one thing from another, one idea from another, and ultimately, one person or group of people from another. Language is nuanced because language is particular and differentiated; the radiating associations of meaning that we have been discussing in this chapter depend on the relationships of speakers and listeners to one another. Speakers and listeners negotiate meaning together actively whenever communicating with one another.

We can think of **nuanced language**, language that positions us in particular relationships to one another, in terms of its relationship to human beings: How do some words and phrases reflect social hierarchies and histories, even by speakers who may not realize these reflections are happening? An example of how the nuances of language position people is the phrase *male* *nurse*. Notice that this phrase spotlights the body of some nurses but—implicitly—not the bodies of other nurses who differ only in that they are female. One implication of this phrase is that nurses who are male are somehow exceptional, which may or may not be true, given that the phrase itself tells us nothing about the nurse *other than* a biological attribute. Other more troubling implications of this phrase are that nurses with female bodies are ordinary and that we should expect, absent special information, for any nurse to be female.

Nuanced and Inclusive Language Is Significant for Public Speakers

Sometimes discussions of nuanced language devolve into talk about "political correctness," the notion that certain ways of using words are shameful or should be policed by the community. Instead, we recommend considering how your language choices differentiate people—including you—from one another. Rather than considering whether it is "correct" or "incorrect" to use the phrase *male nurse*, we encourage you to consider what this phrase signals about *you*, your ideas about the world, and your sense of how you are connected to other people. How might others hear this phrase? Does the phrase encourage forms of thinking that you want to encourage in yourself or in others? Does the phrase bring you closer to others or further from them? Does it make the world more like the one you hope to live in, or less?

Approaching nuanced language from this perspective is especially significant for public speakers given their need to establish and maintain a positive relationship with audiences they hope to influence. Another way language can give an effective public speaker power is through using language, in a subtle manner, to define relationships with audience members. Language used positively in this way is called **inclusive language**. Inclusive language certainly involves being attentive to history, culture, power, and privilege. If you refer to mature females in your audience as *girls*, you are discouraging audience members from conceptualizing themselves as peers capable of making sense of your ideas. If you tell a story that spotlights the racial profile of all characters except White ones, you are discouraging audience members from engaging you within a community of social equity and mutual human respect. This has nothing to do with being "politically correct" and everything to do with meeting your audience members as if you care what they think and feel; each person you fail to include will surely fail to engage your speech and thereby inhibit your success as a speaker.

You can further enhance your relationship to your audience members, and thus further enhance your success as a public speaker, by going beyond language that merely *includes* all of your audience members and *invites* these audience members to think, solve problems, and act along with you. Historically, approaches to rhetoric framed audience members as most readily persuaded by the force of arguments—the more impressive or irrefutable a speaker's argument, the "stronger" the persuasive impact. However, **invitational rhetoric** instead positions audience members as fellow travelers who might join the speaker in engaging the speech topic. When a public speaker uses language carefully to adopt an invitational rhetorical

> "But if thought corrupts language, language can also corrupt thought."
>
> —George Orwell

stance, they emphasize possibility rather than certainty because possibilities spark the interests of listeners, motivating their curiosity. When you develop your own speeches, consider how you might use words that unite you with your audience members. Your chosen words should emphasize what interests and/or concerns you share in common with them. Your chosen words should especially identify and describe tasks you and your audience members can each undertake (such as solving similar problems, taking similar actions, and so on).

Public Speakers Advocate Through Their Uses of Language

As discussed above, when we communicate we do not merely attach words to preexisting things. Through communication, through negotiating meaning in dialogue with others, we make some ideas and some people recognizable while making others less so. We make some actions possible rather than others. We develop some relationships to people and objects while neglecting others. This is why many communication scholars suggest that we actually create reality through our interactions. Scholars differ from one another on the question of whether *all* reality depends on our communication (a perspective framed by the phrase **social construction of reality**) or whether only those aspects of our lives that are social— roles, responsibilities, values, actions—depend on communication (a perspective framed by the phrase **construction of social reality**). In this section, we explore the less radical, more easily defended position—the construction of social reality through communication. "Construction of social reality" is a more easily defended position than "social construction of reality" because social reality is a smaller subset than simply reality; many observers would suggest that at least some aspects of reality that are beyond social reality are materially objective and do not depend on communication—for example, natural processes like oxidation and decay.

Recall that speaking in an impassioned manner is speaking with great feeling, with full commitment to what we say and to how what we say entails a particular relationship to audience members. New York City mayor de Blasio, in the speech we explored earlier in this chapter, attempts to respond to two perhaps incompatible sets of expectations: his role as a public official representing the city's civic institutions—including the police department—on the one hand; and his role as the father of a Black-appearing teenage son concerned about race-based profiling and the threat of police-involved killings of African American men on the other hand. How does he navigate this challenging position, and how do his efforts to do so shape his speech?

Assess the Rhetorical Strategies Used in de Blasio's Speech

In the mayor's speech on the immediate occasion of a grand jury decision important to the city, his words necessarily do more than *express* his response (in favor or against) to that decision; his words also *describe* the reality in which he finds himself at the moment of this speech. In describing reality, de Blasio positions himself as someone who is not at all neutral with respect to the controversial context of the decision, despite his status as a public official. Yet even though he positions himself as nonneutral, the mayor's official status also requires him to consciously address a wide range of audience members whose perspectives might be different from his in complicated ways. Recognizing this, he carefully crafts his language choices using deliberate rhetorical strategies. These language choices demonstrate a nuanced approach to public speaking that embraces his role as someone creating—not merely reacting to, but actively creating—a social reality for New York City and for the nation as a whole.

Connotative meaning. In his speech, de Blasio negotiates connotative meaning when he makes an interesting choice of words to discuss the recent decriminalization of possession of small amounts of marijuana. He says, "The people believed there were too many young people of color arrested and saddled with a record for the rest of their lives." When he says *saddled* here to mean *heavily burdened*, he is using a figure of speech known as a metaphor, and we discuss metaphor and other figures of speech more carefully in the next section. But he chooses this metaphor, we believe, because of its particular connotative meaning, a meaning that depends on several forms of common knowledge: His audience knows that a saddle is literally a piece of equipment used to dress an animal carrying a significant weight. But his audience also knows that the African American community in the United States has been deeply affected by the legacy of slavery in this country. Slavery involved treating human beings like animals who could be held captive, bought, traded, and used to bear heavy burdens of labor without their consent and without compensating them. Treatment of African Americans during slavery, in other words, can be readily associated with treatment of labor animals like those often dressed with a saddle for heavy burdens of work without their consent, because they are property—a camel, a horse, an elephant.

Many African American intellectuals argue that the legacy of slavery, combined with the legacy of constitutional discrimination then the legacy of Jim Crow legislation after the 13th through 15th Amendments, makes it easier even today to justify race-based profiling—due to the persistent association of African American people with less robust human rights as autonomous people. The audience's knowledge of these legacies give de Blasio's choice of the metaphor *saddled* here to mean *heavily burdened* a special power in this speech, and he can access that power with a well-chosen metaphor rather than taking the time to name each of these legacies as we have named them here. In addition to speaking more concisely, he also tacitly acknowledges his awareness of these legacies and his belief that they continue to have importance today, thereby suggesting values he hopes much of his audience will share and that

> "Metaphors hide in plain sight, and their influence is largely unconscious. We should mind our metaphors, though, because metaphors make up our minds."
>
> —James Geary

his audience will use to embrace his ideas. This is an excellent example of why connotative meaning has great significance for public speakers.

Metaphor. One metaphor de Blasio cites in his speech was the one President Obama used in a personal conversation with him; he claims that Obama said, "I know you see this crisis through a very personal lens." This is not a literal reference to de Blasio wearing eyeglasses or contacts or using a visual aid like binoculars; the president instead made use of a common metaphor, a lens, to stand in for a "particular viewing perspective that focuses precisely on some things by narrowing the field of vision and keeping other things in the background or out of sight." Consider what a lengthy phrase the authors constructed to explain the meaning evoked by the use of the everyday metaphor *lens*; this is why rhetorical tropes can have such power, because while they may be less efficient in terms of literal meaning negotiation, they can be exceptionally efficient in terms of depth of meaning.

Metonymy. One instance in which de Blasio uses metonymy is when he contends, "it doesn't come first and foremost, from City Hall, or from One Police Plaza." He is referring here to the demand for change in the relationships of police and the community. Most of his listeners would know that *City Hall* means, in this context, the elected government officials of New York City. Most listeners would also know that *One Police Plaza* means, in this context, the officials of the New York Police Department. He wants to emphasize the institutional nature of these officials and their permanent physical locations, differentiating them in this way from the contingent, shifting nature of New York residents who act without the force of formal authority and thus—for de Blasio—act in more compelling, committed ways that matter more deeply. Metonymy helps him here because the authority of these officials is made rigid, unmoving, and formal by associating it with these buildings.

Synecdoche. Similarly, de Blasio uses synecdoche to help emphasize important qualities. When he cites the police commissioner as having "talked about those who don't live up to the values of the uniform," de Blasio uses synecdoche. Uniforms are inanimate objects and of course are not literally committed to any values themselves. But de Blasio chooses to substitute *uniform*, one visible piece of clothing widely associated with this public role, for the entire police officer, a whole person wearing that uniform who can indeed be committed to values. This is an effective rhetorical trope here because the uniform is perhaps the single most defining quality of a police officer, the item we use to distinguish police officers from civilians even when we cannot clearly see a badge or clearly read lettering. Given that the uniform functions as the defining quality most easily marking police officers as different than civilians, substituting it for the whole office emphasizes that the values de Blasio and the police commissioner expect each officer to hold should also be defining qualities that most easily distinguish police from other people.

Syllepsis. Consider this statement by de Blasio: "And we're grieving, again, over the loss of Eric Garner, who was a father, a husband, a son, a good man—a man who should be with us, and isn't." Here, de Blasio uses the same verb, *to be*, to link several objects to the same subject, Eric Garner. The first three objects all relate Garner to family roles associated with males—*father*, *husband*, *son*. The fourth object links Garner to an idealized description of a male, *good man*. The fifth object, however, is not a role or description of a person; it is instead a prepositional phrase, *with us*, marking Garner's presence (actually, his absence) in the community, yet still using a form of the same verb, *to be*. This is how syllepsis works to surprise listeners, as the meaning of *to be* shifts from *occupy a role* to *exist here and now* simply by which object de Blasio links to the same subject, Eric Garner. He clinches this syllepsis by ending the sentence with "and isn't," underscoring Garner's absence and thereby powerfully reminding listeners—through associating his absence with the absence of those positive male roles just listed—of the significance of that absence.

Antithesis. In his speech de Blasio quotes Martin Luther King Jr.'s claim that "injustice anywhere is a threat to justice everywhere." Two antonyms, *injustice* and *justice*, are closely positioned in this sentence and phrased in parallel with nouns about location, *anywhere* and *everywhere*. King here, through antithesis, emphasizes the connectedness of our quest for justice across multiple local communities, suggesting that one community cannot ignore another community's situation if the first hopes to preserve justice locally. For King, another community's injustice threatens his own community, despite their separation in space.

De Blasio's Speech Uses Inclusive Language

We can explore how inclusive language involves thinking about relationships, rather than thinking about choosing the right labels, by examining de Blasio's careful, nuanced efforts to speak inclusively. In several cases he uses language that signals his concern for the particular positions of various audience members and their interlocking connection to the community he seeks to influence.

- He addresses religious leaders with language that reflects the history some groups have of excluding women from leadership roles: "our brothers and sisters who are members of the clergy, having devoted themselves to comforting and supporting people in all sorts of situations."

- He explicitly acknowledges the shared experience of family love that he believes should unite listeners in empathy for the Garner family: "No family should have to go through what the Garner family went through."

- He strives to show respect for law enforcement and to emphasize his support for their service multiple times in the speech, including: "And that painful sense of contradiction that our young people see first—that our police are here to protect us, and we honor that."

In this photo, NYC protestors are showing solidarity with other protestors in Ferguson and reminding the country that the problems nationwide and in Ferguson affect everyone and need to be stopped.

- He cites the importance of his message for all racial communities by naming communities of color then broadening his claim, though the subjects of his speech are race-based profiling and efforts to confront racism through peaceful demonstrations: "This is not just a demand coming from the African American community. It's not just a demand coming from the Latino community. It's coming from every community."

- He cites, on two occasions, the national response to these same issues and to the also notorious police-involved killing of an African American man in Ferguson, Missouri, Michael Brown, yet he also underscores the centrality of his message for local New Yorkers as particular listeners: "And it conforms to something bigger that you've heard come out in the protests in Ferguson, and all over the country." "The events of Ferguson may have most sharply framed this discussion nationally. For all of us here, what's happened in our own community is what we feel most deeply."

Despite these extensive efforts to include multiple racial communities, highlight shared values, speak as a New Yorker for fellow New Yorkers, and note his support for police work, de Blasio became a flashpoint for criticism and anger when two police officers were shot and killed in their police vehicle 17 days after this speech. How do you make sense of this? Do you find de Blasio's speech successful or not, and how would you describe the reasons for your answer?

"It's All Our Problem—and Anyone Who Believes in the Values of This Country Should Feel Called to Action Right Now"

We have examined many of de Blasio's strategies, but to conclude, we consider one strategy in particular: his choice to frame the current situation as an event—or series of events—that will be written into history. When de Blasio describes "a history that still hangs over us." he suggests that history casts a shadow over our actions that threatens us. De Blasio concludes this series of associations with history by using another metaphor, substituting "chapter" for a noteworthy event: "One chapter has closed, with the decision of this grand jury. There are more chapters ahead." This metaphor takes advantage of the previous uses of *history*, suggesting through the phrase "more chapters ahead" that additional events including and following from the killings of Garner in New York City, Brown in Ferguson, and Tamir Rice in Cleveland will be written into our history books. We ask you to consider, in light of subsequent responses by police and firefighters, de Blasio's efforts: Do you believe that the attempt to emphasize collective responsibility for history, for how the city will be remembered, was effective? Why or why not?

We suggest that one way to answer this question is to consider how de Blasio constructs a social reality through his choice of words. Rather than merely speaking about what *is* happening or what *has* happened, de Blasio implies a vision of a possible future world—of reading a history book—and organizes his ideas around the central value of achieving that world, of bringing it into being. Had he merely spoken about his immediate concerns for the safety of his son, merely demanded immediate accountability from the police department in the absence of a criminal indictment, or merely called on demonstrators to behave in specific ways, his claims would have constructed a reality of passive reaction rather than one of positive action. The difference between these two realities is as small as the difference between a few words in a speech yet could potentially be as large as the difference between civic hostility and civic pride. You, too, can speak successfully even in challenging situations if you attend as carefully as de Blasio to the community with whom you are engaging and to the context that frames your speaking opportunity.

Concepts

antithesis 180
connotative meaning 176
construction of social reality 182
denotative meaning 176
impassioned public speaking 174
inclusive language 181
invitational rhetoric 181
metaphor 178
metonymy 179
nuanced language 180

personification 179
poetic 177
rhetorical frame 175
rhetorical schemes 178
rhetorical tropes 178
simile 178
social construction of reality 182
syllepsis 179
synecdoche 179

Toward Praxis

1. **Reflection:** When have you felt passionately about something or someone? How did that influence your communication? We commonly think about nonverbal communication as a means of communicating emotion, but how do our word choices emerge from our feelings?

2. **Discussion:** A constitutive understanding of communication argues that language creates our reality. Identify examples of language delimiting or opening ways of understanding or acting on an issue of social significance.

3. **Action:** Finish your next speech early enough that you can make conscious and purposeful choices regarding your language use. Who is included and who is excluded by your words? How do your word choices make possible some actions and preclude others? How are your language choices influenced by your position and privilege with respect to the issue you're addressing?

Discussion Questions

1. Consider the connotative and denotative meanings of words that are of consequence to people of varying degrees of power and privilege. For example, what is the difference between *Black Lives Matter* and *All Lives Matter*? *Pro-choice* and *pro-life*? *Physical disability* as opposed to *mental disability*? For whom?

2. To what extent is objectivity essential for being a responsible public speaker?

3. How have language choices played an important role in your own decisions to become more or less involved in an issue?

CHAPTER 10

Public Speaking Is Accountable

In this chapter, we will work together to:

- Identify and evaluate different forms of reasoning public speakers rely on to form strong arguments
- Identify situated reasoning in public speeches
- Detect and correct common errors in reasoning

> Unfortunately, in places like Ferguson and New York City, and in some communities across this nation, there is a disconnect between police agencies and many citizens—predominantly in communities of color.
>
> Serious debates are taking place about how law enforcement personnel relate to the communities they serve, about the appropriate use of force, and about real and perceived biases, both within and outside of law enforcement. These are important debates. Every American should feel free to express an informed opinion—to protest peacefully, to convey frustration and even anger in a constructive way. That's what makes our democracy great. Those conversations—as bumpy and uncomfortable as they can be—help us understand different perspectives, and better serve our communities. Of course, these are only conversations in the true sense of that word if we are willing not only to talk, but to listen, too.
>
> I worry that this incredibly important and incredibly difficult conversation about race and policing has become focused entirely on the nature and character of law enforcement officers, when it should also be about something much harder to discuss. Debating the nature of policing is very important, but I worry that it has become an excuse, at times, to avoid doing something harder.
>
> (Comey, 2015)

On February 12, 2015, Federal Bureau of Investigation (FBI) director James B. Comey spoke to assembled students and faculty at Georgetown University in Washington, D.C. Comey addressed the relationships between law enforcement personnel and their local communities, especially with respect to race, bias, and hostility. Early in his speech, he acknowledges the police shooting–related deaths of Michael Brown (in Ferguson, Missouri) and Eric Garner (in New York City) and the shooting deaths of New York City police officers Wenjian Liu and Rafael Ramos, all in the months before his speech, as a motivation for his remarks. In this speech, Comey calls on law enforcement officials and local community members to work together to build stronger relationships, relationships informed by a sense of history and by attention to the distorted perceptions about race and criminality that we have inherited as a society.

Reasoning, or the process of sharing with listeners the logic you have used to arrive at your argument and what it means for others, is a vital element of a successful speech. When you develop strong reasons for your spoken claims, you show respect for your audience and your connection with them in a given community. Obviously, one very disrespectful way to treat your audience when speaking in public would be to lie to them—giving false citations of scholarly research or testimony, inventing ideas and then stating them as facts, telling a personal story with deep emotional content that you simply fabricate to manipulate the audience's feelings, and so on. But notice how closely this form of disrespect—offering listeners false ideas—parallels another form of disrespect: offering listeners valid information but suggesting a false, or weak, or implausible conclusion based on that information. Flawed or careless reasoning is as dangerous as lying.

When you speak in public, your listeners depend on you to be truthful with your evidence and your emotions. Your audience also relies on you to be truthful—or at least *very* careful—in what you argue your ideas *mean* for them. This chapter will help you use strong reasoning that suits your purpose and audience. You will also learn how to avoid misleading your audience or inadvertently leading them to embrace faulty conclusions. Our primary goal in this chapter, then, is to help you understand how speakers can be *accountable* to their audiences and their relationship if they hold themselves to rigorous standards of reasoning that invite listeners to evaluate and share their conclusions.

Speakers Have a Responsibility to Use Reasoning Appropriately

It is important that we agree at the outset that a speaker cannot simply use a form of reasoning because it is convenient. Instead, a compelling speaker shows respect for the audience by attending to the reasoning forms most widely accepted within the audience's community. We often think of an individual speaker as a solitary person—one who may take up the good of the community in their speech but who makes whatever speaking choices they can effectively execute when planning the speech. This emphasis echoes an understanding of human life common in societies in western Europe, the United States, and Canada, in which each person acts as an individual and is accountable as an individual for the consequences of those actions. Americans, especially those of us from middle-class or aspiring middle-class families with European heritage, are so accustomed to this belief that we might wonder what the alternatives might be. We assume that it would be unfair, for instance, to hold one person accountable for the actions of another person. Yet other non-Western societies conceive of human life and accountability in different ways. For instance, speaking traditions in some societies in Asia and Africa often emphasize the fitness of publicly spoken words for the community. Actions, and our evaluations of their consequences, are conceived not only as affecting a whole community at once but also of emerging *from* a whole community at once. A speaker from such a tradition who spoke in an uneducated or hostile way would not only diminish their own relationship with

In Western cultures it is often common to think of speech as representative of the individual, but in many non-Western cultures a person's publicly spoken words can be taken to be representative of their whole family, community, or culture. What might it be like for someone in a non-Western culture if they said something publicly that embarrassed their family or community? How might the same situation be different in Western culture?

the community, they might diminish their family's relationship to that community, or even the community's sense of itself as a whole.

As our sense of shared responsibility for one another and for the world continues to broaden—even in the West, as we become more aware of our environmental and economic interconnectedness—we can speak more effectively if we become more attentive to the diverse forms of reasoning that engage us in community relationships and that make us accountable to

> "Never have so many been manipulated so much by so few."
>
> — Aldous Huxley

those relationships. You may already be attentive to diverse forms of reasoning, depending on the communities in which you participate. In the rest of this chapter, we will consider what makes for good reasoning in a public speech from a variety of perspectives, so that you can appropriately broaden your own resources for engaging your own and other communities.

Effective Speakers and Listeners Must Understand and Evaluate Different Forms of Reasoning

Reasoning describes a process that speakers use to draw conclusions based on evidence. When reasoning, we gather evidence in different forms depending on the context. We might make direct observations using our own senses, we might investigate questions we cannot easily answer ourselves in a systematic way through primary and/or secondary research, or we might trust the words of others who have some special authority, expertise, or role. Considered in this way, reasoning can include a range of evidence and a variety of conclusions, many of which we will explore in this chapter. Note that *reasoning* according to this definition is not the same as *logic*, even though in everyday conversations we sometimes act as if the two are synonyms. **Logical reasoning** is one form of reasoning; in logical reasoning, two or more ideas are linked to one another through specific relationships; these ideas, because they have a specific relationship to one another, lead to a new idea, a conclusion. Arithmetic is a good example of logical reasoning: In the problem 2 + 3, the numbers 2 and 3 are ideas and addition is a specific relationship among numbers that leads to the conclusion 5. Logical reasoning is just one of the ways, among others, that a person might draw conclusions based on evidence. Here we'll discuss three forms of logical relationships common to arguments in public speeches: deductive logic, inductive logic, and causal logic.

We describe reasoning as a process of drawing conclusions based on evidence because it is important to remember that reasoning is never arbitrary. Sometimes others may not share our conclusions, and we might be tempted to dismiss their ideas—either explicitly to them in dialogue or implicitly in our own lasting perceptions—because we think their reasoning is weak. We might characterize their contrasting ideas as mere opinions or as silly, using labels that suggest the ideas are faulty because they are not defensible conclusions based on evidence—that they are not based in good reasoning. Instead, we recommend taking the position that others' reasoning may be hard for us to grasp, perhaps because they haven't clarified their reasoning for us or perhaps because their reasoning is too deeply embedded, too well hidden, in what they say. It's certainly possible in some cases that others may not carefully examine evidence or may not draw defensible conclusions; we do this ourselves, if we're honest about it, and long-held, untested opinions and weak reasoning affect all of us—all of our efforts to communicate—without exception. But if we begin from the position that reasoning is always based in relationships among evidence, then we can approach arguments by trying to clarify those relationships among evidence even when they are fuzzy or are poorly formed.

Clarifying Reasoning Can Enhance an Argument

Let's take one example from Comey's speech to consider how clarifying reasoning can help enhance an argument. Comey asserts: "The truth is that what really needs fixing is something only a few, like U.S. President Obama, are willing to speak about, perhaps because it is so daunting a task." His next sentence indicates that "what really needs fixing," according to Comey, and what "only a few are willing to speak about," are "the disproportionate challenges faced by young men of color." Some listeners might find the claim that "only a few" have, so far, engaged this topic to be a difficult conclusion to reach. Such listeners, who perhaps live in communities with many young men of color or who work closely with criminal justice programs focused on restorative justice, might dismiss the notion that "only a few" have engaged this topic. Some listeners might even see Comey's claim as evidence of his own racial bias, a bias stemming from his position as a White senior official in a major law enforcement institution, from which position he recognizes the efforts of some speakers while he ignores or remains undereducated about the efforts of others.

Comey could encourage his listeners to more readily accept his claim that "only a few" are addressing this topic if, instead, he added a qualifying phrase that helped his listeners understand his evidence for this claim. Is he considering only those speakers with high-ranking institutional authority, like himself or President Obama? Is Comey contrasting President Obama with other speakers who, in the weeks immediately leading up to this speech, have been widely quoted in mainstream press in response to the shootings in Ferguson and New

In Comey's speech at Georgetown he recognizes President Obama as one of the "few" willing to use his voice to bring attention to the violence happening around the country and in Ferguson, Missouri. But, because Comey's speech comes across as confusing in some parts we are left unsure of what he means and in need of clarification. It is our job as listeners to hold public speakers accountable for their reasoning and it is our job as public speakers to clarify our own language as much as possible when we speak to avoid confusion.

CHAPTER 10 | PUBLIC SPEAKING IS ACCOUNTABLE | 195

York City? Is he including only African American men, or perhaps other men of color, among those speakers in his sample group? Given any of these three frames of the evidence, some listeners might still choose to disagree with Comey's claim that "only a few" are speaking about this topic. Our point is that when we work with Comey to clarify his reasoning, we can much more easily and meaningfully evaluate his conclusions, and we can then hold Comey himself much more accountable in ways that promotes dialogue. It is important for you as a public speaker to support your audience and your speech by clarifying your own reasoning as much as possible through the language you choose during your speech.

Deductive Reasoning Helps Speakers Draw Conclusions From Evidence With Certainty

Deductive logic is a relationship among three kinds of statements: first, a universal statement that would apply to any particular instance of a given category; second, a particular instance of that given category; and third, a conclusion that describes how the particular instance fits the universal claim. You're already familiar with a widely used kind of deductive logic, which is math.

Below is an example of deductive logic in math:

Any odd number, when added to another odd number, will produce an even number
and this:
17 and 85 are both odd numbers
then we can conclude this with certainty:
102, the sum of 17 and 85, is an even number

This example shows how a speaker can develop a conclusion based on deductive logic.

You might notice that the first statement, the universal statement, depends on definitions and/or assumptions. If we were to change the definition of what counts as an odd number in our counting system, then our conclusion might not be strong anymore. This is an important quality of universal statements in deductive logic: They are always founded on some prior terms or rules that are taken for granted within the bounds of the current argument. Thus, conclusions drawn from deductive logic are always *certain* on their own terms. Challenging a conclusion within deductive logic usually involves challenging whether the particular instances fit (perhaps either 17 or 85 is not actually an odd number), challenging agreement on the initial universal statement (by proposing a different counting system), or challenging whether the three parts of the claim are arranged appropriately. These ways of challenging an argument based on deductive logic are available to educated and thoughtful listeners. This is why when you build an argument from deductive logic as a speaker, you must ensure that your argument can withstand challenges like these. A **fallacy** is a weakness in a logical argument, and specific types of fallacies are associated with specific forms of logic.

Avoid Fallacies When Using Deductive Reasoning

When you make an argument using deductive reasoning, you can avoid fallacies first by using the same form described above, beginning with a universal statement and then exploring a particular instance in light of that statement. A common deductive fallacy is **affirming a negative premise**, in which your universal statement is negative but your conclusion, a faulty one, is positive. Consider this fallacy: "I never teach class in shorts; today I am wearing slacks; therefore, I am teaching." Yet this would be leading to a fallacious conclusion because there are many times I wear slacks but do other things besides teaching. If your universal statement is positive, describing a quality that is always true, then your conclusion must also be positive; if your universal statement is negative, describing something that is never true, then your conclusion must also be negative when using deductive logic.

Another way to avoid common fallacies when using deductive logic is to understand why you accept your initial universal statement and why the audience, too, might accept it. Has this universal statement been taken as an initial, agreed-upon set of conditions or definitions which anyone interested in such an argument would have to accept as a starting point, like in our counting system in mathematics? If not, has this universal statement been rigorously and repeatedly tested, as scientific findings often are? In the context of arguments made in societies like those we described earlier in western Europe, the United States, and Canada, these foundations for universal statements are often used in arguments. If, however, you offer a universal statement to your audience as part of your deductive reasoning and that statement is merely widely believed rather than defined or tested, you might be committing the **ad populum fallacy**, meaning that you assert something simply because many other people assert the same thing. Similar fallacies include the **appeal to tradition**, in which you assert a universal truth merely because long-established behaviors or artifacts exemplify it, and the **appeal to nature**, in which you assert a universal truth merely because of given qualities that are taken for granted but not yet well understood. You can examine your deductive reasoning for fallacies like these if you carefully consider how your opening universal statement has been tested and why audiences might accept it.

Interestingly, these last three fallacies of deductive logic would be framed differently if we relied on other forms of reasoning apart from logic. Social values and beliefs about ideas like tradition and nature can be quite significant in situated forms of reasoning.

> "The very nature of deliberation and argumentation is opposed to necessity and self-evidence, since no one deliberates where the solution is necessary or argues against what is self-evident."
>
> —Chaïm Perelman & Lucie Olbrechts-Tyteca

Inductive Reasoning Helps Speakers Draw Probable or Likely Conclusions

We often reason toward a conclusion based on evidence, and relationships among evidence, with much less certainty than the rigorous demands of deductive logic. After all, you cannot be certain, in the sense of deductive logical certainty, of many conclusions that have great importance in your life—for example, conclusions about whom to trust with your physical safety and emotional health, how to choose a college, or how to make a large purchase like a car or a house. As many aspects of our lives involve terms or rules that are not universally applicable, another form of logic becomes significant to public speakers: **inductive logic**. This type of logic involves drawing conclusions based on probability rather than certainty.

The clearest distinction between deductive logic and inductive logic is that a conclusion drawn from an inductive logical relationship is *probable* or *likely* rather than definite or certain, and your language should reflect this when you use inductive logic in a public speech. When you use language consciously in ways that clarify your reasoning, you are more appropriately holding yourself accountable in dialogue with your audience. Instead of starting with a universal statement that audiences accept because of scientific or definitional rigor, a speaker using inductive logic can offer descriptions of a range of evidence about which less is already known, about which we understand fewer universal properties than those like odd and even numbers in our counting system, and argue for a particular relationship among those several items of evidence. Deductive logic, in contrast, only has power when a narrow, precise set of definitions are in place in a given context. We can use inductive logic to draw conclusions from a much wider, more rapidly changing set of ideas—which makes it powerful in a much broader scope of contexts. This is why we use it more often in everyday reasoning.

Inductive reasoning tells you your professor will take roll aloud every class period until the end of the semester because that is how they started the semester. Inductive reasoning is based on a large group of probable instances.

Inductive Reasoning Can Be Based on Large Groups of Instances

We sometimes draw an inductive conclusion because we have access to many instances of evidence. For example, if your public speaking instructor has begun each and every class meeting by taking roll using a handwritten sign-in sheet, you would likely conclude that they will still do so at the start of a particular class near the end of the semester. If a classmate asked you to sign the sheet and thereby cover for an absence, your decision about whether to agree might include lots of factors—your own values like honesty or respect for the instructor, your ability to write in a "disguised" way—but you would likely never consider that the instructor would do something other than take roll the same way they always have. This would not be a provable, certain, deductive conclusion because human behavior varies too much (maybe the instructor has a special plan for class today that led them to skip the sign-in sheet). But it would be a strong inductive conclusion nevertheless.

> "... reason is not always reasonable."
>
> —Christopher Hill

Inductive Reasoning Can Be Based on a Shared Relationship Between Instances

Another way we can draw an inductive claim is to perceive a distinctive or special relationship among particular instances of evidence. Let's say your instructor has worn something colored a very bright, very uncommon shade of yellow on each of the first four class meetings—a different article of clothing, sometimes a shirt, sometimes a hat, but always at least one item colored a very bright, consistent shade of yellow. You might be surprised if they came to class without such a colored item on the fifth meeting, even though "the first four class meetings" is not very much evidence. Your conclusion that your instructor would likely wear something the same shade of yellow, a conclusion that prompted your surprise when they didn't, would have still been reasonable, inductively, if you drew that conclusion based on how few other people you've seen wear that bright, uncommon shade of yellow even one time and how many different clothing options people of your instructor's social class seem to have.

These two forms of inductive reasoning—reasoning from a large group of instances and reasoning from a distinctive shared relationship among instances—are common in everyday life. For this reason, public speakers make use of them very often, much more often than they make use of deductive reasoning. Comey develops one of his key claims—what he labels his "third hard truth"—not merely by *using* inductive reasoning but also by discussing these two forms of inductive reasoning. He shows how they can be easily confused with one another as he develops the claim that these two forms of inductive reasoning do not necessarily lead to strong conclusions in the case of law enforcement officers interacting with community members. We quote this "third hard truth" at length here to explore inductive logic and Comey's analysis of it:

> But that leads me to my third hard truth: something happens to people in law enforcement. Many of us develop different flavors of cynicism that we work hard to resist because they can

be lazy mental shortcuts. For example, criminal suspects routinely lie about their guilt, and nearly everybody we charge is guilty. That makes it easy for some folks in law enforcement to assume that everybody is lying and that no suspect, regardless of their race, could be innocent. Easy, but wrong.

Likewise, police officers on patrol in our nation's cities often work in environments where a hugely disproportionate percentage of street crime is committed by young men of color. Something happens to people of good will working in that environment. After years of police work, officers often can't help but be influenced by the cynicism they feel.

A mental shortcut becomes almost irresistible and maybe even rational by some lights. The two young Black men on one side of the street look like so many others the officer has locked up. Two White men on the other side of the street—even in the same clothes—do not. The officer does not make the same association about the two White guys, whether that officer is White or Black. And that drives different behavior. The officer turns toward one side of the street and not the other. We need to come to grips with the fact that this behavior complicates the relationship between police and the communities they serve.

(Comey, 2015)

Comey here describes one possible use of inductive logic, the one that involves reasoning from a large group of instances, when he discusses the tendency of an interrogating officer to assume that a suspect is lying and again when he discusses the tendency of a patrol officer to focus more carefully on particular citizens based on perceived race. He acknowledges that such conclusions are "maybe even rational by some lights." We agree that from the standpoint of formal inductive logic, the conclusions such officers are drawing—while not certain—might be probable within a very limited contextual frame from which a law enforcement officer might reason. However, while the logic might be strong within that very limited contextual frame, as soon as the frame changes to include factors beyond an officer's immediate need to assess criminal activity, the logic weakens in important ways.

In other words, a formal analysis of inductive logic does not much help us in making law enforcement relationships with the community more just or equitable, as Comey also suggests.

It becomes harmful when law enforcement officers only use their own, or their colleagues', personal experiences when assessing criminal activity in local communities. How might their reasoning become problematic if they don't consider a wider range of factors outside of their personal experiences? How do you think this type of reasoning affects how police officers respond during traffic stops involving "young men of color".

We believe that because the experience of being repeatedly scrutinized on the street by law enforcement can create serious risks to the material and emotional health of a person, such a context demands a more complex use of reasoning than the logic of probabilities (within a limited frame) that Comey describes such officers using. What do you think? Should a law enforcement officer consider a wider range of factors when assessing criminal activity or intent than their own or their colleagues' personal experiences in the local community? Why or why not? How might your answer help you reflect not only on race and law enforcement but on inductive logic and context as elements of strong reasoning?

Comey's analysis of the harmfulness of such probabilistic conclusions also involves his recognition of the second form of inductive reasoning, reasoning from a distinctive shared relationship among instances. In the extended passage above Comey uses the phrase *mental shortcut* to describe something that happens to people in law enforcement. Comey's focus in this passage acknowledges that reasoning about a new context, with two unfamiliar young men in view of a police officer on a given side of the street, can lead to a "behavior that complicates the relationship between communities and law enforcement." The authors suggest that we have a common phrase for this "behavior" in our culture, one Comey does not use in his speech (likely because its use would dissuade many law enforcement members from considering his ideas): racial profiling. If a person is not yet in police custody like those suspects Comey describes in his interrogation example, and if that same person is not yet observed or known by a police officer to be engaged in committing the "hugely disproportionate percentage of street crime" that Comey describes as being committed by "young men of color," then what persuasive explanation could we offer for why "the officer turns toward one side of the street and not the other?" Comey implies, without stating this directly, that the officer has inferred criminal intent—an invisible quality—from just a few visible racial characteristics of the as-yet-unknown two young men. As a use of inductive logic, especially in law enforcement situations that involve less experienced officers or fresh circumstances, this is an example parallel to the one about a very bright shade of yellow discussed above. Remember that in our example, a student might draw a conclusion about the instructor's dress habits based not on a very large series of examples but instead because of distinctive features in a particular group of instances. However, when we consider this form of inductive reasoning in the context of racial profiling, again we would argue that the highly significant context of racial profiling demands a use of reasoning with more rigor than inductive logic can offer, given the serious potential impact on people's lives. In this case, the idea of accountability to a community in public speech acts—whether by law enforcement officers or public speakers—can help us recognize this. Would you agree that a law enforcement officer has a responsibility to consider the impact of their actions on the local community and not only on their supervisors or those directly involved in criminal activity?

Speakers Should Be Careful to Avoid Fallacies When Using Inductive Logic

A different approach to accountability, one that returns to the issue of logical fallacies as they apply to inductive logic, can also help us understand the weakness in the inductive conclusions Comey describes here. If a law enforcement officer devotes more time and attention to potential criminal activity on one side of the street than the other, without additional information beyond visible racial characteristics—as Comey acknowledges some officers might—that officer is committing the **hasty generalization fallacy**. This fallacy draws a conclusion based on inadequate evidence—either too few particular instances of evidence or too thin a texture of shared characteristics among particular instances. Even if racial profiling somehow did not put the material or emotional health of a person at risk, a community might still criticize an officer for using faulty inductive logic because we might conclude that the attribution of criminal intent is a rather hasty generalization based on shared characteristics as arbitrary as perceived race.

You can strengthen your own inductive logic when speaking in public by considering whether the evidence you offer is adequate to convince your chosen audience of the probable conclusion you offer. Do you provide enough examples so that your audience can see that they are related to one another—not by chance but by some underlying common features?

This can help you avoid a hasty generalization. Do you provide examples that, in each case, are clearly parallel to one another in scope and in their most important features? This can help you avoid another fallacy of inductive logic, the **fallacy of the single cause**. This fallacy stems from suggesting to your audience a single explanation for outcomes or phenomena that could instead be explained by several possible influences. Identifying possible causes for something we observe is an important aspect of logical reasoning, and we turn our attention to causal relationships in the next section.

Causal Logic Can Offer Solutions to Problems, If Well Supported

Another way to propose logical relationships among statements is to suggest a cause–effect relationship. **Causal logic** specifies a logical relationship among two or more elements in which one element is a necessary effect whenever a preceding element, the cause, is present. Causal logic is a special form of deductive logic in which the elements have a logical relationship to one another that is not necessarily permanent and persistent; instead it depends on time (because an effect *follows after* a cause). This reasoning can be especially useful when you offer a speech that identifies a problem and offers a solution to that problem, because if your audience agrees with the cause–effect relationship you describe, you can predict positive effects that will help solve the problem by enhancing positive effects if we take the steps that will cause them. Similarly, if your audience agrees then you can also predict negative effects that, if we bring their causes under control or change the processes that perpetuate those causes, will be eliminated and thereby help solve the problem by removing its negative aspects.

In his speech Comey offers a simple, direct claim about causation when he says, "Demographic data regarding officer-involved shootings is not consistently reported to us through our Uniform Crime Reporting Program. Because reporting is voluntary, our data is incomplete and therefore, in the aggregate, unreliable." His claim here is that, in effect, unreliable statistical data about officer-involved shootings nationwide has a single cause: the fact that departments report the data on a voluntary, rather than a mandatory, basis. He does not offer citations for this evidence, expecting his audience to trust his unique position as the director of the FBI to accept this claim.

When you speak, you will be in a more difficult position if you try to ascribe a single direct cause to a single effect. You will likely need to cite not only the source of your information but also testimony from an authority figure about the cause being the only relevant one. However, causal reasoning can be much more useful to you as a public speaker when you consider how more complex ideas about causes and effects can help you make arguments.

Comey develops these more complex cause–effect relationships in his speech, so let's examine how he does this in order to suggest how you might do so. He builds on the simple cause–effect claim above, the claim about unreliable data on officer-involved shootings, in this way:

> Without complete and accurate data, we are left with "ideological thunderbolts." And that helps spark unrest and distrust and does not help us get better. Because we must get better, I intend for the FBI to be a leader in urging departments around this country to give us the facts we need for an informed discussion, the facts all of us need, to help us make sound policy and sound decisions with that information . . . we—especially those of us who enjoy the privilege that comes with being the majority—must confront the biases that are inescapable parts of the human condition. We must speak the truth about our shortcomings as law enforcement, and fight to be better. But as a country, we must also speak the truth to ourselves. Law enforcement is not the root cause of problems in our hardest hit neighborhoods.
>
> (Comey, 2015)

Comey's argument here depends on his distinction between a **necessary cause** of the effect he advocates—healthier relationships between law enforcement and local communities—and a **sufficient cause** of that same effect. Let's discuss these in greater detail.

Comey's claim is that healthy relationships between law enforcement and local communities are only possible if policy makers have "the facts we need for an informed discussion." We know he believes these facts are necessary to achieve this effect because he asks, "How can we address concerns about 'use of force,' how can we address concerns about officer-involved shootings if we do not have a reliable grasp on the demographics and circumstances of those incidents?" Comey implies that we cannot do so otherwise, maintaining in the very next sentence: "We simply must improve the way we collect and analyze data to see the true nature of what's happening in all of our communities." So we know that for Comey, more comprehensive data about officer-involved shootings are a necessary cause of the effect he describes, the healthier relationships.

Yet we also know that Comey considers this data inadequate by itself to achieve the desired effect. We know this because he follows this analysis by insisting that "law enforcement is not the root cause of problems in our hardest hit neighborhoods." His only immediate reference here to other possible "root causes" after this claim is that the effects of such root causes, the problems he names, are "the product of problems that will not be solved by body cameras." He implies here that he is referring back to an earlier passage in his speech, which he summarized in this way: "Young people in 'those neighborhoods' too often inherit a legacy of crime and prison." In other words, he argues—though indirectly—that systemic poverty and the related lack of education and job opportunities must also be addressed, in addition to the behavior of law enforcement officials. This means that gathering and using more comprehensive statistical data about officer-involved shootings, while necessary for achieving an intended effect, is not sufficient for achieving that effect. This is why Comey's argument depends on a distinction between a necessary cause and a sufficient cause.

One additional possibility that Comey's argument structure could have left open, had he chosen a different approach, is the possibility that the data gathering he advocates is a **contributory cause** of the desired effect. This would be true if gathering this data could help bring about healthier relationships, but if law enforcement agencies ignore the data-gathering need, then healthy relationships might happen in some other way. We have already seen that Comey does not agree; he argues that such agencies "simply must improve" their data gathering. So for Comey, improved data gathering is a necessary cause, not merely a contributory cause.

Distinguish Necessary, Sufficient, and Contributory Causes

Necessary, sufficient, and contributory causes can be distinguished from one another if we more precisely describe cause–effect relationships: If an effect (let's call that effect E to make things simpler) exists, then a necessary cause (let's call it N) must exist also. But the reverse is not true: If we know that N exists, we don't know yet whether E exists—remember, according to Comey, other causes are part of the desired effect he advocates. In shorthand, if E exists, then N must exist; but if N exists, we don't yet know if E exists. It might, but it might not. In the case of a sufficient cause (let's call it S), however, we can say something different: If E exists, then S must exist, and if S exists, then E must exist—that tight relationship is what we mean when we label something a sufficient cause. A sufficient cause is in itself enough to achieve the effect. In the case of a contributory cause (let's call it C), we cannot say anything quite so certain: The existence of C does not mean that E exists, and the existence of E does not mean that C exists.

This pile of potentially confusing symbols points to one major insight that matters most when you make cause–effect claims in your own speaking: Be sure you understand how vital each cause is if you make an argument about causes. Is a cause you identify sufficient all by itself to establish an effect? If so, then say so, because that gives you great power to advocate that cause if your audience embraces the desired effect. If not, then show your audience that you are ready to be accountable to them by acknowledging, as Comey does, that more than just one single cause must be your audience's focus, and what each of those relevant causes might mean.

Strongly Defined Cause–Effect Relationships Can Help Speakers Avoid Fallacies

Strongly defined cause–effect relationships can help you avoid other reasoning fallacies as well. One common causal fallacy is the **post hoc fallacy**, in which one event or outcome follows another, and therefore, a person makes an argument that falsely assumes that the first event caused the second. The way to avoid this fallacy is to ensure not only that two sequential events are related but that they are *causally related*. Consider this: Suppose that in the next few years, most law enforcement agencies adopt a more mandatory, careful system of documenting officer-involved shootings and then, some years later, media channels begin to widely report and celebrate a huge drop in the number of such shootings. Can we argue that the more careful system of documentation caused the drop? We cannot. As Comey observes, such factors as training procedures, perceptual prejudice, and community relationships and trust also play important roles, which should lead us to be wary of attributing a single cause to an effect as profound as a drop in the number of such shootings.

Another fallacy related to causation is the **slippery slope fallacy**. This fallacy results from predicting a series of increasingly negative effects from a single negative cause, which is weak causal reasoning. As we have discussed, Comey directly argues in his speech that the current voluntary, haphazard system of documenting officer-involved shootings makes policy formation and deep understanding difficult. Suppose he had gone on to claim a series of consequences that he predicted from our failure to change this system, such as a persistently high number of controversial officer-involved shootings; increased hostility directed toward law enforcement by local communities; and a deterioration of the ability of officers to effectively combat crime in the future. Could he justify this based on the evidence he provided in the speech? He could not; he would need to introduce and develop additional cause–effect relationships for each step in this predicted series of future effects, ensuring that he established each such relationship as carefully as he did the previous one. Otherwise, his hypothetical argument would have been weakened by the slippery slope fallacy. You can also avoid this fallacy by linking each effect you describe, carefully, to a specific cause or set of causes.

Speakers May Also Reason by Making Meaningful Comparisons Called Analogies

A form of reasoning related to but distinct from logical reasoning is reasoning from analogy or **analogical reasoning**. When we do analogical reasoning, we draw conclusions based not on the *relationships between statements*, as we do in logical reasoning in the ways described above. Instead, we encourage our audience to embrace a conclusion because they *associate* a given complex experience—an experience they know well or understand fully—with one that is new to them or questionable for them.

Early in his speech Comey uses an analogy to draw a conclusion. He offers this:

> As a society, we can choose to live our everyday lives, raising our families and going to work, hoping that someone, somewhere, will do something to ease the tension—to smooth over the conflict. We can roll up our car windows, turn up the radio and drive around these problems, or we can choose to have an open and honest discussion about what our relationship is today—what it should be, what it could be, and what it needs to be—if we took more time to better understand one another.
>
> (Comey, 2015)

Comey uses the analogy of driving around with windows rolled up to help listeners understand what they are metaphorically doing when they avoid difficult topics and conflict. Does this seem like an effective analogy to you?

Here, Comey expects that enough of his audience members are familiar with driving a car that they will reflect on both the actions they can choose in that situation—"roll," "turn up," "drive"—and the sensory and emotional memories of what flows from those actions. He implies that when we drive a car, we often put ourselves into a place of isolation, cut off from the sounds and smells of the environment and the people in it, and that when we do so

Speakers often use analogies to make meaningful comparisons. For example, the analogy of learning to ride a bike is often tied to how we understand and don't forget concepts that have become so ingrained (like bike riding). How might this analogy be different for someone who doesn't know how to ride a bike?

it is a way of taking a stance, of adopting a position about that environment and those people. He wants his audience to recall these driving experiences and associate this position and its feelings to the position and feelings of a person who expects the tension and conflict between law enforcement and local communities to simply dissolve or be handled by someone else. The authors consider this a highly effective analogy not only because Comey chooses a common experience that is a good fit for his conclusion, reminding us of the distinctive, aloof ways we position ourselves in the community when we drive generally, but also because the common experience itself—driving with windows up and music shutting out other sounds—is closely related to Comey's chosen subject matter. After all, we the authors have ourselves made these exact choices before—the closed windows and the musical barrier—when driving in areas of great poverty visible on surface streets. Have you done this as a driver? What do you think it means? Do you consider this an effective analogy? Why or why not?

Like inductive reasoning, analogical reasoning is something we do often in everyday life. We have common phrases in our culture like, "It's like learning to ride a bike: you'll never forget" or "they ran the class like a drill sergeant." When we develop an analogy, we expect our audience to be familiar with a complex process, something that often involves multiple parts or extended personal experience to understand well. We are encouraging our listeners to reflect on their experiences and judge our association of that experience with a new or questionable idea. This is also why an effective analogy, one that will encourage your audience to embrace your conclusion, depends on your choice of an experience that audience members widely share and on which they can reflect at length to the benefit of your conclusion.

Analogies can be powerful as reasoning processes, because they connect with direct experience grounded not just in thought but in past, embodied actions that your listeners will recall in profound ways. But analogies, given this same quality, can also be weak forms of reasoning that are weakened by social hierarchies and privilege if you use them unreflectively. Consider our two examples above: One of the authors learned to ride a bike as a thirty-something adult yet was asked to appreciate the "ride a bike" analogy as something they had done during childhood. Neither of our authors has a history of military service. If you were in our position, writing this book, would these two analogies be useful in making an argument? Which readers might find them compelling? Which readers find them unclear or even demeaning, something that leads not to profound, embodied reflection but to negative feelings of exclusion? You can be accountable to your audience when using an analogy if you consider the fitness of the analogy for audience members whose experiences, histories, and relationships might differ from your own. This is another example of how public speaking itself, as a communicative act, creates community by embracing connections among speakers and listeners, and another example of why a public speaker who is attentive to these connections and treats them with respect can speak effectively.

As you strive to use analogies effectively, you must consider, as we have discussed, two questions: How widely shared in this particular community is the process or experience you expect your audience to already know? How strong is the fit, the span of common features, between that known experience and the new, questionable one you want your audience to better grasp along with you? If you consider both of these questions you can avoid a fallacy known as a **false analogy**, which results from poor fitness between the two items you bring together by association.

Ethical, Inclusive Speakers Attend to Situated Reasoning

Each of the approaches to reasoning that we have explored so far in this chapter share a view of "good reasons" consonant with values about human life, relationships, and nature most common, historically, in mainstream Western institutions. These approaches to reasoning typically organize themselves around rules, or principles, of logical organization (Hicks & Langsdorf, 2011). In this section, we consider an approach to reasoning that depends on relationships rather than rules.

Such an approach can be characterized by the phrase **situated reasoning**. This term helps identify one central feature, common to several forms of reasoning marginalized in Europe, Canada, and the United States, that distinguishes those forms from the dominant forms: They embrace reasons grounded in particular times and places. They derive their force (and thus the strength of their conclusions, when speakers offer conclusions) from knowledge based in immediate relationships. This is in contrast to the abstract rules and procedures that apply universally—in other words, regardless of time or place—within the structures of logic or causality that we discussed above.

We will continue to reflect on the subject of Comey's speech, officer-involved shootings of people of color, as we offer an example of situated reasoning. Suppose you are in public, in the midst of a chaotic and potentially violent environment, and you hear or see an order from a police officer to do something with your body, immediately. Perhaps you have learned

Situated reasoning might cause some people to comply when police officers pull them over or tell them to put their hands up where they can be seen, but it might also make other people run or react violently. The same situation can have different affects on different people.

that when such an authority figure gives you this kind of order, you must comply because it is "right," and complying makes you a "good" citizen.

Perhaps, instead, you have learned within your community that you must comply because it is dangerous *not* to comply—the officer might use force on you if you don't comply. The threat of force being used against your body might be the strongest factor leading you to comply, stronger than a sense of what is "right." Perhaps, in our hypothetical example, you are not alone in this environment when the officer gives you an order—perhaps a close family member who depends on you is with you in this moment. Perhaps you fear for the safety of this close family member and worry that if you comply with the officer's order, that family member may be gravely harmed. Under these circumstances, you might decide it is reasonable to ignore or disobey the order given by the officer, even knowing that doing so puts your own safety at risk, because you would not hesitate to put yourself in harm's way to protect your family member. In our hypothetical example, attempting to explain why you *should* comply based on logic or causality, or even based on a simple adding up of past experiences (a kind of inductive logic), would not be enough to change your mind. You might argue that your decision to not comply was based in your community's history, your perception of the immediate situation, and your care for your family member. You might argue that these factors carry greater weight for you than rules or principles determined in advance, in the abstract, could do.

Our writing about situated reasoning, given the force of this approach to reasoning, necessarily reflects our own partial, situated histories and cultures: Both of the authors are

White Americans, one is a woman and one is a man, and both have been deeply influenced by masculine philosophies predominant in the academy. We urge you, as you read this section, to consider your own history, culture, and decision-making processes in light of our claims here: Which of these forms of situated reasoning do people use when developing and organizing ideas within your family? Your neighborhood? Your spiritual community?

Forms of situated reasoning have been historically marginalized in the predominant discourses within many Western cultures. When we observe this, we are not suggesting that situated reasoning is absent or necessarily confusing or misunderstood throughout Europe, Canada, and the United States. What makes these forms marginal is that these Western cultures have, for centuries, framed key decisions in government, law, and other important social processes within the context of logic and causation. This persistent framing elevates the status of logic and causation. This creates a social reality in which logic and causation become, in practical contexts, often viewed as "better" reasons than those reasons flowing from situated forms of reasoning. As a result, logic and causation acquire increasing power over time, and speakers (and other communicators) who emphasize logic and causation find it much easier to marshal resources and shape action according to their wishes. We have explored logic and causation in the depth we have in this chapter because no matter what approach to reasoning you find compelling, the playing field of effective reasoning is not level. You will, for the foreseeable future, speak with greater power if you can use logic and causation successfully. However, you can effect change in your communities if you can also use situated forms of reasoning successfully.

"We Must Account for That Inheritance"

When we speak on issues that affect us all, and for whom the consequences are greater for those with the least power, privilege, and security in our communities, we bear a responsibility to be diligent and respectful in our argumentation. To do so, we cannot only think of our own convenience as speakers, of what might be easiest or would help us "win" our arguments. Our communication exists in a web of relationships that is strengthened or damaged by our efforts to articulate how we understand the world (some process, policy, issue, or experience). We can work toward stronger arguments, and stronger relationships, by remembering this interconnectedness and inviting it to challenge our thinking.

Concepts

ad populum fallacy 197
affirming a negative premise 196
analogical reasoning 206
appeal to nature 197
appeal to tradition 197
causal logic 202
contributory cause 204
deductive logic 195
fallacy 196
fallacy of the single cause 202

false analogy 208
hasty generalization fallacy 202
inductive logic 197
logical reasoning 194
necessary cause 204
post hoc fallacy 205
reasoning 191
situated reasoning 209
slippery slope fallacy 206
sufficient cause 204

Toward Praxis

1. **Reflection:** Consider a time when you were moved to make an argument that was deeply important to you. What strategies did you call on to persuade your listener(s)? Which were most effective? How so?

2. **Discussion:** Consider the politics of reasoning. Which forms of reasoning are most effective, and with whom? How is that effectiveness or lack thereof the result of historical, cultural, and economic relationships between groups of people?

3. **Action:** Learn about other situated forms of reasoning. Who is empowered or marginalized by each? How might you draw on these insights in your next speaking occasion?

Discussion Questions

1. How have you encountered the different forms of reasoning in your daily lives? Which are most compelling for you and why?

2. For whom do you speak? What are the consequences of your messages for the people others see as identified with you?

3. What sorts of fallacies, or errors in argumentation, have you observed recently? Here you might consider political candidates' speeches, advertisements, or what you encounter in the news.

CHAPTER
11

Public Speaking Is Evolving

In this chapter, we will work together to:

- Identify and distinguish between traditional communication contexts and computer-mediated communication contexts, especially the way each context affects public speaking

- Identify factors that shape how speakers create, distribute, and receive responses to messages in computer-mediated environments, especially public contexts

- Describe effective strategies for public advocacy within computer-mediated communication contexts

One out of every five women will be sexually assaulted or raped before she reaches the age of 18. That women of color, if they're raped or sexually assaulted before the age of 18, are 66-percent more likely to be raped or sexually assaulted again. Seventy percent of girls who are sexually trafficked are girls of color. They are coming out of the foster care system, they are coming out of poverty. It is a billion-dollar industry. When they go into the sex trafficking business—and they call it a business, trust me—more than likely, they are gang raped.

I am speaking today, not just for the #metoos, because I was a #metoo, but when I raise my hand, I am aware of all the women who are still in silence. The women who are faceless. The women who don't have the money, and who don't have the constitution, and who don't have the confidence, and who don't have the images in our media that gives them a sense of self-worth enough to break their silence that's rooted in the shame of assault. That's rooted in the stigma of assault.

. . . [E]very single day your job as an American citizen, is not just to fight for your rights; it's to fight for the rights of every individual who is taking a breath.

(Davis, 2018)

On January 10, 2018, Viola Davis, a Hollywood actor, addressed demonstrators assembled in Los Angeles for the Women's March, a movement initially organized in January 2017 to protest the inauguration of Donald Trump as U.S. president. In her speech, Davis noted the history of governmentally legislated discrimination against citizens of color in the United States that deprived these citizens of a range of rights. She linked this history to the focus in the Women's March on the forms of gender-based discrimination and assault perpetrated against women in employment contexts such as the local film and television industry—her own. Davis named the #MeToo movement as a force driving public attention to sexual abuses of power by men in this industry, underscoring the ways that African American women's foundational work in constructing this particular form of resistance resulted in great personal costs to these women.

Viola Davis, Selection from "Women's March Speech." Copyright © 2018 by Viola Davis.

> **If you've been sexually harassed or assaulted write 'me too' as a reply to this tweet.**
>
> Me too.
>
> Suggested by a friend: "If all the women who have been sexually harassed or assaulted wrote 'Me too.' as a status, we might give people a sense of the magnitude of the problem."

Alyssa Milano gained national attention with her #metoo hashtag. The #metoo movement is an ongoing hashtag campaign that has brought popular and cultural awareness to sexual assault and everyday gendered violence. This campaign is an example of a computer-mediated context.

In this chapter, we consider Davis's speech as an example of public speaking as ever evolving. In particular, she suggests that the mediated environments allowing the #MeToo movement to rapidly accelerate its visibility and impact, including image-based media and social media, might also have other, negative or limiting consequences when it comes to transforming communities. Specifically, her discussion of mediated messages and her selective citation of influential leaders are important speaking choices. Both of these speaking choices draw our attention to the fact that communication, even in computer-mediated contexts like those of the #MeToo movement, is powerfully shaped by the features of how our human bodies appear to one another in face-to-face, media-rich contact with another. Davis argues that we must take care to note racial and gender features as movements like the #MeToo campaign gain momentum in ways that can distort or lessen our recognition of social responsibility.

Davis's claim that socially mediated messages like the #MeToo hashtag depend on face-to-face experiences is an interesting and powerful claim for communication studies scholars. In this chapter, we begin by considering how computer-mediated communication contexts are and are not like face-to-face contexts. We explore how computer-mediated contexts relate to public discourse, which historically involved a different kind of access to speakers in public settings. We consider some ways that computer-mediated speakers might continue to effectively engage their communities and advocate for positive change, even when communities are linked primarily through digital channels.

Communication Is Mediated—Often in Ways We Don't Notice

On one level, we can define **computer-mediated communication (CMC)** in a straightforward manner as any communication that occurs through a channel that requires the use of a computer to send and/or receive messages. CMC is important because it has allowed us to take special advantage of the symbolic nature of communication, which has allowed us to create and read messages across great distances in space and time. With CMC, we can communicate

In our current society, individuals can communicate with anyone at any time. Think of what it was like before cell phones existed. How would you have kept in touch with your friends during the day?

across huge spatial divides without a huge time cost. Think of how different it is to text with a friend far away, rather than having to write a letter and wait days (or longer) for a reply.

There are, however, some complications involved with our straightforward definition of CMC. First, we need to keep in mind that *computer* in contemporary technological conditions very often means a device that does not usually go by that name. The phones that many of us carry in our pockets and use as our most frequent method of engaging in communication (through texting or using other applications such as Twitter, Instagram, Snapchat, or WhatsApp) are also computers. We cannot send or receive messages of any of these types without computers and this fact has significant consequences for communication that we discuss below. Second, several historically important channels of communication that were not considered CMC, and were not studied in that way by scholars, are now converging with CMC because they are most often accessed through computers, phones, and other devices like tablets that have CMC features. Clear examples of this convergence are television and film (now often viewed on personal devices rather than in groups assembled around a screen) and news media (now often viewed through online e-distribution requiring a computer). Convergence is exciting but it also blurs the distinctions between CMC and non-CMC forms of communication, which means that we have to be increasingly thoughtful about the complex ways we communicate with one another if we hope to harness the power of communication.

"Facebook is not your friend. It is a surveillance engine."

—Richard Stallman

CHAPTER 11 | PUBLIC SPEAKING IS EVOLVING | 217

Computer-mediated devices have changed how we enjoy TV/movies. Have you ever been in the same room with someone while you are both watching different TV shows on separate iPads? These elements of communication are quite different when you watch a film on a personal device versus in a movie theater.

How do you usually watch television programs or feature films? Do you usually watch alone? Do you sometimes use headphones if family members or roommates are nearby? These questions highlight why CMC contexts can be so distinct from traditional, non-computer-mediated contexts. Even if you watch a feature film in a commercial movie theater, for instance, and even if you are still and silent as you do so, the reactions of others around you (their excitement, their laughter, their fidgeting, their bodies' impact on the temperature and air flow in the room) may change your experience of the film. These elements of communication are quite different when you engage a film on a personal device, and thus communication changes.

CMC Is Meaningfully Different

Other differences are also evident between CMC and non-CMC forms of communication. Some forms of CMC include exclusively verbal/visual symbols and have no nonverbal elements in their messages—such as text messaging. Please note: Emoji, which commonly picture nonverbal gestures, are not considered nonverbal communication because they are communicated solely through symbols, the way letters are communicated. When we use CMC that does not rely on nonverbal elements to communicate with one another, this affects how we make meaning of messages because we cannot rely on the nonverbal cues we use in face-to-face or oral/aural (like phone calls) contexts. Depending on the message and on the situation, we might find

FaceTime and other video chat programs are examples of synchronous communication. This type of communication involves interacting with one another at the same time.

it more difficult to achieve clarity without nonverbal cues. Furthermore, some forms of CMC involve communicators interacting with one another at the same time—FaceTime and other video chat platforms are good examples of this, which is called **synchronous communication**. Other forms of CMC involve communicators interacting with one another at (potentially) widely separated times, which is called **asynchronous communication**. E-mail is a good example of asynchronous communication.

Many forms of CMC fall somewhere between these two extremes, as our separation from one another in time varies depending on how each of us chooses to engage with one another. As professors, the authors sometimes receive e-mails from students that include apologies for e-mailing us at a given time, such as 2:00 a.m. Notice, though, that unless we have our e-mail sending us push notifications involving vibrations or ring tones, we will probably read these e-mails the next day during regular business hours—meaning that the apology by the student makes an assumption based in synchronous communication, when in fact we as professors choose to use e-mail in more asynchronous ways.

Email is a good example of asynchronous communication, which involves interacting with one another at (potentially) widely separated times.

CHAPTER 11 | PUBLIC SPEAKING IS EVOLVING

These negotiations between communicators of the time dimension of CMC are always in play, and they affect communication. Would you consider it a negative message if your closest friend, who hadn't told you they were going anywhere special anytime soon, didn't reply to a text for a full day? Would you consider it a negative message if a professor offered to receive messages via text but didn't reply to your text for a full day? As a public speaker, you will be most effective if you consider how your messages are perceived and interpreted by audience members according to their assumptions and orientation to your speech.

CMC Is Relevant for Public Speakers

The ubiquity of CMC for contemporary communicators has at least two consequences, then, for you as a public speaker. First, your speech will have greater impact if you take into account the ways that listening to and watching your speech, in a single assembled group like a class, differs from what your audience members usually experience as communicators in CMC environments. Will we expect you to use short, concise phrases because our ability to quickly decode meaning has been shaped by our routine engagement of the short, concise phrases of text messages and Instagram captions? Will we learn best if we have opportunities for immediate feedback, such as web-based instant polls you offer us during your speech, because our phones routinely provide us with immediate feedback on our curiosity in most instances?

Second, your opportunities to engage in dialogue within your communities may be much more widespread, and have much more impact, if you search for innovative ways to reach community members that range beyond the group of people who happen to share the immediate space and time with you. The #MeToo movement noted by Davis gives us one example of how CMC can enhance the reach and impact of public messages.

CMC Can Enhance the Reach and Impact of Public Messages

The phrase *MeToo* was initially used by Tarana Burke in 2006. Burke is an activist who was striving for a way to create "empowerment through empathy" for women of color, initially young women and girls in the southern United States, who survived sexual violence (Ohlheiser, 2017). It began in a socially mediated context, Myspace, so from its inception it was an example of an effort to raise awareness across space and time through CMC channels. Burke's avowed interest was in raising the profile of acts of sexual violence that affected women of color, and the phrase was designed to encourage survivors of these acts of violence to acknowledge their reality and the ways their lives continued to be affected over time. At its inception, then, one value of the phrase *MeToo* is that it could help resist the culture of shame that can discourage women from reporting sexual assault or that can lead women to blame themselves for having been sexually assaulted. A second value is that it could help show, in its focus on enduring effects over a person's life, how sexual violence deployed against women of color

A grassroots version of the "me too" movement was initiated 10 years earlier by activist Tarana Burke to aid sexual assault survivors in underprivileged communities "where rape crisis centers and sexual assault workers weren't going," Milano's celebrity allowed the conversation to travel more broadly.

can work to sustain systems like racism and sexism that prevent women of color from having access to power in job settings and in other institutions by stoking fear and undermining these women's confidence.

In October 2017, the *MeToo* phrase was popularized as a hashtag in a tweet by Alyssa Milano, a White-appearing actor, in response to allegations that Harvey Weinstein, an influential film executive, committed several sexual assaults and created an enduring climate of sexual harassment within the professional film industry. The hashtag soon went viral and became an umbrella handle describing a series of efforts by social media users to publicly identify themselves as survivors of sexual assault and/or harassment. In broadening the reach of the movement, the experiences that unite women of color specifically may be lost.

When Davis names the #MeToo movement in her speech, one goal she accomplishes is creating a bond of community—of solidarity—with those in attendance at the Women's March in Los Angeles. This event, on the 1-year anniversary of the Women's March in 2017, emerged as a form of protest of the inauguration of Donald Trump as the 45th president of the United States. Media coverage of Trump's campaign had prominently featured questions about his past public messages about women and his acts of sexual violence and degradation; the Women's March signaled outrage at the seating of this man in the chief executive office. Davis, by citing the #MeToo campaign, invokes on this anniversary event a more recent, high-profile instance of public discourse that addresses similar concerns about abuses of power that involve sexual violence and degradation and that are especially deployed against women. In doing so, she symbolizes her solidarity with assembled listeners who share her outrage at these abuses of power. This is a compelling act of connecting herself with her audience's beliefs and values, grounding what she has to say for audience members in a common ethical frame. Her choice of the #MeToo movement is also a significant indexing of local concerns, in that Los Angeles is the most prominent city in the film industry, the industry that the movement identified as a principle example of a hostile workplace for women.

Davis is in an interesting position here, situated in both traditional and mediated speaking contexts. She is speaking as a person using a microphone to communicate over loudspeakers with an audience assembled around her. Yet when she selects her primary and most frequently used method of creating a common ethical frame for audience members to make sense of her messages, she does not choose their shared interest in the 1-year-old Women's March. Instead, she emphasizes a socially mediated movement dependent on CMC channels. This might seem like a surprising choice, the choice to highlight the immediate, face-to-face sense of shared community by making repeated references to the much more abstract, much less immediate bond of the #MeToo campaign. Why do you think she made this choice? We the authors believe that one reason she did so is to make good use of the timeliness of this campaign. You can use this as a guide when you make your own choices for creating shared systems of value with your audience members as a speaker, by deliberately emphasizing current, widely discussed themes and examples.

But we also find Davis's choice interesting for an additional reason: It reminds us of the tangled ways that CMC and traditional, face-to-face communication contexts cannot be easily distinguished from each other anymore. Consider that most of the listeners assembled in front of Davis at the Women's March likely learned when and where the demonstration would occur through some form of CMC—especially through social media posts but also through online news sources, text messages, and other direct messages from friends, and so on. The attendees may well also be more committed to the Women's March as a meaningful use of their time because similar CMC-based channels—especially social media—persuade them of its relevance, reach, and impact. So the fact that Davis builds a common foundation of ethical community in a face-to-face setting, with primary emphasis on a CMC-based movement is perhaps right on target for this reason as well: She acknowledges that she is speaking to a group of listeners whose very presence together depends to a large extent on our contemporary CMC-based environment. She can potentially best activate their motivations as allies by speaking within a CMC frame, even when face-to-face with them. We encourage you to consider how you, too, can acknowledge your audience's impulses, experiences, and motivations—through your language choices, through your choice of appropriate examples, and through challenging us to examine these impulses, experiences, and motivations when you think it can support your efforts to enhance life in your communities.

Traditional Public Speaking Concepts Both Deepen and Adapt in Mediated Contexts

The complex situation of Davis's public speech can help us trace some questions about how public speaking concepts apply when speakers use CMC to reach audiences. It's possible that some of these concepts will continue to apply well to CMC-based public speaking contexts, but it's also possible that some of these concepts will need to be extended or modified to account for how discourse works in CMC contexts.

Consider, for instance, that Davis spoke in front of only a portion of a crowd in Los Angeles, that sources estimate to have consisted of approximately 500,000 demonstrators. Her speech was recorded, though, and can now be viewed in the form of a video recording by hundreds of millions of people who were not able to see and hear her live, greatly enhancing its potential impact. This relies on technologies that, in their form, are not based in CMC. The public speeches of government officials and other key political figures, for instance, have been recorded and repeatedly viewed for many decades. We suspect that each person reading this can recall seeing Dr. Martin Luther King Jr. speak in a recorded form, for example. But CMC changes the potential impact of Davis's speech in important ways related to space and time that are not available to us without digital media.

CMC Changes the Impact of a Speech Related to Space and Time

First, in terms of space, Davis's speech is accessible to a much wider range of audience members who can view it at any time they choose, from any place with sufficient Internet connectivity and associated computer viewing tools. The authors' first opportunities to view a video recording of Dr. King speaking took place in classrooms (a kind of shared space) with all class members viewing his speech on televisions. In our contemporary CMC environment, however, we (and you) can view him speaking on our own personal devices at any time. This means that Davis, like other public speakers in our contemporary CMC environment, is engaging audience members whose bond with

In this photo a student is reading an essay she wrote about Martin Luther King Jr to an audience on Martin Luther King Day. Video from his life plays in the background. Nowadays, students can watch or listen to his famous speech on their computer-mediated devices whenever they want. Computer-mediated devices can enhance the reach and impact of public messages, like that of Dr. King.

> "First of all, I *know* it's all people like you. And that's what's so scary. *Individually* you don't know what you're doing *collectively*."
>
> —Dave Eggers

one another does not depend on our shared spaces. Even though she is speaking in the daylight in Los Angeles in January 2018, Davis is in certain respects vital to community transformation when she is "delivering her speech" to a person sitting in bed at night in India a week or a month later.

How should this great spatial reach shape Davis's speaking choices, given what you now know about audience analysis, organizing a speech, developing examples, using effective language, and delivery? Should she select examples that anticipate this great spatial reach? Should she organize her speech differently, or choose different language, based on this concern? Should you take these concerns into account when speaking, if you know your classroom speech is being video recorded and could be posted online if someone chose? Such concerns for extended audiences are challenging to manage with precision and can be taken too far, as neither you nor Davis could make much progress in developing your speeches without beginning somewhere. As we have discussed, Davis begins in the appropriate place—her immediate community—as demonstrated by her concern for local audience members, their likely reasons for gathering together at the Los Angeles Women's March, and their shared interest in challenging climates hostile to women. You, too, should anchor your speaking choices in the local community first.

But in subtle ways, Davis does make choices that allow her speech to have a stronger chance to affect viewers in spatially remote areas and that are sensitive to our contemporary CMC environment. Note that by emphasizing the #MeToo movement more fully than the Women's March itself, she potentially broadens her reach beyond those viewers invested in the United States and its 45th president. Also, as we discuss in the next section, her citation of several African Americans and their claims and struggles throughout her speech gives the speech a relevance for those interested in diminishing the power of racist systems—some of whom may feel that their interests are well represented by those in attendance at the Women's March, but others of whom may not feel this way. These are two strategies Davis uses to simultaneously anchor her speech in the shared community of the Los Angeles Women's March demonstration and anticipate more spatially diverse audiences who may engage her speech. You may choose some public speaking topics and settings that are clearly linked to broader contexts that extend beyond your local community, while you may choose other topics and settings with less clear links to more remote communities. If you take the time to explore and, when appropriate, clarify such links within your speech as you analyze your audience, organize your speech, choose examples, and choose language and delivery style, then you are appropriately addressing our contemporary CMC environment.

Second, in terms of time, Davis's speech has the opportunity to increase significantly in impact as a result of the power of CMC to accelerate the rate at which we share information.

We can understand this through her own central topic, the #MeToo movement: She makes reference to this movement in ways that take for granted her audience's widespread recognition of the movement and acknowledgment of its great impact, despite the fact that Milano's initial tweet preceded Davis's speech by only about 14 weeks. The #MeToo hashtag has been described in the press as having gone viral (Ohlheiser, 2018), a reminder that in a CMC environment 14 weeks is actually a very long time and that some messages reach millions of audience members only hours after they are first shared online. Furthermore, the algorithms at the root of most social media platforms amplify this temporal spike in relevance, as these algorithms enhance the social media visibility of messages based not only on how frequently they are shared but on how recently they have been shared. What this means to public speakers like Davis (and you) is that CMC profoundly compresses the feedback loops that historically existed between public speakers and audience members. Audience responses in CMC environments are bewilderingly rapid and the more rapid they are, the more rapid still they become when shared online because of social media algorithms.

The compression of the time dimension and related feedback loops in CMC environments can offer us several benefits as public speakers. Many forms of information, and many different perspectives in any area of discourse, are available to us and to our audiences when we speak publicly. As a result, we have a heightened obligation to carefully cite our sources, to use compelling examples and reasoning, and to strive to understand our audience members' existing orientation to our topics. Otherwise, our public speech will have a vanishingly small impact on audience members within the din of contemporary CMC-influenced environments.

Communication Expectations Are Evolving

How, then, can we as speakers signal to our audiences that we have developed a public speech that is worthy of their selective attention? How can we sustain their interest in face-to-face environments, using the tools we have explored in this book—tools that draw attention to us and our topic, that identify the pedagogically rich elements of a speaking situation and that engage our audiences in ways parallel to interpersonal conversation? One way to begin to answer these questions is to explore an example related to how communication expectations are evolving in our lives.

When using the phone, do you assume that a person who has recently given you their phone number, perhaps just an acquaintance or a potential study partner from class, expects you to text them before you make a voice call? The authors have learned over the course of our lives that this is the expectation amid the present-day culture of smartphones, despite the fact that for most of our lives, the purpose of a phone number exchange (either exclusively or, later, primarily) was to enable voice calling. The "rule" (rarely explicitly stated as a rule, but understood by communicators seeking to avoid misjudgment or negative consequences) might be stated as "Before making a voice call, you must text a person to arrange such a call unless the

Communications expectations are evolving. Students expect their teachers and speakers will use varied modes of engagement. If communication needs aren't met, students often become distracted.

person is a close friend or family member." This would be an example of a **regulative rule of communication**; such rules organize communication, helping us recognize when, where, with whom, and why we can acceptably communicate and anticipate reliable, positive responses from others. A **constitutive rule of communication**, in contrast, tells us the meaning of a given message. Staying with our texting/voice calling example, if you were to respond "'kay" orally, as a shortened version of "okay," most listeners would accept that as a signal that you understand what they are saying to you and are still listening, yes? But the authors have learned that simply texting back the letter *k* as a response in a text exchange, which might seem reasonable as a symbolic equivalent of *'kay*, can be interpreted as rude or short-tempered. This interpretation would be explained by a constitutive rule of communication.

Connecting these two types of rules to public speaking, we have observed that "traditional" public speaking contexts, in which a group of assembled listeners have arrived and expect to sit quietly with their full attention on one single speaker for several minutes, are increasingly rare, even in institutional settings that have historically emphasized these forms of communication—such as schools or political rallies. For instance, each of us has modified our teaching over time because the regulative rules determining appropriate lengths of turns at talk—even for teachers—are changing, as are regulative rules about the speed of **feedback loops**, which are patterns of messages shared from one communicator to another in which each message is affected by the previous messages in the exchange. Similarly, the constitutive rules determining **modes of address** (how we should refer to one another) between students and teachers are changing, as are constitutive rules about using certain forms of formal academic language in

226 | EMPOWERING PUBLIC SPEAKING

essays. An effective public speaker must now recognize that audience members will likely expect more varied modes of engagement, beyond merely oral/aural exchange, and will likely experience our public speech as just one element in an ongoing fluid stream of ideas at any given time.

If you consider the context in which Davis speaks, you might note that the standards for success in the Women's March context are not primarily directed toward stoking commitment to the cause among those locally assembled; they include Davis's goals of changing awareness of the racialized dimensions of sexual violence, patriarchy, and economic power—an awareness that depends on her reach extending beyond the local setting through CMC-based channels such as tweets and other digital platforms for sharing both her original speech and the ideas she offers. She can speak successfully because she sculpts her speech using her knowledge of the regulative and constitutive rules of the #MeToo campaign and the Women's March, as our explication of her speech below shows.

Effective Speakers Communicate in Ways That Give Rise to Lasting Change

The distinctive elements of mediated communication and their impact on public advocacy shape Davis's speech at the level of her chosen focus. She begins the speech by highlighting

Rules of public speaking are constantly evolving and have been significantly effected by the rise of computer-mediated devices. Now we can watch *The Today Show* on TV live or watch it later online. We can also share video clips from the show that we liked on social media. The use of all of these mediums allow speakers to affect many people with their words, so the burden put on speakers to give rise to change or make an impact on society has increased.

> "Every generation expands its definition of equality. Previous generations fought for the vote and civil rights. They had the New Deal and Great Society. Now it's our time to define a new social contract for our generation."
>
> —Mark Zuckerberg

the history of racist laws in the United States and the importance of those who fought to change these laws. She then moves through acknowledgment of the impact of the #MeToo movement online to naming particular African American women who experienced rape as a means of violence directed at them based not only on their gender but also on their race, then to addressing the hashtag's origins (with Burke) in the effort to support African American survivors of sexual assault. Why would Davis so strongly emphasize race in her speech to those assembled to resist sexism? Her turn at the end of the speech helps us answer this question and helps us understand how sensitive her speech is to our contemporary CMC environment.

Davis closes her speech by emphasizing the cost paid by many women, especially women of color, who have preceded her—not only in the film industry but in many areas of American life, economically and socially. She insists that the primary outcome of the embrace of the #MeToo movement among those assembled should not merely be public celebration of a common slogan. In this, she is attending to a criticism of online advocacy summarized satirically as **slacktivism** (Funnell, 2017), in which the rapid feedback loops that we discussed above allow online users to signal commitment to a given cause that begins and ends with repeating—through readily available mediated modes such as retweets and shares—a single, viral message. The criticism is that advocacy in these contexts begins and ends with the mediated message sharing, without any change in the user's local engagement with their face-to-face community. Davis explicitly calls for audience members not to follow this pattern with her closing line: "It's about keeping it rolling once you go home." In closing this way, she marks the potential distance between CMC and traditional communication contexts in terms of social action and responsibility. This distance for Davis is not merely a casual difference (e.g., a different channel for communication), given her themes of racialized and gendered bodies in history. A dimension of the "slacktivism" critique that Davis offers here is that the #MeToo movement, when it accelerates its temporal reach and amplifies its spatial reach, can become ever more distant from its origins in the pain and struggle of the African American women at its roots. She uses her speaking opportunity to advocate for recognition and preservation of that history, reminding us as she does that even as public speaking is evolving in a digital age, our persistent obligations to our local, physically shared communities are not minimized but perhaps heightened.

"It's About Keeping It Rolling Once You Go Home"

Effective speakers do what they can to make the most of the interplay between more traditional and mediated public speaking settings. Comparing one against the other can help us better understand the importance of carefully shaping a message for both particular and perhaps unexpected audiences. This requires both commitment to one's values and a willingness to adapt and grow. It also requires speakers to attend to their own power and privilege, taking care to understand the historical context of any messages or campaigns we wish to critique or advance so that we do not engage in co-optation or misrepresentation.

Effective speakers understand the value of **alliances**, of building connections with others who share experiences, values, and objectives. Alliances are relationships that entail being "associated, connected, and joined in a unified front . . . where parties are interdependent and responsible for and to each other" (Collier, 2003, p. 2). To this end, effective speakers do not presume to speak for others, but rather alongside others in ways that respect the dignity and meaning of others' positions. Finding ways to meaningfully connect with and ally with others will entail both face-to-face and mediated means of communication.

Concepts

alliances 229
asynchronous communication 219
constitutive rule of communication 226
feedback loops 226
modes of address 226

regulative rule of communication 225
slacktivism 228
synchronous communication 219
computer-mediated communication (CMC) 216

Toward Praxis

1. **Reflection:** What is or has been the role of social media in your own efforts to become better informed about and involved in issues that affect the communities to which you belong?

2. **Discussion:** How involved should an effective public speaker be in social media campaigns, whether as a means to better understand an issue or community or as a way to reach listeners beyond a traditional face-to-face speaking setting? How is this complicated or enabled by our perceptions of privacy or the lack thereof in mediated settings?

3. **Action:** Experiment with limiting your social media consumption for a period of time, for example, 1 week (or if that's too long, 48 hours). How did this experience affect you? Your relationships? Your awareness of what is timely and relevant to know? Who profits or loses in your participation in social media, and how so?

Discussion Questions

1. How do you feel about the ways that communication media, including social media, shape your understanding and experience?

2. How do the various social media platforms shape how you communicate? What role do these media play in your efforts to be a compelling public speaker?

3. What are the regulative and constitutive rules of communication at play in the public speaking opportunities available to you in this course?

CHAPTER

12

Public Speaking Is Empowering

In this chapter, we will work together to:

- Explore public speaking as essential to personal growth, civic engagement, and social transformation
- Define and practice reflexivity
- Identify advocacy tactics for transformation that help resist exhaustion and nihilism

> ... love is at the root of our resistance.
>
> It is our love for 12-year-old Tamir Rice. ... It is our love for Philando Castille ...
>
> It is our love for Stephon Clark ... that will not allow us to stop until we achieve liberation for our people.
>
> Our love is not an individualized love—it is a collective love. A collective love that is constantly combating collective forms of racialized hate ...
>
> But I am hopeful. I am inspired.
>
> This is why we have to protest ... We protest because we love ourselves, and our people.
>
> (Kaepernick, 2018)

Public speaking is empowering. It is within our communication with others that we are able to transform others and ourselves. The power of public protest is one such example. Colin Kaepernick, former quarterback for the San Francisco 49ers, chose to sit through the American national anthem during the third preseason game of the National Football League (NFL) season. He did so to call attention to police violence against people of color, to protest a government that failed to protect all citizens equally under the law. As he described in a postgame interview:

> I am not going to stand up to show pride in a flag for a country that oppresses black people and people of color. To me, this is bigger than football and it would be selfish on my part to look the other way. There are bodies in the street and people getting paid leave and getting away with murder.
> (Wyche, 2016)

Kaepernick would later kneel during the anthem in a show of respect to current and former U.S. military, helping give rise to the #takeaknee movement, which trended on social media with many athletes and entertainment figures taking a knee in support of both Kaepernick and Black Lives Matter, an organization and movement that explicitly addresses systemic racism and oppression in the United States (Willingham, 2017). This decision would prove to be yet another flashpoint in race relations in the United States.

There is also nothing inherently empowering about public speaking. Certainly it does not always feel empowering. President Trump cast Kaepernick's actions as disloyal and unpatriotic, asking participants at a political rally, "Wouldn't you love to see one of these NFL owners, when somebody disrespects our flag, to say, 'Get that son of a bitch off the field right now. Out! He's fired. He's fired!'" (Graham, 2017). Beyond aspersions about his patriotism, Kaepernick has faced a barrage of racist epithets, anti-Islam rhetoric, and

---

Colin Kaepernick, Selection from "Amnesty International's Ambassador of Conscience Award Speech." Copyright © 2018 by Colin Kaepernick.

death threats across a variety of social media platforms. Public speaking is not without consequence. Public speaking is always already imbued with power and privilege, a fraught environment where people of varying degrees of influence will attempt to shape our perceptions—and who will, at least in some measure, succeed. We have no choice but to navigate this environment. Communication is as ubiquitous as air; we breathe it in and it fills us, changes us.

It has been our hope, as authors, to explore with you the relationship between public speaking and power. We do not believe that in order to do so meaningfully we must see eye to eye. It may be that you perceive Kaepernick's gesture as unforgivably rude, or it may be that you see his actions as brave. Still, we can all agree that his actions have shaped a national conversation about racism, violence, and justice. Whether words or gestures, tweets or speeches, interpersonal conversations or political rallies, communication is constitutive. Communication creates. *Your* communication creates. We could choose to take this as inevitable, shrug our shoulders and not give it another thought. But in doing so, we would fail to attend to how our communication is a significant way in which power moves in and through us as a vehicle for social change.

Through Public Speaking, We May Empower Ourselves and Each Other

Public speaking is a transformative act of communication. This book is full of examples of prominent figures who, through their communication in a variety of settings, have affected us all—perhaps even in ways we don't yet realize. This is a common understanding of and motivation for public speaking. Through communication, we can effect change to our classrooms, our schools, our organizations, our neighborhoods, our communities, and our cultures. At some level, the question is "What sort of transformation is occurring?" Public speakers may, if they speak in ways that reflect that they are feeling bored or dismissive, quell our curiosity and even limit our understandings and imaginations. However, in raising our voices in volume and clarity, with passion and preparedness, we may become agents of change. We become people who, as social justice educator–scholar Freire suggests, act on the world in order to transform it for the better. This is one

Dr. Martin Luther King inspired social change through his speeches and empowered people all over to the U.S. to stand up against racial inequality.

Community organizers do not just choose a cause because it matters to them or only affects them, they want to change the world for the better. In order to be successful, community organizers must work toward their goals with their listeners in mind.

way to think of becoming empowered. When Kaepernick says "but I am hopeful. I am inspired," he suggests that he believes in the power that he has to transform the world for the better. But speakers are not the only ones who may be empowered by public speaking.

As speakers attempt to change the world for the better, they must always do so with their listeners in mind. They must consider what is "better" for whom, and at what cost? As we've argued throughout this book, an effective public speaker does not simply choose a topic that matters to them or that affects only them. They choose topics, form arguments, and consult sources that invite their listeners into agency with respect to issues that affect the community they build in speaking with each other. Kaepernick, for example, did not choose to become a public speaker directly advocating for racial justice; he chose instead to use his own body in ways that responded to a social expectation that he stand as part of a public patriotic ritual. This use of his body, an entirely nonverbal choice, resulted in widespread discussion topics as diverse as patriotism, racial justice, and the role celebrities might play in political debate. In other words, where speakers open spaces for others to join in dialogue, we may say they are empowering.

In this way, public speaking is a meaningful form of communication for civic engagement and social transformation. Public speaking, as you've seen throughout this book, constitutes our classrooms and courtrooms, boardrooms and branches of government. It is often how we name our challenges and advance possible solutions, but also how we remember the dead and celebrate the living. Public speaking is often what unites and divides us. As a uniquely human endeavor, public speaking is what shapes and defines our bonds with one

Public speaking happens in classrooms and courtrooms, boardrooms and branches of government.

another—bonds that will inevitably be tested by our relationship to one another along lines of power and privilege.

Finally, it is important to note that through public speaking, we engage in personal transformation as well. One of your authors, Keith, witnessed a demonstration on his campus in which students occupied a public space and spoke about their opposition to the continued enrollment of a fellow student in the same university who was a widely known advocate for White supremacy. This was a brave choice by the speakers in the situation—first, because they knew in advance that they were directly opposing a decision made by the university president (putting their own educations at risk in some implicit ways), and second, because many (though not all) of the speakers were students of color who were thereby targets of the hate speech propagated by White supremacy. When you call attention to and speak into issues that matter to you and people you care about, you are taking a risk. You become vulnerable—yet paradoxically, you become strong. We often encourage others to "take a stand," and when we do, we may mean this both literally (as in stand up and refuse to tolerate something anymore) and figuratively (as in arguing for your own beliefs, for what you know to be true). The vulnerability we often experience in articulating and sharing our perspectives, our stories, our fears, and our solutions is powerful and scary, but it is an opportunity. With vulnerability comes the opportunity to learn what others think of what we've said, and in that moment, we ourselves learn. Learning from and acting on the insights others so generously share with us, as speakers and as listeners, is what makes public speaking so transformative.

Empowering Public Speakers Practice and Encourage Reflexivity

In the rush to do "all the things" in the course of a semester (or year, or life), it is all too easy to overlook how we are (or often are not) practicing **reflexivity**, or the practice of discerning and better understanding how we are both products and producers of cultural phenomena. Yet a necessary and meaningful element of what empowering public speakers do is become reflexive about how their participation in communication creates humane or dehumanizing social worlds. We refer to reflexivity as a practice because it requires attention and effort, in much the same way one practices meditation, martial arts, or yoga.

Reflexivity as a concept has its roots in research investigation, but its implications are lasting for learning both in and beyond the classroom. Communication scholars Fassett and Warren (2007) note that "reflexivity is . . . something we practice, not an end result, but rather a process; reflexivity is not simply about ourselves, but about locating ourselves in relation to the phenomena we investigate" (p. 50). You now recognize that communication does more than represent things in the world, whether ideas or objects. Communication creates the world around us by giving rise to social organization, from the way we shape our identities in relation to one another to the way we contribute to the creation, maintenance, and dissolution of families, organizations, and other cultures. Further, our communication, as philosophers Lakoff and Johnson (1980) and others have long argued, is metaphorical. Our use of a

Reflexivity is the practice of discerning and better understanding how we are both products and producers of cultural phenomena. We can practice reflexivity by considering our role in how we shape ourselves and others in ways that are both humanizing and harmful.

> "Hope is the thing—That perches in the soul—And sings the tune without the words—And never stops—at all . . ."
>
> —Emily Dickinson

particular word or gesture opens some ways of seeing and being and masks others—remember Lakoff and Johnson's example of argument as war, as compared to argument as dance? How we speak with ourselves about ourselves and with each other about each other gives rise to the cultures and communities that nurture and sustain us. Reflexivity as a process challenges us to consider our role in this interpretive process—how we shape ourselves and others in ways that are both humanizing and harmful. Did the discussion of Kaepernick's choice to kneel during performances of the national anthem lead you to consider, even if briefly, how you use your own body during such public performances that you attend? Do you place your hand over your heart? Do you look at the closest American flag, directly and without breaking your gaze? Do you remove your hat, and if you do, is this choice to remove your hat related to your gender? Questions like these, when prompted for you by the actions or comments of another person, are examples of reflexivity because they go beyond merely *reflecting* (in your mind) and extend to *acting* in specific ways in the world.

Practicing Reflexivity Provides Benefits

There are several benefits to practicing reflexivity: First, we help model and examine with our listeners how communication is constitutive of culture. Second, in illuminating how communication is constitutive of culture, speakers and listeners may better understand their participation in social systems of power, privilege, and oppression—as both reaffirming and challenging such structures. Each of us sits at the nexus of different cultural experiences, some valorized and some marginalized. One may be White and working class; another may be cisgender, male, and disabled; and still another may be a queer woman of color who is highly educated and Christian. Here it may help to explore the concept of privilege.

We may already have a variety of connotative definitions of **privilege** involving access, opportunity, and advantage. Privileges may be earned, as in the rights and responsibilities you receive when you earn your degree in a given discipline or field of study. We may also benefit from (or see others around us benefit from) unearned privileges. Such unearned privileges are those that stem from structural inequities in our sociocultural relationships. Feminist and antiracist scholar Peggy McIntosh's (1990, 2012) landmark essays on White and male privilege help identify the unearned privileges experienced by White people and males. She famously describes privilege as "an invisible weightless knapsack of special provisions, assurances, tools, maps, guides, codebooks, passports, visas, clothes, compass, emergency gear, and blank checks" (2012, p. 1). For example, a White person may experience privileges such as "I can go shopping alone most of the time, pretty well assured that I will not be followed or harassed" or "I can worry about racism without being seen as self-interested or self-seeking." Someone who appears to be a cisgender heterosexual man may experience privileges such as "On average, I am taught to fear walking alone after dark in average public spaces much

How might a working mother with kids navigate the corporate world in a way that her male colleagues (with kids) might not? What privileges do you think her male colleagues have that they are unaware of? By becoming more reflexive about ourselves we can examine our privileges, implicit biases, and assumptions.

less than my female counterparts are" or "If I have children and a career, no one will think I'm selfish for not staying at home" (Deutsch, 2018). Fassett (2010) applies this same inquiry to ability privilege, observing unearned privileges such as "No one has ever told me that I should be satisfied with my achievements because most people like me never made it this far" (p. 468) and "My differences in ability are not amplified or stigmatized by mass mediated representations" (p. 467). Our goal in surfacing these examples of privilege is not to suggest that they are universally true or positive. It is often the case that people who receive unearned privilege do so at a cost, as in the unreflective sexism that stay-at-home fathers face when they choose to provide care to their children instead of work outside the home. It is also possible to be possessed of some earned and unearned privileges at the same time other aspects of one's identity are marked by stigma.

What Does Becoming Reflexive Mean?

Becoming more reflexive entails examining our implicit biases and assumptions and how these influence our actions in the world (including our communication). This can seem daunting, especially since it requires us to explore and challenge assumptions about our own and others' identities. McIntosh, a scholar who studies assumptions about race, reminds us that, rather than attempting to identify individual bad actors (e.g., so and so is a racist), we should focus instead on the social systems we all participate in, from health care to education to the law, and how those privilege some at the expense of others in ways that perpetuate inequality and dehumanization (McIntosh, 1997). (For an excellent overview of how social structures disproportionately harm people of color, in contexts ranging from health care to criminal justice, see education scholar Robin DiAngelo's (2016) book *What does it mean to be White?: Developing White racial literacy*.) Though enduring and seemingly solid institutions, social systems exist because we (re)enact them. This is one truth highlighted by Kaepernick's decision first to sit (and later to kneel) during the performance of the national anthem at NFL games: The uniqueness and valor of the United States are not permanent qualities of our country but instead qualities we do work to consistently sustain through our actions. His naming of "a collective love that is constantly combating collective forms of racialized hate" suggests that for him, our collective actions (whether loving or hateful) are what form and reform our nation, each day. The authors believe that it is possible to change institutions and systems through our actions, but we must be committed to exploring how our actions and their outcomes are intertwined and have consequences for ourselves and others.

Empowering Public Speakers Practice Advocacy

Reflexivity sounds (and sometimes is) exhausting. It is also worrying, embarrassing, and painful to consider that we have acted (and will, even still, sometimes continue to act) in ways that

What do you think it means to use your privilege for good? These women are suggesting that some people need a regular reminder that they are privileged and that they should use their advantages to help others.

are harmful to others. This can lead to a kind of emotional fatigue that can take the form of cynicism or nihilism. **Cynicism** is the sense that nothing will ever change, that our efforts won't matter for much in the long run. Feeling cynical diminishes our sense of agency, leading us to become overly critical of someone's efforts to effect change or even causing us to remain silent so as to not "waste our effort." **Nihilism** is even more bleak: This is a sense of hopelessness from which it is very difficult to emerge. When our actions seem meaningless in the face of oppression, why act at all? We act because we can choose hope and humanity and change—even if it is slow and hard-won. Here we offer strategies for how to remain resilient and communicate to make a difference.

Practice Advocacy Through Reflexivity

Reflexivity is the foundation for our communication. Though a practice of compassionately exploring how our communication may be humanizing and/or dehumanizing for ourselves and others, we can become more accountable for how we enable or resist oppression. This will also help us hold others accountable for their actions and inactions. What we learn in the classroom isn't preparation for "the real world," it *is* already meaningful interaction in the world. Classrooms are among our earliest sites of (un)fairness and abuse of power, and examining why we did or didn't speak up, file a grievance, or walk out can be revelatory for how we navigate our participation in other structures of power.

Classrooms are among our earliest sites of inequality and power struggle. Understanding how we respond to unfairness and abuses of power in a classroom setting can be revelatory for how we navigate our participation in other structures of power.

> "I believe in this country. I believe in the American people. I believe that people are more good than bad. I believe tragic things happen. I think there's evil in the world, but I think at the end of the day, if we work hard and if we're true to those things in us that feel true and feel right, that the world gets a little better each time."
>
> —*Barack Obama*

Practice Advocacy Through Dialogue

As we have argued throughout this book, communication at its most empowering is dialogic and invitational. Advocacy seems more possible for you as a speaker if you see yourself as (a) joining a conversation that precedes and coexists with you and (b) inviting others into (or acknowledging others already present in) this conversation in ways that respect them as people with good reasons for feeling and behaving as they do (even, and perhaps especially, if you don't agree). In other words, acknowledging the role of power as a speaker means doing all you can to understand how others (including institutions and social systems) are speaking through you and shaping the lives of your listeners. Some questions to consider are: Whose voices are marginalized in or missing from this dialogue? Are those conversations happening elsewhere? Have you earned the right to participate in those conversations? How is your own communication perpetuating or resisting the inequities that shape your life and those of your listeners? Entering into dialogue doesn't mean a calm, convenient, and apolitical exchange of words. It may mean listening both compassionately and critically to ideas and experiences that are difficult for you to hear. Dialogues may be fraught, and it may be that your listeners do not feel as though your invitation is genuine. Allow these moments to nurture your continued reflexivity.

While we often think of textbooks as objective and authoritative, as the authors mentioned at the start of the book, they are not. Each author has their own biases that they bring to the text when writing. In addition, publishing companies and customers also bring their own ideologies to their assessment of a textbook.

Practice Advocacy Through Critical Literacy

Effective advocacy as a speaker and a listener means taking nothing at face value (even this book). **Critical literacy** refers to reading texts for their foundational values and assumptions. Here it is important to note that reading can also refer to interpreting in general (including listening and viewing), and texts can come in a variety of forms, from newspaper articles and other sources to songs and stories. Ask yourself: whose agenda or interests are served by this communication? Is the source credible? To whom? Textbooks are an interesting example of communication that seems objective and authoritative. Their job, presumably, is to help a teacher teach and a student learn. We often presume that textbooks contain facts and details that are worthy of memorization and recitation. However, textbooks are also often a battleground for power interests—see, for example, the controversial decision to remove both Hillary Clinton, former U.S. secretary of state and presidential nominee, and Helen Keller, deaf-blind American activist and labor rights advocate from the Texas social studies curriculum (Strauss, 2018). Education researcher James Loewen (2018) effectively demonstrates how textbooks are neither impartial nor objective, but rather replete with lies and misrepresentations as suit the authors, publishers, customers, and their ideologies.

> Usually when I'm asked, "What's the biggest lie?" I put my hand out in front of me slanting upward and to the right. And what I mean by that is the overall theme of American history is we

Alliances often unite people from different identities. In this photo Straight Allies protest at the Seattle March for Marriage Equality.

started out great and we've been getting better ever since kind of automatically. And the trouble with that is two things. First of all, it's not always true. . . . And the second part is what it does to the high school student. It says you don't need to protest; you don't need to write your congressman; you don't need to do any of the things that citizens do, because everything's getting better all the time. (Kamenetz, 2018)

It is important for us as speakers and listeners to actively and critically evaluate the communication in our worlds.

Practice Advocacy Through Alliance Building

Alliances are, at their most basic, relationships. Communication studies scholar Mary Jane Collier (2003) defines them as "a relationship in which parties are interdependent and responsible for and to each other" (p. 2). In our present moment in the United States, we often talk about alliances where they unite people from different identities (such as White women and women of color). An oft-circulated meme on Facebook asks if one can be an ally (to the LGBTQ community) if one's partner is homophobic. This perhaps helps illuminate how challenging it can be to develop meaningful alliances, especially across differences in power and privilege. However, that this can be challenging isn't a reason to stop. As Chicana feminist cultural studies scholar Gloria Anzaldúa (2009) argues, alliances give rise to "powerful, meaning-making experiences" (p. 141)—alliances are activist in how they bridge together different people. They challenge us to navigate power and privilege in thoughtful ways, to "move across and through *power lines*" (Carillo Rowe, 2010, p. 216, emphasis original).

Taken together, all four forms of advocacy (listed above) may preserve our resilience and our creativity and sense of agency in the face of what may seem like insurmountable challenges.

> "Please remember, especially in these times of group-think and the right-on chorus, that no person is your friend (or kin) who demands your silence, or denies your right to grow and be perceived as fully blossomed as you were intended."
>
> —Alice Walker

"But I Am Hopeful. I Am Inspired."

Your communication matters. It makes some idea or action (more) real for you and for your listeners. Kaepernick's choice to take a knee—and his subsequent framing of this action—drew attention to the role of police violence against people and communities of color. His actions inspired some, but also drew scrutiny and criticism from others, creating space for dialogue and dissent with respect to free speech in the United States. While our speech may be free in that we may speak our own truths, our speech is not free from consequences,

Colin Kaepernick's choice to take a knee—and his subsequent framing of this action—drew attention to the role of police violence against people and communities of color. His actions inspired many, like these female college basketball players at Rutgers to also take a knee and continue to spread awareness of the issues of police violence in the African American community. By kneeling and placing a hand on one another's shoulders, these players demonstrate solidarity with one another and with their community. While our words are significant in moving listeners, our nonverbal gestures—and our silences—are powerful means of communication.

and that matters too. When we allow others to genuinely challenge our thinking, our ideas are stronger as a result. We also, in such moments of struggle, learn resilience. Resilience is a quality we often associate with flexibility and the ability to bounce back; it is a skill that public speakers can practice as they reflexively advocate change with others. We hope this responsibility leaves you feeling inspired: What issues will you speak into? And with whom? What do you hope to achieve? What will you do next?

Concepts

alliance 244
critical literacy 243
cynicism 241

nihilism 241
privilege 238
reflexivity 237

Toward Praxis

1 **Reflection:** In what aspects of your identity do you experience marginalization or stigma? In what aspects of your identity do you experience unearned privilege? What do you make of these tensions/paradoxes?

2 **Discussion:** When and how have you allied with others? What have you accomplished? In what ways did/do you struggle? What are the qualities of a meaningful alliance?

3 **Action:** Explicitly and intentionally trace the power lines associated with an upcoming speech you are preparing. Who benefits by the arguments and sources you advocate? With whom do you advocate? Whose voices are missing or marginalized? With what consequence?

Discussion Questions

1. What do you do to stay motivated when you're feeling exhausted and overwhelmed? What do you say to others to help them stay resilient?

2. In what ways have you felt transformed—for better or worse—as a speaker or listener?

3. How might your speeches open up spaces for dialogue and transformation in your community?

Glossary

A

Abstract: The idea that a given word or gesture is not the thing itself, but rather represents the item, idea, or experience. One cannot drink the word *coffee*, nor is the word *run* the act of running.

Academic Integrity: One's efforts as a learner to engage in ethical research, from data collection and analysis to how they share their insights with others aloud or in print.

***Ad Populum* Fallacy**: A fallacy in which something is asserted simply because many other people assert the same thing.

Advantage–Disadvantage: An organizational pattern that sets two (or more) ideas against one another such that all the comparisons and contrasts involve an assessment of what is worthy or useful about each idea in comparison or contrast to the next.

Advocacy: Entails speaking alongside less privileged groups so as to amplify their voices. An effort to speak on behalf of a position or cause such that others join one in that effort.

Affirming a Negative Premise: A fallacy in which the universal statement is negative but the conclusion, a faulty one, is positive. For example, "I never teach class in shorts; today I am wearing slacks; therefore, I am teaching."

Agency: Refers to a person's ability to feel as though they can take action in the world that is meaningful. The capacity to transform oneself, learn, grow, and effect change in one's own life and in the world.

Alliances: The act of building connections with others who share experiences, values, and objectives.

Ambiguous: The idea that a word or gesture one might express may not be what another imagines, though there will likely be some overlap. The word *coffee*, for example, can evoke, variously, the type of roast, a hot or cold drink, something bitter that you may not like, and so on.

Analogical Reasoning: A type of reasoning that encourages an audience to embrace a conclusion because they *associate* a given complex experience—an experience they know well or understand fully—with one that is new to them or questionable for them.

Anecdotal Evidence: A brief example from one's own or others' experience that humanizes or lends a personal connection to something that may be complex.

Antithesis: Involves closely positioning two opposing ideas to frame how their opposition includes more than just their definitional distinction but additional elements as well. For example, "I play poker like it's fun, but I play blackjack like it's serious."

APA: A specific style guide managed by the American Psychological Association.

Appeal to Nature: A fallacy in which a universal truth is asserted merely because of given qualities that are taken for granted but not yet well understood.

Appeal to Tradition: A fallacy in which a universal truth is asserted merely because long-established behaviors or artifacts exemplify it.

Arbitrary: The idea that people could, given a word or gesture, choose a different word or gesture to represent the same thing or concept. For example, some may choose to refer to coffee as *joe*, *kahvi* (Finnish), or even *burnt tea* or some such.

Articulation: Refers to the ways you use your mouth and breath to form and project each sound with your voice.

Artistic Appeals: The intentional and artful use of language to persuade.

Artistic Proofs: Persuasion that requires a speaker's craft and skill to be successful through appealing to ethos, pathos, and logos.

Asynchronous Communication: Communication in which communicators interact with one another at the different times. For example, E-mail.

Attention Getter: The act of engaging the audience by asking a question, illustrating a theme via a visual, dramatizing or acting out a theme, using a different communication mode such as shouting, or invoking humor.

Audience Analysis: A meaningful process of learning the needs, values, and goals of groups about which we care and whom we respect.

Aural Communication: Communication perceived through the ears.

B

Banking: An educational approach that treats teachers as experts who share their knowledge with passive students who lack knowledge and who gradually become more and more knowledgeable through the actions of teachers sharing their knowledge.

Bias: Distortion of reality in communication based on one's assumptions or beliefs.

Biased: Favoring one perspective, focus, or outcome over others based on existing perceptions or assumptions.

Brainstorm: The act of preparing one's mind to *generate* ideas, and then listing a large number of ideas that are connected to one big, central idea.

C

Calling: The idea of being motivated to speak into a given issue or concern. Sometimes people describe this as listening to a higher power, and sometimes people describe this as delving deeply inward to acknowledge and pursue their own best qualities.

Care: Using phrases that stablish a caring relationship to the audience while speaking by engaging whenever possible in taking perspective.

Causal Logic: Specifies a deductive logical relationship among two or more elements in which one element is a necessary effect whenever a preceding element, the cause, is present.

Cause–Effect: An organizational pattern that shows that one idea or set of ideas, usually ideas that have very strong evidence to support them or that are well-known to audience members, will necessarily and directly lead to an effect or series of effects (usually this series of effects are the key ideas in the speech, the ones newest to audience members).

Ceremonial Speech: A speech in which the speaker's primary purpose is to highlight for audience members the distinctive important elements of a special person or occasion.

Change the Focus: Involves deliberately disrupting an audience's sense that they know what one will say and do next. A sense that they will only get what they expect can dull audience members' attention and lead them to listen, look, and think less carefully.

Change the Frame: A way of changing the focus that involves altering how an audience filters out some communication or treats it as less relevant than other communication. For instance, a person's perspective might change depending on if they were told an agitated professor had a family member hospitalized, versus if they were told that agitated professor was new to campus and teaching their first class.

Character: Using phrases that highlight a shared relationship to the audience and the wider community to be effective in a public speaking situation.

Chronologically: Describing ideas arranged as they developed over time.

Citation: The process of acknowledging others' work.

Clincher: A final, memorable closing remark to a speech.

Communication Anxiety: A feeling of aversion to engaging in communication with others; for many people, this feeling of aversion is specific to a certain type of communication, such as speaking in public to an assembled audience.

Communication as Representation: A model or way of thinking that invites people to see words as symbols or representations for things in the world, such as the word *coffee* standing in for the drink one may be holding in their hand.

Communication Is Constitutive: To argue that communication shapes and even creates our social reality. In this model, our words do not simply *represent* individuals, organizations, and cultures. Instead our words *make* those individuals, organizations, and cultures.

Communication Mode: The manner or style in which one addresses others (for example, by sharing words in writing or orally; by using *we* language, *I* language, or *you* language when stating ideas; by using an angry or a silly voice).

Compare–Contrast: An organizational pattern that sets two (usually; occasionally there are more than two) distinct ideas against one another, allowing the speaker to best illustrate and complicate each idea by showing which elements one idea has in common with the other and which elements make one idea meaningfully different from the other.

Compassion: Entails empathy and acknowledgment of why someone has chosen to speak; the effect of those words on the speaker and others. Requires tempering one's inclination to judge, pausing to consider the conditions that made a given speaker's utterance possible and, if possible, trying to intimately imagine those conditions in one's life.

Competence: Using oral citations, personal expertise, and precise language to be effective in a public speaking situation.

Computer-Mediated Communication (CMC): Any communication that occurs through a channel that requires the use of a computer to send and/or receive messages.

Connotative Meaning: The cloud of ideas suggested by a word or phrase. This cloud of ideas cannot be understood by reference to definitions and rules but only by a shared set of experiences and/or knowledge. Through connotation with words, speakers create and sustain with the audience a common understanding of their shared lives and how far that sharing extends.

Constitutive: The idea that one's communication is the means by which one accesses the world and recognizes it as meaningful for oneself and for others.

Constitutive Rule of Communication: A communication rule that tells us the meaning of a given message. For example, the interpretation of *k* in a text exchange as rude or short-tempered.

Construction of Social Reality: The idea that those aspects of people's lives that are social—roles, responsibilities, values, actions—depend on communication.

Contextualize: To provide meaningful background and interpretations for sources when you cite from them.

Contributory Cause: A type of argumentative relationship described by the statements: The existence of C does not mean that E exists, and the existence of E does not mean that C exists.

Coordination: The process of developing ideas that are comparable and parallel.

Credibility: The perception of one's qualifications and character.

Critical: Describes listening to and thinking about a speaker's ideas so that one evaluates their merit, recognizing what the speaker has done well and where the speech may still be lacking.

Critical Literacy: Refers to reading texts for their foundational values and assumptions, taking nothing at face value.

Cynicism: The sense that nothing will ever change, that one's efforts won't matter for much in the long run. Feeling cynical diminishes one's sense of agency, leading people to become overly critical of someone's efforts to effect change or even causing people to remain silent so as to not "waste our effort."

D

Deductive Logic: A form of logic that describes relationship among three kinds of statements: first, a universal statement that would apply to any particular instance of a given category; second, a particular instance of that given category; and third, a conclusion that describes how the particular instance fits the universal claim.

Deliberative Speeches: Speeches that address events that have not yet occurred. In this way, such speeches attempt to show effects in the future. Good examples of deliberative speeches include political speeches calling for policy changes (which anticipate specific community needs and propose solutions to those needs) and advocacy speeches (which urge listeners to take voluntary action to enhance their future lives or those of others).

Delivery: Refers to how one performs or enacts public communication—that is, *how* one shares a message with listeners. Successful delivery involves balancing verbal communication with nonverbal communication.

Demographics: Refers to statistical patterns one can identify in populations of people along different characteristics—for example, age, ability, economic class, education level, ethnicity/race, geographic location, gender identity/expression, income, language of origin, military status, nationality, political affiliation, religion, or sexual orientation.

Demonstration Speech: A speech in which the speaker's primary purpose is to allow audience members to develop the ability to accomplish a precise, narrowly defined task.

Denotative Meaning: The literal meaning of a word or phrase. This type of meaning can easily be accessed in a dictionary or checked by reference to a grammar textbook. Through denotation with words, speakers create and sustain with the audience a common understanding of the world and their place in it.

Descriptive/Narrative Evidence: Refers to examples that are extended and detailed. Such examples help a speaker fully describe how a given topic or phenomenon affects someone's life.

Dialogic: Describes when two or more people are engaged in a mutual sharing of ideas.

Dialogic Communication: Describes communication in which meanings are cocreated by the speaker and the listeners.

Dialogue: Defined by Martin Buber (1970/1996) as a respectful engagement between speaker and listener characterized by remaining open-minded even (and perhaps especially) when they don't agree.

Direct Quote: Sharing a source's language word for word, contained in quotation marks.

Docile Bodies: The idea that by restricting how one attends to or calls attention to one's body through frequent and unreflective repetition, institutions teach people to conform to their expectations. One learns to blend in, to minimize the differences in thinking that emerges from different bodies, and to comply with those in power.

Dynamics: Refers to the volume of voice when a speaker speaks.

E

Empirical Evidence: A focus on providing and interpreting broad predictive patterns in events, beliefs, and/or behaviors. Further, this type of data emphasizes facts (information that can be verified), such as dates, policy decisions, and so forth.

Ephemeral: An idea or process that only exists for a very short time frame.

Epideictic: Describes a type of speech that addresses a present event, such as a demonstration or celebration speech.

Epideictic Speeches: Speeches that address events in the present. In this way, such speeches attempt to show how we currently stand in relation to one another in the community. Good examples of epideictic speeches include toasts at weddings (which highlight bonds of family and friendship) and award nomination and acceptance speeches (which establish the worthiness of those receiving or presenting an award).

Epistemic: Describes when something has an effect on how one forms knowledge.

Ethic of Care: The idea that efforts at advocacy must be informed by a dialogue and relationship with the people who will be affected by communication. In adopting the premise that one should care for others with communication, one hopes to emphasize the importance of engaging with others to learn more about them and oneself.

Ethos: Refers to a speaker's efforts to appear credible: qualified, trustworthy, and confident. For example, the speaker may call on or cite other sources in a speech or share their own prior experience with the topic.

Extemporaneous Speaking: When a speaker carefully prepares in advance to speak about a topic, typically developing a brief set of notes or a speaker's outline. Then the speaker works from occasional references to the notes or outline as they deliver the speech, focusing on the audience and choosing most words in the moment rather than precisely choosing each word in advance

Expert Testimony: Involves someone knowledgeable and credible sharing their understanding and experience of the issue at hand.

F

Facial Expressions: The ways people use the muscles in their faces to create meaning.

Fallacy: A weakness in a logical argument.

Fallacy of the Single Cause: A type of fallacy that stems from suggesting to an audience a single explanation for outcomes or phenomena that could instead be explained by several possible influences.

False Analogy: A type of fallacy that results from poor fitness, or the span of common features between a known experience and a new one, between the two items brought together by association.

Feedback Loops: Patterns of messages shared from one communicator to another in which each message is affected by the previous messages in the exchange.

Focused Attention: The act of selecting and privileging some points of focus rather than others.

Forensic Speeches: Speeches that address events that have already occurred in the past. In this way, such speeches attempt to show causes for effects we are currently experiencing. Good examples of forensic speeches include attorney statements in courtrooms (which attempt to assign responsibility) and scientific speeches (which analyze events in the natural world).

Frame: A way one interprets messages, using an idea about what matters most to filter out some communication or treat it as less relevant than other communication.

Full-Sentence Outline: A collection of full sentences that helps one remember essential information and the logic that links it meaningfully to the listeners.

Fully Memorized Speech: When a speaker has a speech timed in advance (in rehearsal after rehearsal), at the cost of not choosing their words as they speak.

G

Gestures: The ways that people move their hands and arms to create meaning.

Google Scholar: A specialized search engine that can point one to a range of scholarly sources about topics of broad scope.

Gross Bodily Movement: How people use the larger part of their body—shoulders, hips, and legs—to create larger movements that change their relationship to the space around them.

H

Hasty Generalization Fallacy: A type of fallacy that draws a conclusion based on inadequate evidence—either too few particular instances of evidence or too thin a texture of shared characteristics among particular instances.

Hegemony: Refers to how we grant others the power and privilege to shape our worldviews, attitudes, beliefs, expectations, and actions. This is, in a sense, a process of domination by consent; one consents to others' influence, even when that influence may be harmful.

I

Impassioned Public Speaking: Speaking both with strong feeling, with attention to the felt sense of your words and their impact, and with transformative power, with the capacity to enact change through words.

Implicit Bias: An unreflective or unconscious belief or stereotype about a particular group of people.

Impression Management: Efforts to shape one's own and other people's perception of who one is.

Impromptu Speaking: When a speaker does not develop a speech prior to the speaking context; they receive a topic (often one not of their own choosing) only once they are within the speaking context.

Inclusive Language: Involves using language that is attentive to history, culture, power, and privilege. For example, referring to mature females as *women* instead of *girls*, because the word *girls* discourages audience members from conceptualizing themselves as peers capable of making sense of ideas.

Inductive Logic: A type of logic involves drawing conclusions based on probability rather than certainty. A conclusion drawn from an inductive logical relationship is *probable* or *likely* rather than definite or certain.

Informative Speech: A speech in which the speaker's primary purpose is to educate audience members about a topic

Interpersonal: Describes a mutual sharing of ideas that depends on the particular histories and perspectives of each person in dialogue.

Invitational Rhetoric: Rhetoric that positions audience members as fellow travelers who might join the speaker in engaging the speech topic.

K

Keyword Outline: A collection of key words and phrases that helps one remember essential information and the logic that links it meaningfully to the listeners.

L

Lay Testimony: The perspective of the average person who is affected by the issue at hand. For example, to better explain the issue of why faculty members might choose to go on strike, one might include information from an interview with faculty members about how they are affected by a lack of cost-of-living salary increase.

Listening: An active process of making meaning by, ideally, communicating that one understood not only the content but the intent of a message and that one has integrated that information meaningfully with respect to a broader context—whether of an issue or within one's life.

Logical Reasoning: A form of reasoning in which two or more ideas are linked to one another through specific relationships; these ideas, because they have a specific relationship to one another, lead to a new idea, a conclusion. For example, in the arithmetic problem 2 + 3, the numbers 2 and 3 are ideas and addition is a specific relationship among numbers that leads to the conclusion 5.

Logos: Refers to the speaker's efforts to demonstrate the sound logic or reasoning of the speech. For example, the speaker would work to establish the connective tissue between evidence and the conclusions they've drawn from that evidence, demonstrating unequivocally for the listeners that the argument is valid.

M

Maslow's Hierarchy of Needs: Defined by Abraham Maslow (1943) as a series of human needs set in a five-level hierarchical relationship. From the most basic or elemental human need to the most complex, they are physiological, security, belongingness, esteem, and self-actualization.

Metaphor: Involves substituting one word or phrase for another in order to highlight the quality or character of an idea, even though our substitute word or phrase does not fit the literal meaning of the idea. "This classroom is an oven today" is an example of a metaphor.

Metaphorical: As defined by George Lakoff and Mark Johnson (1980), the idea that people often use one concept to understand and explain another. For example, to "fight" for our ideas or defend them from attack evolves from the metaphor of argument as war.

Metonymy: Involves substituting a widely known quality or characteristic of something for the literal name of the thing itself. A common example of metonymy is using a building in which a government office resides to refer to that office itself—such as using *the White House* to refer to the Office of the President of the United States.

MLA: A specific style guide managed by the Modern Language Association.

Modes of Address: How one should refer to another person.

Monologic: Communication that suggests that only one person's voice is present and matters.

Monroe's Motivated Sequence (MMS): An organizational pattern that challenges a speaker to more fully and explicitly meet the needs of their listeners. There are five steps to MMS: attention, need, satisfaction, visualization, and action.

Mythical Norm: As described by Frankenburg (Lorde, 1984), the idea that being color evasive has helped create a situation where White cultural norms have shaped race relations in the United States.

N

Narration Sickness: Defined by Paulo Freire (1970/1993) as the idea that educators have tended to focus on transmission of knowledge rather than helping students join in the process of knowledge construction.

Necessary Cause: A type of argumentative relationship described by the statements: If E exists, then N must exist; but if N exists, we don't yet know if E exists.

Nihilism: A sense of hopelessness from which it is very difficult to emerge. An idea exemplified by the question "when our actions seem meaningless in the face of oppression, why act at all?"

Nonverbal Communication: Those elements of public communication that go beyond the words of a message. Nonverbal communication is embodied, encompassing voice, facial expressions, gestures and movements, and even use of time and space.

Nuanced Language: Language that positions people in particular relationships to one another. For example, the phrase "male nurse."

O

Oral Communication: Communication with the mouth.

Order: The act of putting ideas into sequences that listeners will find logical or effective.

Organizational Patterns: A guide for how to arrange one's ideas.

Outlining: The process of organizing ideas so that they are precisely related to one another in terms of both appropriate sequence and level of importance.

P

Paraphrasing: Entails a restatement or summary of a source's ideas in one's own words.

Pathos: Refers to a speaker's efforts to draw on listeners' emotions, helping them connect with a person or issue in personal ways. For example, this might include sharing an extended and emotionally fraught story.

Pedagogical: An adjective indicating that something involves learning about the world and also connotes that, in the process of learning, changes our understanding of the world as a result of this new learning.

Pedagogy: An act that communicates ideas as well as a specific relationship *to* those ideas, *among* the community, all at once.

Performance: Describes how a public speaker says and does certain things in certain ways for certain reason.

Personification: Involves using words that attribute human qualities (movement, thought, intention, feeling) to nonhuman objects. For example, "my car's not going to put up with that" or "fortune smiled upon me."

Persuasive Speech: A speech in which the speaker's primary purpose is to convince audience members to take a particular action.

Pitch: Refers to the frequency of the oscillating sound waves that listeners hear in a speakers voice; people refer to pitches with a higher frequency of sound waves as *high-pitched* and those with a lower frequency as *low-pitched*.

Poetic: A usage of language that attends to the *feeling* of words in addition to their literal meaning.

Post Hoc Fallacy: A type of fallacy in which one event or outcome follows another, and therefore, a person makes an argument that falsely assumes that the first event caused the second.

Praxis: Defined by Freire (2005) as "reflection and action on the world in order to transform it."

Prestige Testimony: Refers to the sort of commentary a celebrity might provide on an issue. As a speaker, one might choose to share how a celebrity feels about a given issue, even if they don't have direct experience with it or expertise on it.

Preview Statements: An introduction that shares the organizational structure of a speech with an audience, usually following the thesis.

Primacy Effect: The idea that the first thing a listener hears will shape their perception of a speech.

Privilege: A concept involving the differing levels of access, opportunity, and advantage of individuals and groups of people. Some of these levels of access, opportunity, and advantage might be earned, as is the case when someone earns a degree in a given field of study, or unearned, as is the case with structural inequalities in sociocultural relationships.

Problem Posing: An educational approach in which students' existing knowledge and experiences help motivate their active learning as they work together with teachers to solve problems that enhance their ability make sense of the world

Problem–Solution: An organizational pattern that presents strong evidence to frame a problem that must be solved in order for the community to be whole and successful.

Public Speaking Anxiety: A discomfort associated with speaking before a large group of people.

Q

Quality of Sources: A factor that determines whether evidence in a speech is compelling that depends on the reputability of the publishing organization and the source's scope and timeliness.

R

Rate: Refers to how quickly these vowel sounds pass through your mouth as you move from syllable to syllable, from word to word, and from phrase to phrase.

Reasoning: The process of sharing with listeners the logic a speaker has used to arrive at their argument and what it means for others.

Recency Effect: The idea that the last thing a listener hears will continue to resonate after a speech is complete.

Reciprocity: Mutual interdependence in communication as a process of cocreation of meaning that requires each person to enter into sustained and thoughtful contact with one another.

Reflexivity: The capacity to see oneself as part of the problem, issue, or situation one is working to describe. Speakers who are reflexive are aware of how they are implicated in the issue they are addressing, and that their communication shapes their own and others' understandings of and actions with respect to that issue.

Reframing: The process of turning an idea or an experience into something else. For instance, one can reframe fear by changing it into an opportunity—something powerful and meaningful.

Regulative Rule of Communication: A communication rule that organizes communication, helping people recognize when, where, with whom, and why one can acceptably communicate and anticipate reliable, positive responses from others.

Rehearsal: The time a speaker spends intentionally performing and reperforming their communication.

Relational: Described a concept created at the intersection of personal and communal interests.

Review Statement: A statement that revisits and underscores earlier main points.

Rhetoric: Defined by Aristotle as "uncovering, in any given situation, the available means of persuasion" (Rapp, 2010; Sachs, 2008), or "the faculty of observing in any given case the available means of persuasion" (Aristotle, *Rhetoric*, book I, chapter 2, para. 1).

Rhetorical Frame: The way a speaker focuses their words in relationship to a given time, place, set of values, and immediate needs.

Rhetorical Schemes: Involves arranging words in unusual patterns to create surprise and draw attention to a relationship among ideas.

Rhetorical Tropes: Involves substituting one word or phrase for another to freshly illuminate an idea.

S

Scope: Refers to both the breadth and depth of a topic:

Sequentially: Describing ideas arranged as steps in a process.

Simile: Involves linking two ideas in a substitution by using the word *like* or the word *as*. For example, "this classroom is like an oven today" or "this classroom's hot as an oven today."

Situated Reasoning: A type of reasoning that embraces reasons grounded in particular times and places. It derives its force (and thus the strength of its conclusions, when speakers offer conclusions) from knowledge based in immediate relationships.

Slacktivism: A concept defined by Funnel (2017) as a form of online advocacy in which rapid feedback loops allow online users to signal commitment to a given cause that begins and ends with repeating—through readily available mediated modes such as retweets and shares—a single, viral message. The criticism is that advocacy in these contexts begins and ends with the mediated message sharing, without any change in the user's local engagement with their face-to-face community.

Slippery Slope Fallacy: A type of fallacy that results from predicting a series of increasingly negative effects from a single negative cause, which is weak causal reasoning.

Social Construction of Reality: The concept that *all* reality depends on communication.

Social Significance: Describes items that are relevant or meaningful for some culture or group.

Sonic Messages: A type of temporary message that involves receiving the message through vibrations of air molecules.

Sources: The original materials one uses to locate others' work.

Spatially: Describing ideas arranged by where they are located in space or on a map.

Speaker Preparation: Refers to all of the ways one spends time ensuring that they speak effectively—from researching evidence to choosing appropriate language to rehearsing with notes and visual aids.

Speaking Contexts: Entire communities with diverse values, interests, histories, and areas of expertise.

Speaking For: Parallel to the banking model of education in that a speaker can approach a public speaking opportunity as if they are already as knowledgeable as they need to be on their topic, as if their task is merely to share this knowledge with a passive, waiting audience.

Speaking from a Manuscript: When a speaker has written their entire speech word for word, using their rehearsal time to deliver the speech as written and doing this often enough that they can eventually speak while only occasionally referring to the manuscript.

Speaking Occasion: The reason that attendees come together to witness someone speaking to a public group. These events are only sometimes within the speaker's control. The occasions or events then prompt effective speakers to consider how the context or speaking occasion can help them shape the speech in ways they *can* control.

Speaking Purpose: The primary reason for the opportunity (whether by invitation, obligation, or choice) to speak to a group of listeners. The speaker also identifies the type of speech expected in this occasion, one that acknowledges the needs and values of the community in this time and place. The speaker then selects a general topic based on how the type of speech intersects with their own interests and expertise. Finally, the speaker begins to work with this general topic as a researcher; they assemble information and organize ideas.

Speaking With: Parallel to the problem-posing model of education in that a speaker can approach a public speaking opportunity as a means of deepening their understanding of the current conditions of a community and a chance to work together with that community to support its growth.

Structure: The effort to place ideas or objects in a meaningful order.

Style Guide: A specific citation format contained in a special academic format. Examples include APA and MLA.

Subordination: The process of discerning which ideas are more significant to an argument than others.

Sufficient Cause: A type of argumentative relationship described by the statements: If *E* exists, then *S* must exist, and if *S* exists, then *E* must exist.

Supporting Materials: The information and ideas that are called on to develop arguments.

Syllepsis: Using more than one different object for the same single verb; doing so often subtly shifts the meaning of the verb, creating surprise for listeners and encouraging them to carefully consider the shadings of meaning carried by the verb. For example, "I like to play basketball, and the saxophone, and poker, and sometimes student."

Synchronous Communication: Communication in which communicators interact with one another at the same time. For example, FaceTime or another video chat program.

Synecdoche: Involves substituting one single part of something in place of the literal name of the whole thing itself. Common examples would be referring to a professional mercenary as a *hired gun* or to an automobile as *my wheels*.

Syntax: The lengths of sentences; the arrangement of sentence elements like noun phrases, verb phrases, and modifying or qualifying phrases.

T

Tactile Messages: A type of enduring message that involves receiving the message through indentation of the skin.

Testimonial Evidence: Involves sharing someone's experience with or perspective on an issue. Just as a juror may be called to provide their testimony in a court case, testimony in a speech functions to lend insight from people with positions on that topic.

Thesis Statement: A precise, unique, direct, and argumentative topic that helps one understand how to organize the work of creating the rest of the elements of one's speech.

Timeliness: The particular moment the speech originates and by how the speaker and audience share a particular relationship as community members at that moment.

Topic: The main idea being discussed in a public speech.

Transitions: Essential components of forming a compelling argument that bind one idea or main point to the next.

U

Unearned Privilege: Refers to those benefits someone receives simply because they match the mythical norm.

V

Verbal Communication: When the focus is on the words that make up a message.

Visual Messages: A type of enduring message that involves receiving the message through light entering one's eyes.

W

Working Outline: The stages and layers of an outline as one thinks through what one hopes to accomplish with a speech.

References

Adams, S. (2012, December 17). President Obama's speech in Newtown: Leadership at its best. *Forbes*. https://www.forbes.com/sites/susanadams/2012/12/17/president-obamas-speech-in-newtown-leadership-at-its-best/#456e7cd181ee

Alter, C., Haynes, S., and Worland, J. (2019). *Time* Person of the Year: Greta Thunberg. *Time*. Available: https://time.com/person-of-the-year-2019-greta-thunberg/

Anzaldúa, G. (2009). Bridge, drawbridge, sandbar, or island: Lesbians-of-color hacienda alianzas. In A. Keating (Ed.), *The Gloria Anzaldúa reader* (pp. 140–155). Duke University Press.

Aristotle, Roberts, W. R., Bywater, I., & Solmsen, F. (1954). *Rhetoric*. Modern Library.

Aristotle. (1991). *On rhetoric* (G. A. Kennedy, Trans.). Oxford University Press.

Barzun, J. (1945). *Teacher in America*. Liberty Press.

Bever, L. (2016). "You took away my worth": A sexual assault victim's powerful message to her Stanford attacker. *The Washington Post*. https://www.washingtonpost.com/news/early-lead/wp/2016/06/04/you-took-away-my-worth-a-rape-victim-delivers-powerful-message-to-a-former-stanford-swimmer

Brooks, A. (2014). Get excited: Reappraising pre-performance anxiety as excitement. *Journal of Experimental Psychology, 143*(3), 1144–1158.

Brown, D. (1984). I was dumb now I speak. *Times Daily*, p. 13A.

Buber, M. (1996). *I and thou*. Touchstone. (Original work published 1970)

C-SPAN. (2018). Arizona senator Jeff Flake condemns President Trump's "fake news" attacks on the media. https://www.c-span.org/video/?c4708744/arizona-senator-jeff-flake-condemns-president-trumps-fake-news-attacks-media

Carillo Rowe, A. (2010). Entering the inter: Power lines in intercultural communication. In T. K. Nakayama & R. T. Halualani (Eds.), *The handbook of critical intercultural communication* (pp. 216–226). Wiley-Blackwell.

Chang, K. (2012, March 12). Life on Mars? Funds to find answer fade. *The New York Times*. https://www.nytimes.com/2012/03/13/science/space/life-on-mars-funds-for-nasa-to-find-the-answer-fade.html?_r=0

Chomsky, N. (2017). *It is the responsibility of intellectuals to speak the truth and to expose lies*. The New Press.

Chomsky, N. (2018). 2018 media bias chart: Still wildly off. Reddit.com. https://www.reddit.com/r/chomsky/comments/7yk4vw/2018_media_bias_chart_still_wildly_off_source

CNN Staff. (2018). Florida student Emma González to lawmakers and gun advocates: "We call BS." *CNN*. https://www.cnn.com/2018/02/17/us/florida-student-emma-González-speech/index.html

Coakley, C., & Wolvin, A. (1997). Listening in the educational environment. In M. Purdy & D. Borisoff (Eds.), *Listening in everyday life: A personal and professional approach* (2nd ed., pp. 179–212). University Press of America.

Collier, M. J. (2003). Negotiating intercultural alliance relationships: Toward transformation. In M. J. Collier (Ed.), *Intercultural alliances: Critical transformation* (pp. 1–16). SAGE.

Comey, J. (2015). Hard truths: Law enforcement and race. Federal Bureau of Investigation. http://www.fbi.gov/news/speeches/hard-truths-law-enforcement-and-race

Committee to Protect Journalists. (n.d.). Our research. https://cpj.org/about/research.php

Conaway, M. S. (1982). Listening: Learning tool and retention agent. In A. S. Algier & K. W. Algier (Eds.), *Improving reading and study skills* (pp. 51–63). Jossey-Bass.

Davis, V. (2018). Viola Davis' full speech at Women's March. *CNN*. https://edition.cnn.com/videos/us/2018/01/20/viola-davis-full-speech-womens-march-la.cnn

de Blasio, B. (2014). Transcript: Mayor de Blasio holds media availability at Mt. Sinai United Christian Church on Staten Island. NYC. http://www1.nyc.gov/office-of-the-mayor/news/542-14/transcript-mayor-de-blasio-holds-media-availability-mt-sinai-united-christian-church-staten

de León, C. (2019). You know Emily Doe's story. Now learn her name. *New York Times*. https://www.nytimes.com/2019/09/04/books/chanel-miller-brock-turner-assault-stanford.html

DeGeneres, E. (2003). Here and now. HBO.

Delpit, L. (1995). *Other people's children: Cultural conflict in the classroom*. The New Press.

Deutsch, B. (n.d.). The male privilege checklist: An unabashed imitation of an article by Peggy McIntosh. http://www.csueastbay.edu/dsj/files/docs/popular-media/dsjguide-male-privilege.pdf

DiAngelo, R. (2016). *What does it mean to be White? Developing White racial literacy*. Lang.

Dickinson, E. (1960). Poem 254. In T. H. Johnson (Ed.), *The complete poems of Emily Dickinson*. Little, Brown.

Dwyer, K. K., & Davidson, M. M. (2012). Is public speaking really more feared than death? *Communication Research Reports, 29*, 99–107.

D'Angelo, C. (2016). Watch members of Congress read Stanford rape victim's full statement. *Huffington Post*. https://www.huffpost.com/entry/congress-stanford-rape-statement_n_5762122fe4b05e4be860e2d5

Eggers, D. (2013). *The circle*. Vintage Books.

Elbow, P. (1998). *Writing with power: Techniques for mastering the writing process* (2nd ed.). Oxford University Press.

Eller, C. (2018). Emma González opens up about how her life has changed since Parkland tragedy. *Variety*. https://variety.com/2018/politics/features/emma-González-parkland-interview-1202972485

Emerson, R. W. (1904/2013). *The Complete Works*. Houghton, Mifflin. www.bartleby.com/90/1103.html

Emerson, R. W. (2001). *The later lectures of Ralph Waldo Emerson 1843–1871* (Vol. 2, R. A. Bosco & J. Myerson, Eds.). University of Georgia Press.

Eno, B. (1996). *A year with swollen appendices: Brian Eno's diary*. Faber and Faber.

Ethics of Care. (2011). Carol Gilligan. https://ethicsofcare.org/carol-gilligan

Fassett, D. L. (2010). Critical reflections on a pedagogy of ability. In T. K. Nakayama & R. T. Halualani (Eds.), *The handbook of critical intercultural communication* (pp. 461–471). Wiley-Blackwell.

Fassett, D. L., and Warren, J. T. (2007). *Critical communication pedagogy*. SAGE.

Foucault, M. (1977). *Discipline and punish: The birth of the prison* (A. Sheridan, Trans.). Vintage Books.

Frankenberg, R. (1993). *White women, race matters: The social construction of Whiteness*. University of Minnesota Press.

Freire, P. (2003). *Pedagogy of the oppressed: 30th anniversary edition*. Continuum. (Original work published 1970)

Freire, P. (2005). *Pedagogy of the oppressed—30th anniversary edition*. Continuum. (Original work published 1970)

Funnell, A. (2017). From slacktivism to "feel-good" protests, activism is broken: Here's how to fix it. *ABC*. http://www.abc.net.au/news/2017-10-25/activism-is-broken-heres-how-we-fix-it/9077372

Geary, J. (2011). Metaphors in mind. Macmillan dictionary blog. http://www.macmillandictionaryblog.com/metaphors-in-mind

Golden, J. L., Berquist, G. F., Coleman, W. E., and Sproule, J. M. (2011). *The rhetoric of western thought*. Kendall-Hunt.

González, E. (2018). Emma González's powerful March for Our Lives speech in full [Video file]. *The Guardian*. https://www.theguardian.com/us-news/video/2018/mar/24/emma-Gonzálezs-powerful-march-for-our-lives-speech-in-full-video

Gottfried, J., & Grieco, E. (2018). Younger Americans are better than older Americans at telling factual news statements from opinions. Pew Research Center. http://www.pewresearch.org/fact-tank/2018/10/23/younger-americans-are-better-than-older-americans-at-telling-factual-news-statements-from-opinions

Graham, B. A. (2017, September 23). Donald Trump blasts NFL anthem protesters: 'Get that son of a bitch off the field.' *The Guardian*. https://www.theguardian.com/sport/2017/sep/22/donald-trump-nfl-national-anthem-protests

Graham, M. (2015, October 20). An athlete of God. *This I Believe* [Podcast]. http://thisibelieve.org/essay/16583

Gramsci, A. (1971). *Selections from the prison notebooks*. International.

Greenfield, D. (2014). NYPD officers turn backs to de Blasio at police funeral. *Frontpage Magazine*. http://www.frontpagemag.com/2014/dgreenfield/nypd-officers-turn-backs-to-de-blasio-at-police-funeral

Haas, J. W., & Arnold, C. L. (1995). An examination of the role of listening in judgments of communication competence in co-workers. *Journal of Business Communication, 32*(2), 123–139.

Haddon, M. (2003). *The curious incident of the dog in the night-time*. Vintage Books.

Hicks, D., & Langsdorf, L. (2011). Argumentation in the affective dimension: An inquiry into the presuppositions of joint deliberation. In R. C. Rowland (Ed.), *Reasoned argument and social change* (pp. 129–136). American Communication Association.

Hill, J. B. (2011). Thomas Acquinas. In M. A. De La Torre & S. M. Floyd-Thomas (Eds.), *Beyond the pale: Reading theology from the margins* (pp. 55–62). Westminster John Knox Press.

hooks, b. (2010). *Teaching critical thinking: Practical wisdom*. Taylor and Francis.

Huxley, A. (1958). *Brave new world revisited*. Harper and Bros.

Jung, C. G. (1969). *The archetypes and the collective unconscious* (2nd ed., R. F. C. Hull, Trans.). Princeton University Press.

Kaepernick, C. (2018). Amnesty International's Ambassador of Conscience Award transcript of speech.

Amnesty International. https://www.amnesty.nl/content/uploads/2018/04/Colin-Kaepernicks-Speech-Ambassador-of-Conscience-Final.pdf?x66178

Kamenetz, A. (2018). "Lies my teacher told me," and how American history can be used as a weapon. *NPR*. https://www.npr.org/2018/08/09/634991713/lies-my-teacher-told-me-and-how-american-history-can-be-used-as-a-weapon

Keneally, M., & Margolin, J. (2014). Eric Garner case: NYPD officer not indicted in choke hold death. *ABC News*. http://abcnews.go.com/US/nypd-officer-indicted-eric-garner-choke-hold-death/story?id=27341079

Kimmel, M. (2005). *The history of men: Essays on the history of American and British masculinities*. State University of New York Press.

Kristof, N. D., & WuDunn, S. (2009). *Half the sky: Turning oppression into opportunity for women worldwide*. Knopf.

Lakoff, G., & Johnson, M. (1980). *Metaphors we live by*. University of Chicago Press.

Lao Tzu. (4th c. BCE?). *Tao Te Ching*.

LaPierre, W. (2012, December 21). Text of the N.R.A. speech. *The New York Times*. http://www.nytimes.com/interactive/2012/12/21/us/nra-news-conference-transcript.html?_r=0

Lash, J. P. (1980). *Helen and Teacher: The Story of Helen Keller and Anne Sullivan Macy*. Delacorte Press/Seymour Lawrence.

Lockhart, P. R. (2018). Living While Black and the criminalization of Blackness. *Vox*. https://www.vox.com/explainers/2018/8/1/17616528/racial-profiling-police-911-living-while-black

Loewen, J. W. (2018). *Lies my teacher told me: Everything your American history textbook got wrong*. New Press.

Lorde, A. (1984). *Sister outsider*. Crossing Press.

Lorde, A. (2007). *Sister outsider*. Ten Speed Press. (Original work published 1984)

Lorde, A., & Rich, A. (1981). An Interview with Audre Lorde. *Signs*, *6*(4), 713–736. http://www.jstor.org/stable/3173739

Mandela, N. (1990, June 23). Speech to Madison Park High School, Boston, MA.

Marcus, A., & Hays, G. (2002). *Meditations*. Modern Library.

Maslow, A. H. (1943). A theory of human motivation. *Psychological Review*, *50*(4), 370–396.

McCroskey, J. C., & Richmond, V. P. (1991). *Quiet children and the classroom teacher*. ERIC Clearinghouse on Reading and Communication Skills.

McCroskey, J. C., & Teven, J. (1999). Goodwill: A reexamination of the construct and its measurements. *Communication Monographs*, *66*, 90–103.

McCroskey, J. C., Anderson, J. F., Richmond, V. P., & Wheeless, L. R. (1981). Communication apprehension of elementary and secondary students and teachers. *Communication Education*, *30*, 122–132.

McIntosh, P. (1990, Winter). White privilege: Unpacking the invisible knapsack. *Independent School*, 31–36.

McIntosh, P. (1997). White privilege and male privilege: A personal account of coming to see correspondences through work in women's studies. In R. Delgado & J. Stefancic (Eds.), *Critical White studies: Looking behind the mirror* (pp. 291–299). Temple University Press.

McIntosh, P. (2012). White privilege and male privilege: A personal account of coming to see correspondences through work in women's studies. In M. Anderson & P. H. Collins (Eds.), *Race, class, and gender: An anthology* (9th ed., pp. 94–105). Wadsworth.

Monroe, A. H. (1943). *Monroe's principles of speech* (military edition). Scott, Foresman.

Morrison, T. (1994). *The Nobel lecture in literature, 1993*. Knopf.

Noguchi, Y. (2018). Starbucks training focuses on the evolving study of unconscious bias. *NPR*. https://www.npr.org/2018/05/17/611909506/starbucks-training-focuses-on-the-evolving-study-of-unconscious-bias

Obama, B. (2012, December 16). President Obama's speech at prayer vigil for Newtown shooting victims (full transcript). *The Washington Post*. https://www.washingtonpost.com/politics/president-obamas-speech-at-prayer-vigil-for-newtown-shooting-victims-full-transcript/2012/12/16/f764bf8a-47dd-11e2-ad54-580638ede391_story.html?utm_term=.bfc8c73e3bdc

Obama, B. (2017, January 18). Obama's last news conference: Full transcript and video. *The New York Times*. https://www.nytimes.com/2017/01/18/us/politics/obama-final-press-conference.html?_r=0

Office of the State's Attorney. (2013). Report of the State's Attorney for the Judicial District of Danbury on the shootings at Sandy Hook Elementary School and 36 Yogananda Street, Newtown, Connecticut on December 14, 2012. Judicial District of Danbury (CT). http://www.ct.gov/csao/lib/csao/Sandy_Hook_Final_Report.pdf

Office of the UN Special Envoy for Global Education. (2014). Emergency coalition for global action. http://educationenvoy.org/the-emergency-coalition-for-global-education

Ohlheiser, A. (2017, October 19). The woman behind "Me Too" knew the power of the phrase when she created it—10 years ago. *The Washington Post*.

Ohlheiser, A. (2018, January 22). How #MeToo really was different, according to data. *The Washington Post.* https://www.washingtonpost.com/news/the-intersect/wp/2018/01/22/how-metoo-really-was-different-according-to-data/?utm_term=.8f66397b4560

Orwell, G. (1946). Politics and the English language. *Horizon, 13*(76), 252–265.

Palmer, P. (2001, March 31). Now I become myself. *Yes! Magazine.* https://www.yesmagazine.org/issues/working-for-life/now-i-become-myself

Palmer, P. (2011). *Healing the heart of democracy: The courage to create a politics worthy of the human spirit.* Jossey-Bass.

Palmer, P., & Scribner, M. (2007). *The courage to teach: Guide for reflection and renewal* (10th anniversary edition). Wiley.

Perelman, C. H., & Olbrechts-Tyteca, L. (1991). *The new rhetoric: A treatise on argumentation.* The University of Notre Dame Press.

Pew Research Center. (2008). U.S. religious landscape survey. Religious affiliation. https://www.pewforum.org/2008/02/01/u-s-religious-landscape-survey-religious-affiliation

Plato. (2001). Gorgias. In P. Bizzell and B. Herzberg (Eds.), *The rhetorical tradition* (2nd ed.). Bedford/St. Martin's.

Plato. (n.d.). Gorgias (B. Jowett, Trans.). http://classics.mit/plato/gorgias

Plutarch. (1992). On listening. In *Essays by Plutarch* (R. Waterfield, Trans.). Penguin Classics.

Queen Rania. (2016). Queen Rania's speech at UN Summit for Refugees and Migrants—NY, USA. https://www.queenrania.jo/en/media/speeches/queen-ranias-speech-un-summit-refugees-and-migrants-ny-usa

Quintilian. (1856). *Quintilian's Institutes of Oratory; Or, Education of an Orator.* J. S. Watson (Ed.). G. Bell and Sons.

Rapp, C. (2010, Spring). Aristotle's rhetoric. In E. N. Zalta (Ed.), *The Stanford encyclopedia of philosophy.* http://plato.stanford.edu/archives/spr2010/entries/aristotle-rhetoric/

Rather, D., & Kirschner, E. (2017). *What unites us: Reflections on patriotism.* Algonquin Books.

Richmond, V., & McCroskey, J. C. (1998). *Communication: Apprehension, avoidance, and effectiveness* (5th ed.). Gorsuch Scarisbrick.

Roosevelt, E. (1963). *Tomorrow is now.* Harper and Row.

Sachs, J. (Ed.). (2008). *Plato's Gorgias and Aristotle's Rhetoric.* Focus Publishing/R. Pullins Company.

Scholars at Risk Network. (n.d.). Retrieved from https://www.scholarsatrisk.org

Shaull, R. (2005). Foreword. In P. Freire, *Pedagogy of the Oppressed: 30th Anniversary edition.* Continuum.

Shear, M. D. (2012, December 19). Obama vows fast action in new push for gun control. *The New York Times.* https://www.nytimes.com/2012/12/20/us/politics/obama-to-give-congress-plan-on-gun-control-within-weeks.html

Spano, S. J. (2001). *Public dialogue and participatory democracy: The Cupertino project.* Hampton Press.

Srinivasan, S., & Kandavel, S. (2012, February 7). Facebook is a surveillance engine, not friend: Richard Stallman, Free Software Foundation. *The Economic Times.* https://economictimes.indiatimes.com/opinion/interviews/facebook-is-a-surveillance-engine-not-friend-richard-stallman-free-software-foundation/articleshow/11786007.cms

Strauss, V. (2018, September 15). Texas moves to remove Hillary Clinton from social studies curriculum. Really. *The Washington Post.* https://www.washingtonpost.com/education/2018/09/15/texas-moves-remove-hillary-clinton-social-studies-curriculum-really/?noredirect=on&utm_term=.42268093b14f

Tropp, L. R., & Godsil, R. D. (2015, January 23). Overcoming implicit bias and racial anxiety. *Psychology Today.* https://www.psychologytoday.com/us/blog/sound-science-sound-policy/201501/overcoming-implicit-bias-and-racial-anxiety

Turner, V. (1982). *From ritual to theatre: The human seriousness of play.* PAJ.

Twain, M. (1917/2012). *Mark Twain's Letters, volume 2.* London: Forgotten Books.

Tyson, N. (2012). Written testimony submitted to the U.S. Senate Committee on Commerce, Science, and Transportation. https://www.haydenplanetarium.org/tyson/commentary/2012-03-07-past-present-and-future-of-nasa.php

United Nations High Commissioner for Refugees. (2018). Global trends: Forced displacement in 2017. http://www.unhcr.org/5b27be547.pdf

United Nations. (2015). Universal Declaration of Human Rights. https://www.un.org/en/udhrbook/pdf/udhr_booklet_en_web.pdf

Walker, A. (2004). *In search of our mothers' gardens.* Harvest Books.

Warren, J. T., & Hytten, K. (2004). The faces of Whiteness: Pitfalls and the critical Democrat. *Communication Education, 53,* 321–339.

What are Americans afraid of? (1973, July). *The Bruskin Report*, 53.

Willingham, A. J. (2017). The #takeaknee protests have always been about race. Period. *CNN.* https://edition.cnn.com/2017/09/27/us/nfl-anthem-protest-race-trump-trnd/index.html

Winans, J. A. (1915). *Public speaking: Principles and practice*. Sewell.

Wink, J. (2004). *Critical pedagogy: Notes from the real world* (4th ed.). Pearson.

Wittgenstein, L. (1922). *Tractatus logico-philosophicus* (C. K. Ogden, Trans.). Kegan Paul, Trench, Trubner.

Woodward, A., and De Luce, I. (2019, September). How 16-year-old Greta Thunberg became the face of climate-change activism. *Business Insider*. https://www.businessinsider.com/greta-thunberg-bio-climate-change-activist-2019-9

Wyche, S. (2016). Colin Kaepernick explains why he sat during national anthem. NFL.com. http://www.nfl.com/news/story/0ap3000000691077/article/colin-kaepernick-explains-protest-of-national-anthem

Yousafzi, M. (2013). Speech at the Youth Takeover of the United Nations. http://www.aworldatschool.org/pages/the-text-of-malala-yousafzais-speech-at-the-united-nations

Yousafzi, M., & Lamb, C. (2013). *I am Malala: The girl who stood up for education and was shot by the Taliban*. Little, Brown.

Zuckerberg, M. (2017, May 25). Mark Zuckerberg's commencement address at Harvard. *The Harvard Gazette*. https://news.harvard.edu/gazette/story/2017/05/mark-zuckerbergs-speech-as-written-for-harvards-class-of-2017/

Quotation Credits

Aurelius, M. (2008). *Meditations*. Project Gutenberg. http://www.gutenberg.org/files/2680/2680-h/2680-h.htm

Barzun, J. (1945). *Teacher in America*. Liberty Press.

Chomsky, N. (2017). *It is the responsibility of intellectuals to speak the truth and to expose lies*. The New Press.

Churchill, W. (1941). *Great Contemporaries*. London: The Reprint Society. https://archive.org/details/in.ernet.dli.2015.13535/page/n5

DeGeneres, E. (2003). *Here and now* [Film]. HBO.

Dickinson, E. (1960). Poem 254. In T. H. Johnson (Ed.), *The complete poems of Emily Dickinson*. Little, Brown and Company.

Eggers, D. (2013). *The circle*. Vintage Books.

Emerson, R. W. (2013). *The complete works*. Houghton, Mifflin & Co. www.bartleby.com/90/1103.html (Original work published 1904)

Emerson, R. W. (2001). *The later lectures of Ralph Waldo Emerson 1843–1871, Vol. 2* (R. A. Bosco & J. Myerson, Eds.). University of Georgia Press.

Eno, B. (1996). *A year with swollen appendices: Brian Eno's diary*. Faber & Faber.

Geary, J. (2011). Metaphors in mind. *Macmillan dictionary blog*. http://www.macmillandictionaryblog.com/metaphors-in-mind

Graham, M. (2015, October 20). An athlete of God. *This I believe* [Audio podcast]. http://thisibelieve.org/essay/16583

Haddon, M. (2003). *The curious incident of the dog in the night-time*. Vintage Books.

Hill, J. B. (2011). Thomas Aquinas. In M. A. De La Torre & S. M. Floyd-Thomas (Eds.), *Beyond the pale: Reading theology from the margins* (pp. 55–62). Westminster John Knox Press.

Huxley, A. (1958). *Brave new world revisited*. Harper and Bros.

Jung, C. G. (1969). *The archetypes and the collective unconscious* (R. F. C. Hull, Trans.; 2nd ed.). Princeton University Press.

Lakoff, G., & Johnson, M. (1980). *Metaphors we live by*. University of Chicago Press.

Lao T. (2012). *Tao Te Ching* (D. Goddard & H. Borel, Trans.). John Wiley & Sons.

Lash, J. P. (1980). *Helen and teacher: The story of Helen Keller and Anne Sullivan Macy*. Delacorte Press/Seymour Lawrence.

Lorde, A. (2007). *Sister outsider*. Ten Speed Press. (Original work published 1984)

Lorde, A., & Rich, A. (1981). An interview with Audre Lorde. *Signs*, *6*(4), 713–736.

Mandela, N. (1990, June 23). Speech to Madison Park High School, Boston, MA. https://www.nytimes.com/1990/06/24/us/the-mandela-visit-education-is-mighty-force-boston-teen-agers-are-told.html

Obama, B. (2017, January 18). Obama's last news conference: Full transcript and video. *The New York Times*. https://www.nytimes.com/2017/01/18/us/politics/obama-final-press-conference.html?_r=0

Orwell, G. (1946). Politics and the English language. *Horizon*, *13*(76), 252–265.

Perelman, C. H., & Olbrechts-Tyteca, L. (1991). *The new rhetoric: A treatise on argumentation*. The University of Notre Dame Press. (Originally work published 1971)

Plutarch. (1992). On listening (R. Waterfield, Trans.). In *Essays by Plutarch*. Penguin Classics.

Rather, D., & Kirschner, E. (2017). *What unites us: Reflections on patriotism*. Algonquin Books.

Roosevelt, E. (1963). *Tomorrow is now*. Harper and Row.

Shaull, R. (2005). Foreword. In P. Freire, *Pedagogy of the oppressed: 30th anniversary edition*. Continuum.

Srinivasan, S. & Kandavel, S. (2012, February 7). Facebook is a surveillance engine, not friend: Richard Stallman, Free Software Foundation. *The Economic Times*. https://economictimes.indiatimes.com/opinion/interviews/facebook-is-a-surveillance-engine-not-friend-richard-stallman-free-software-foundation/articleshow/11786007.cms

Tyson, N. G. (2012). *Reddit AMA*. https://www.reddit.com/r/IAmA/comments/631eem/i_am_neil_degrasse_tyson_your_personal/

United Nations. (2015). *Universal declaration of human rights*. https://www.un.org/en/udhrbook/pdf/udhr_booklet_en_web.pdf

Walker, A. (2004). *In search of our mothers' gardens*. Harvest Books.

Wink, J. (2004). *Critical pedagogy: Notes from the real world* (4th ed.). Pearson.

Wittgenstein, L. (1922). *Tractatus logico-philosophicus* (C. K. Ogden, Trans.). Kegan Paul, Trench, Trubner & Co.

Zuckerberg, M. (2017, May 25). Mark Zuckerberg's commencement address at Harvard. *The Harvard Gazette*. https://news.harvard.edu/gazette/story/2017/05/mark-zuckerbergs-speech-as-written-for-harvards-class-of-2017/

Image Credits

Table of Contents

Fig. 0.1: Copyright © 2019 Newscom/Mike Stocker.

Fig 0.2: Copyright © by DFID - UK Department for International Development (CC BY 2.0) at https://commons.wikimedia.org/w/index.php?search=Malala+Yousafzai+speaking&title=Special%3ASearch&go=Go#/media/File:Malala_Yousafzai_speaks_to_DFID_staff_-_2017_(33990606651).jpg.

Fig 0.3: Source: https://commons.wikimedia.org/wiki/File:President_Obama_Speaks_on_the_Shooting_in_Connecticut_(2012-12-14).jpg.

Fig 0.4: Copyright © by Michael Vadon (CC BY-SA 4.0) at https://commons.wikimedia.org/wiki/File:NRA_Wayne_LaPierre_at_CPAC_2017_on_February_24th_2017_a_by_Michael_Vadon_04.jpg.

Fig. 0.5: Source: https://www.thecut.com/2016/06/stanford-rape-victim-statement-house-floor.html.

Fig. 0.6: Source: https://www.youtube.com/watch?v=LH9sIeK2nV8.

Fig 0.7: Copyright © by Jeff Flake (CC BY-SA 2.0) at https://commons.wikimedia.org/wiki/File:Jeff_Flake_(21188573650).jpg.

Fig 0.8: Copyright © by Sarah Elliott (CC BY 2.0) at https://commons.wikimedia.org/wiki/File:Tyson-speaking_to_Business_Horizon_Retreat_attendees.jpg.

Fig 0.9: Copyright © by Thomas Good (CC BY-SA 4.0) at https://commons.wikimedia.org/wiki/File:Bill_DeBlasio.jpg.

Fig 0.10: Source: https://commons.wikimedia.org/wiki/File:FBI_Director_Attends_Civil_Rights_and_Law_Enforcement_Conference_(26646831163).jpg.

Fig 0.11: Copyright © by Gage Skidmore (CC BY-SA 2.0) at https://commons.wikimedia.org/wiki/File:Viola_Davis_(27983785894).jpg.

Fig. 0.12: Copyright © 2019 Newscom/Nhat V. Meyer.

Chapter 1

Fig. 1.1: Copyright © 2019 Newscom/Mike Stocker.

Fig. 1.2: Copyright © 2016 Depositphotos/monkeybusinessimages.

Fig. 1.5: Text from Joann Keyton and Stephenson Beck, "Building Relationships In Groups," *Communicating in Groups and Teams: Strategic Interactions*, p. 94. Copyright © 2017 by Cognella, Inc.

Fig. 1.6: Copyright © 2017 Depositphotos/monkeybusinessimages.

Fig. 1.7: Copyright © 2018 iStockphoto LP/chpua.

Fig. 1.8: Copyright © by Angela Radulescu (CC BY-SA 2.0) at https://commons.wikimedia.org/wiki/File:Toni_Morrison_2008-2.jpg.

Fig. 1.9: Source: https://commons.wikimedia.org/wiki/File:Plato_and_Aristotle_in_The_School_of_Athens,_by_italian_Rafael.jpg.

Fig. 1.10: Copyright © 2013 Depositphotos/monkeybusiness.

Fig. 1.11: Copyright © 2018 Depositphotos/SeventyFour.

Fig. 1.12: Copyright © by Neon Tommy (CC BY-SA 2.0) at https://commons.wikimedia.org/wiki/File:Kamala_Harris_(5122897990)_(cropped2).jpg.

Fig. 1.13: Copyright © by Lorie Shaull (CC BY-SA 2.0) at https://commons.wikimedia.org/wiki/File:Thoughts_and_Prayers_Don%27t_Save_Lives,_student_lie-in_at_the_White_House_to_protest_gun_laws_(40369207261).jpg.

Chapter 2

Fig. 2.1: Copyright © by DFID - UK Department for International Development (CC BY 2.0) at https://commons.wikimedia.org/wiki/File:Malala_Yousafzai_speaks_to_DFID_staff_-_2017_(33990606651).jpg.

Fig. 2.2: Copyright © 2016 Depositphotos/monkeybusinessimages.

Fig. 2.3: Copyright © 2018 iStockphoto LP/FatCamera.

Fig. 2.4a: Copyright © 2018 iStockphoto LP/Django.

Fig. 2.4b: Copyright © 2019 iStockphoto LP/monkeybusinessimages.

Fig. 2.5: Copyright © 2014 Depositphotos/monkeybusiness.

Fig. 2.6: Source: https://www.youtube.com/watch?v=bd972Rxiie0.

Fig. 2.7: Copyright © 2013 Depositphotos/londondeposit.
Fig. 2.8a: Source: https://commons.wikimedia.org/wiki/File:Abraham_Lincoln_April_10_1865.jpg.
Fig. 2.8b: Copyright © by Marc E. (CC BY 2.0) at https://commons.wikimedia.org/wiki/File:Adele_2016.jpg.
Fig. 2.9: Copyright © by Southbank Centre (CC BY 2.0) at https://commons.wikimedia.org/wiki/File:Malala_Yousafzai_-_13008047525.jpg.

Chapter 3

Fig. 3.1: Source: https://commons.wikimedia.org/wiki/File:President_Obama_Speaks_on_the_Shooting_in_Connecticut_(2012-12-14).jpg.
Fig. 3.2: Copyright © by Maureen (CC BY 2.0) at https://commons.wikimedia.org/wiki/File:Dalai_Lama_at_Buffalo_faculty_dialogue.jpg.
Fig. 3.3: Source: https://commons.wikimedia.org/wiki/File:Plato_Aristotle_della_Robbia_OPA_Florence.jpg.
Fig. 3.4a: Copyright © 2013 Depositphotos/PabloDamonte.
Fig. 3.4b: Source: https://www.goodfreephotos.com/united-states/wisconsin/madison/wisconsin-madison-graduation-billboard.jpg.php.
Fig. 3.5: Source: https://archive.defense.gov/news/newsarticle.aspx?id=50402.
Fig. 3.6: Copyright © 2013 Depositphotos/albund.
Fig. 3.7a: Copyright © (CC BY-SA 4.0) at https://myusf.usfca.edu/student-life/intercultural-center/check-your-privilege.
Fig. 3.7b: Copyright © by (CC BY-SA 4.0) at https://myusf.usfca.edu/student-life/intercultural-center/check-your-privilege.
Fig. 3.8a: Copyright © 2017 iStockphoto LP/asiseeit.
Fig. 3.8b: Copyright © 2014 iStockphoto LP/Joel Carillet.
Fig. 3.9: Copyright © 2019 Depositphotos/fizkes.
Fig. 3.10: Source: https://www.flickr.com/photos/obamawhitehouse/8390810296/in/photolist-dH38eD-dMt6z3-dV625m-dCYiYo-eazmgj-dUZsrB-dH38UX-dH8zXo-iLNn7H-iLQbKf.

Chapter 4

Fig. 4.1: Copyright © by Michael Vadon (CC BY-SA 4.0) at https://commons.wikimedia.org/wiki/File:NRA_Wayne_LaPierre_at_CPAC_2017_on_February_24th_2017_a_by_Michael_Vadon_04.jpg.
Fig. 4.2: Copyright © Bahudhara (CC BY-SA 4.0) at https://commons.wikimedia.org/wiki/File:Victoria_Bannon_eulogy.JPG.
Fig. 4.3: Copyright © by Will Folsom (CC BY 2.0) at https://commons.wikimedia.org/wiki/File:Bill_Nye_at_Tech6.jpg.
Fig. 4.4: Copyright © by (CC BY-SA 2.0) at https://www.flickr.com/photos/102627552@N04/25184039395.
Fig. 4.5: Copyright © by Gage Skidmore (CC BY-SA 3.0) at https://commons.wikimedia.org/wiki/File:Bernie_Sanders_by_Gage_Skidmore.jpg.
Fig. 4.6: Copyright © 2011 Depositphotos/monkeybusiness.
Fig. 4.7a: Source: https://commons.wikimedia.org/wiki/File:Kennedy_Nixon_Debat_(1960).jpg.
Fig. 4.7b: Source: https://www.youtube.com/watch?v=yeoXblp_Nbo.
Fig. 4.8: Copyright © 2013 Depositphotos/londondeposit.
Fig. 4.9a: Copyright © by LGEPR (CC BY 2.0) at https://commons.wikimedia.org/wiki/File:LG_Dios_Built-In_Cooking_Class_with_Kim_Ho-Jin.jpg.
Fig. 4.9b: Copyright © by roanokecollege (CC BY 2.0) at https://commons.wikimedia.org/wiki/File:%22The_Magic_of_Chemistry%22_(8074314491).jpg.

Chapter 5

Fig. 5.1: Source: https://www.thecut.com/2016/06/stanford-rape-victim-statement-house-floor.html.
Fig. 5.2: Copyright © 2019 Depositphotos/Rawpixel.
Fig. 5.3: Copyright © 2018 iStockphoto LP/2511photos.
Fig. 5.4: Copyright © 2016 Depositphotos/Rawpixel.
Fig. 5.5: Copyright © 2014 Depositphotos/kasto.
Fig. 5.6: Copyright © 2018 iStockphoto LP/SolStock.
Fig. 5.7: Copyright © by Pax Ahimsa Gethen (CC BY-SA 4.0) at https://commons.wikimedia.org/wiki/File:Families_Belong_Together_SF_rally_20180623-3706.jpg.
Fig. 5.8: Copyright © 2013 iStockphoto LP/adamkaz.
Fig. 5.9: Copyright © 2019 iStockphoto LP/kali9.
Fig. 5.10: Copyright © by Frank Schulenburg (CC BY-SA 4.0) at https://commons.wikimedia.org/wiki/File:Stanford_University_campus_in_2016.jpg.

Chapter 6

Fig. 6.1: Source: https://www.youtube.com/watch?v=LH9sleK2nV8.
Fig. 6.2: Copyright © 2017 iStockphoto LP/vm.

Fig. 6.3: Copyright © by (CC BY 2.0) at https://commons.wikimedia.org/wiki/File:Jason_Manford_comedy_masterclass_(8434366175).jpg.

Fig. 6.4: Copyright © 2017 Depositphotos/KrisCole.

Fig. 6.5: Copyright © 2017 iStockphoto LP/PeopleImages.

Fig. 6.6: Source: https://www.obamalibrary.gov/sites/default/files/P120910PS-0935.jpg.

Fig. 6.7a: Source: https://pxhere.com/en/photo/210351.

Fig. 6.7b: Copyright © 2015 Depositphotos/Rawpixel.

Fig. 6.8: Copyright © by (CC BY-ND 2.0) at https://search.creativecommons.org/photos/84e846f4-c221-412e-8b32-9f218cbd104d.

Chapter 7

Fig. 7.1: Copyright © by Jeff Flake (CC BY-SA 2.0) at https://commons.wikimedia.org/wiki/File:Jeff_Flake_(21188573650).jpg.

Fig. 7.2: Source: https://commons.wikimedia.org/wiki/Helen_Keller#/media/File:Helen_Keller25.jpg.

Fig. 7.3: Copyright © 2014 Depositphotos/Serg64.

Fig. 7.4: Copyright © 2018 Depositphotos/monkeybusinessimages.

Fig. 7.5: Copyright © 2018 Depositphotos/nd3000.

Fig. 7.6: Copyright © 2017 iStockphoto LP/andresr.

Fig. 7.7: Copyright © 2016 iStockphoto LP/valentinrussanov.

Fig. 7.8: Copyright © by Google.

Fig. 7.9: Copyright © 2014 Depositphotos/nanka-photo.

Chapter 8

Fig. 8.1: Copyright © by Sarah Elliott (CC BY 2.0) at https://commons.wikimedia.org/wiki/File:Tyson_speaking_to_Business_Horizon_Retreat_attendees.jpg.

Fig. 8.2: Source: https://obamawhitehouse.archives.gov/blog/2012/05/12/first-lady-michelle-obama-addresses-virginia-tech-graduates.

Fig. 8.3: Copyright © 2011 iStockphoto LP/Joan Vicent Cantó Roig.

Fig. 8.4: Copyright © by TonyTheTiger (CC BY-SA 3.0) at https://commons.wikimedia.org/wiki/File:20081102_Obama-Springsteen_Rally_in_Cleveland.JPG.

Fig. 8.5: Source: https://commons.wikimedia.org/wiki/File:ChesterMysteryPlay_300dpi.jpg.

Fig. 8.6: Copyright © by Steve Jurvetson (CC BY 2.0) at https://commons.wikimedia.org/wiki/File:Edward_Snowden%27s_Surprise_Appearance_at_TED.jpg.

Fig. 8.7: Source: https://commons.wikimedia.org/wiki/File:SENATE_JUDICIARY_HEARING_(38848578625).jpg.

Fig. 8.8: Copyright © by Karl Gruber (CC BY-SA 4.0) at https://commons.wikimedia.org/wiki/File:Teleprompter_3716.JPG.

Fig. 8.9: Copyright © 2013 Depositphotos/monkeybusiness.

Fig. 8.10: Source: https://commons.wikimedia.org/wiki/File:White_House_Press_Briefing_(46629242574).jpg.

Fig. 8.11: Copyright © 2013 Depositphotos/szefei.

Fig. 8.12: Copyright © 2018 iStockphoto LP/Mikolette.

Fig. 8.13: Copyright © 2006 iStockphoto LP/Thomas Northcut.

Chapter 9

Fig. 9.1: Copyright © by Thomas Good (CC BY-SA 4.0) at https://commons.wikimedia.org/wiki/File:Bill_DeBlasio.jpg.

Fig. 9.2: Copyright © 2018 Depositphotos/wolterke.

Fig. 9.3: Copyright © 2015 Newscom/Shannon Stapleton.

Fig. 9.4: Copyright © by AFGE (CC BY 2.0) at https://commons.wikimedia.org/wiki/File:Keeping_the_Promise_Rally_-_Milwaukee_(30062494444).jpg.

Fig. 9.5: Copyright © 2014 Depositphotos/monkeybusiness.

Fig. 9.6: Copyright © by Matt H. Wade (CC BY-SA 3.0) at https://commons.wikimedia.org/wiki/File:WhiteHouseSouthFacade.JPG.

Fig. 9.7: Copyright © 2013 Depositphotos/aijohn784.

Fig. 9.8: Copyright © by The All-Nite Images (CC BY-SA 2.0) at https://commons.wikimedia.org/wiki/File:NYC_protester_in_solidarity_with_Ferguson_Missouri.jpg.

Chapter 10

Fig. 10.1: Source: https://commons.wikimedia.org/wiki/File:FBI_Director_Attends_Civil_Rights_and_Law_Enforcement_Conference_(26646831163).jpg.

Fig. 10.2a: Copyright © by Ahmedmack9 (CC BY-SA 4.0) at https://commons.wikimedia.org/wiki/File:Feast_day_speech.jpg.

Fig. 10.2b: Copyright © 2017 Depositphotos/Wavebreakmedia.

Fig. 10.3: Source: https://obamawhitehouse.archives.gov/blog/2014/11/24/president-obama-delivers-statement-ferguson-grand-jurys-decision.

Fig. 10.4: Copyright © 2013 Depositphotos/bradcalkins.
Fig. 10.5: Copyright © by versageek (CC BY-SA 2.0) at https://commons.wikimedia.org/wiki/File:New_Jersey_State_Police_Traffic_Stop.jpg.
Fig. 10.6: Copyright © 2013 Depositphotos/logoboom.
Fig. 10.7: Copyright © 2018 iStockphoto LP/hadynyah.
Fig. 10.8: Copyright © 2015 Depositphotos/lucidwaters.

Chapter 11

Fig. 11.1: Copyright © by Gage Skidmore (CC BY-SA 2.0) at https://commons.wikimedia.org/wiki/File:Viola_Davis_(27983785894).jpg.
Fig. 11.2: Source: http://criticalmediaproject.org/metoo/.
Fig. 11.3: Copyright © 2017 Depositphotos/Gladkov.
Fig. 11.4: Copyright © 2015 iStockphoto LP/svetikd.
Fig. 11.5: Copyright © 2014 Depositphotos/mark@rocketclips.com.
Fig. 11.6: Copyright © 2016 Depositphotos/Rawpixel.
Fig. 11.7: Copyright © 2019 Newscom/Albin Lohr-Jones.
Fig. 11.8: Source: https://www.andersen.af.mil/News/Photos/igphoto/2001335935/.
Fig. 11.9: Copyright © 2015 iStockphoto LP/LeoPatrizi.
Fig. 11.10: Source: https://en.wikipedia.org/wiki/File:Today_logo_2013.png.

Chapter 12

Fig. 12.1: Copyright © 2019 Newscom/Nhat V. Meyer.
Fig. 12.2: Source: https://commons.wikimedia.org/wiki/File:Martin_Luther_King_-_March_on_Washington.jpg.
Fig. 12.3: Copyright © by (CC BY-SA 2.0) at https://commons.wikimedia.org/wiki/File:Families_Belong_Together_-_San_Rafael_Rally_-_Photo_-_50_(29069624788).jpg.
Fig. 12.4: Copyright © 2018 iStockphoto LP/HRAUN.
Fig. 12.5: Copyright © 2017 iStockphoto LP/PeopleImages.
Fig. 12.6: Copyright © 2015 iStockphoto LP/Mlenny.
Fig. 12.7: Copyright © by Elvert Barnes (CC BY-SA 2.0) at https://commons.wikimedia.org/wiki/File:DearWhiteFriends.BaltimoreMD.20January2018_(39801807722).jpg.
Fig. 12.8: Copyright © 2019 iStockphoto LP/skynesher.
Fig. 12.9: Copyright © 2017 iStockphoto LP/Jacob Ammentorp Lund.
Fig. 12.10: Copyright © by Ryan Georgi (CC BY 2.0) at https://commons.wikimedia.org/wiki/File:Straight_Allies_protesting.jpg.
Fig. 12.11: Copyright © by Joel Plummer.

Index

A

Abstract, 9–10
Abuses of power, 9, 215, 221–222, 241
Academic integrity, 128–129
Academic Search Premiere, 74–75
Accountable public speaking, 190–213
Action, in Monroe's motivated sequence, 115
Adele, 35
Ad populum fallacy, 197
Advantage–disadvantage, 115
Advocacy, 240–244
    alliance building and, 244
    critical literacy and, 243–244
    defined, 18–19
    dialogue and, 242
    empowerment and, 240–244
    ethic of care and, 46–47
    persuasion as, 45–46
    public speaking as, 42, 43–47
    reflexivity and, 241
    social significant, 16–19
    through use of language, 182–186
    voices amplified by, 18–19
Aesthetic performance, 145–147, 161
Affirming a negative premise, 197
Agency
    defined, 17
    power and, 48
    problem-posing approaches, 30
Agenda, set by public speakers, 82–83
Alliance, 229, 244
Ambiguous, 10
Analogical reasoning, 206–209
Anecdotal evidence, 131
Antithesis, 180, 185
Anzaldua, Gloria, 244
APA, 7, 137
Appeal to nature, 197
Appeal to tradition, 197
Arbitrary, 9
Argumentative thesis statement, 75
Argument, clarifying reasoning to enhance, 195–196
Aristotle, 13–14, 15, 43, 45, 61, 63, 72
    on speaking occasions, 61–64, 72
    persuasive appeals identified by, 14–15, 45
    rhetoric defined by, 13–14, 43, 45
    Rhetoric written by, 13
Articulation, 162–163
Artistic appeals, 14
Artistic proofs, 14, 45. *See also* Persuasive appeals
Asynchronous communication, 219
Attention getter, 95–100
Attention-getting strategies, 93–100. *See also* Change the frame
    ask a question, 96
    different communication mode, 98
    dramatize key idea or theme, 97–98
    humor, 98–99
    illustrate key idea or theme, 96–97
Audience. *See* Audience analysis
    change the frame for, 94–95
    communication and, 151–152
    credibility and, 89
    giving time/taking time and, 157, 159–160
    identifying learning needs, 90–91
    primary, 149–151
    role of public speakers relative to, 84–86
    social reality and, creating and maintaining, 145–146
    speaker's credibility with, 85
    speaker's relationship and understanding of, 85–86
Audience analysis, 51–54
    defined, 51
    demographics and, 51–54
    Maslow's hierarchy of needs and, 54
Aural communication, 151–152
Aurelius, Marcus, 65

B

Banking, 24–25, 28–30
Becoming reflexive, 239–240
Belongingness, 54
Beloved (Morrison), 11
Bias, 138–139
    defined, 6
    implicit, 53–54
    in sharing source material, 138–139
"Birdies for the Brave" program, 46
The Bluest Eye (Morrison), 11

Black Lives Matter, 171–172, 233
Body, delivery and, 146, 164–165
Brainstorm, 70–71
Branden, Nathaniel, 128
Brown, Gordon, 24
Brown, Michael, 186, 187, 191
Buber, Martin, 28, 51–52
Burke, Tarana, 220, 221–222, 228–229

C

Calling, public speaking as, 42–43
Care, 92–93
Causal logic, 203–205
Cause–effect, 115
    causal logic and, 203–205
    fallacies and, 206
    necessary, sufficient, contributory causes and, 205
    relationships, 203–206
    transitions to identify, 119
Celebration speeches, 153
Ceremonial speeches, 61, 68
Change the focus, 94
Change the frame, 94–95, 99–100. *See also* Attention-getting strategies
Character, 92
Chomsky, Noam, 132, 139
Chronologically, 115
Churchill, Winston, 24
Citation, 130, 137–138
Civic engagement, 235
Claims made by speaker, 119
Clarifying reasoning, 195–196
Clincher, 111, 120, 131, 159
Clinton, Hillary, 66, 243
Closing statement, 26, 111–112, 120, 159–160
Collier, Mary Jane, 244
Comey, James B., 191, 195–196, 199–208, 209
Communication. *See also* Computer-mediated communication (CMC)
    as public speaking, 147–153
    as public speaking, characteristics of, 148–150
    as representation, 9
    asynchronous, 219
    audience and, 150–151
    aural, 151–152
    complexity of, 174
    constitutive, 2–21
    constitutive rule of, 226
    dialogic, 24, 27–28
    ephemeral speech and, 153
    expectations of, evolving, 225–227
    gestures in, 9–10
    interpersonal, 24, 25–28
    monologic, 26–27
    non-CMC forms of, 217, 218–220
    oral/aural communication and, 151–152
    reciprocity in, 34
    regulative rule of, 226
    relational, 11–16, 22–39
    rhetoric and, 12–16
    slacktivism and, 228
    social constructionist model of, 173
    social reality created by, 10–11
    synchronous, 219
    technologies of shared, 149
    timeliness and, 152–153
    words in, 9–10
Communication anxiety, 35–36
Communication mode, 98
Community relationships
    ceremonial speeches and, 68
    demonstration speeches and, 68–69
    informative speeches and, 64–66
    knowledge levels and, 64–66
    persuasive speeches and, 66–67
    speaking occasions defined by, 63–64
Compare–contrast, 115
Compassionate listening, 33
Competence, 91
Computer-mediated communication (CMC), 214–231
    defined, 216–218
    distinguished from non-CMC, 218–220
    for change, 227–228
    public messages enhanced by, 220–222
    relevancy of, for public speakers, 220
    speech related to space and time impacted by, 223–225
Computer-mediated devices, 218, 223, 227
Conclusions, 120–121
Connotative meaning, 10, 176–177, 183–184
Constitutive communication, 2–21, 32
Constitutive rule of communication, 226
Construction of social reality, 182
Contextualize, 136
Contradictory writing, 7
Contributory cause, 205
Coordination, 113
Credibility, 85
    audience and, 89
    audience learning needs and, 89
    informative speaking shaped by speaker's, 85
    in impact statement, 103
    introduction and, 117–118
    introductions to establish, 117–118
    speaker preparation to enhance, 87–93

Credible recall, 103
Critical listening, 33–34. *See* Compassionate critical listening
Critical literacy, 243–244
Critical thinking, 128
C-SPAN, 125
Cynicism, 241

D

Dalai Lama, 42
Databases, 74–75, 133, 134–135
Davis, Viola, 215–216, 220–225, 227–228
De Blasio, Bill, 171–173, 182–278
Deductive logic, 196–197
DeGeneres, Ellen, 165
Deliberative speeches, 63
Delivery
    body and, 164–165
    defined, 144
    modes of, 154–161
    voice and, 162–164
Demographics, 51–54
Demonstration speeches, 61, 68–69, 153
Denotative meaning, 10, 176–177
Descriptive/narrative evidence, 131
Dialogic communication, 24, 27–28
Dialogue
    advocacy and, 242
    audience analysis and, 51–54
    defined, 28
DiAngelo, Robin, 240
Dickinson, Emily, 238
Direct quote, 137
Direct thesis statement, 74–75
Docile bodies, 48–49
Doe, Emily, 81, 83, 100–103
Dramatize key idea or theme, 97–98
Durant, Kevin, 62, 63
Dynamics, 163–164

E

Echo chambers, 134
Eggers, Dave, 224
Email, 219
Emerson, Ralph Waldo, 45, 61
Empirical evidence, 130–131
Empowerment, through public speaking, 232–247
    advocacy and, 240–244
    reflexivity and, 237–240
Ephemeral, 153
Epideictic speeches, 62–63, 153
Epistemic, 48–49

Esteem, 54
Ethic of care, 46–47
    advocacy and, 46–47
    defined, 47
    reflexivity and, 47
Ethos, 14–15, 45, 128
Expertise
    in impact statement, 103
    to establish competence, 91
Expert testimony, 131
Extemporaneous speaking, 154–157
    defined, 154–155
    prepared and practiced, 155–156
    time in, importance of, 156–157

F

Facebook, 23, 37, 64, 217, 244
FaceTime, 219
Facial expressions, 165
Fake news, 134
Faking, 145–146
Fallacy
    ad populum, 197
    appeal to nature, 197
    appeal to tradition, 197
    cause–effect relationships to avoid, 206
    deductive, 197
    defined, 196–197
    false analogy, 209
    hasty generalization, 202–203
    inductive, 202–203
    of the single cause, 203
    post hoc, 206
    slippery slope, 206
Fallacy of the single cause, 203
False analogy, 209
Fassett, D. L., 237, 239
Fear of public speaking
    communication anxiety and, 35–36
    reframing, 36–37
Feedback loops, 225, 226–227
Finchem, Tim, 46
Flake, Jeff, 125–126, 139
Focused attention, 83
Forensic speeches, 61–62, 153
Foucault, Michel, 48
Frame, 94. *See also* Change the frame
Frankenberg, Ruth, 49
Freire, Paulo, 24–25, 28, 29, 30, 31, 47, 50, 234
Full-sentence outline, 112, 155
Fully memorized speeches, 157–158

G

Garner, Eric, 171–172, 185, 187, 191
Geary, James, 184
Geographically, 115
Gestures, 165
    abstract, 9–10
    ambiguous, 10
    arbitrary, 9
Goals of speech
    conclusion and, 120
    conclusions to share, 120
    structure and, 108–109
González, Emma, 3–4, 7, 14–15, 18, 19, 63
Google Scholar, 134–135
Gorgias, 13
Graham, Martha, 74
Gramsci, Antonio, 48
Gross bodily movement, 165

H

Haddon, Mark, 115
Hasty generalization fallacy, 202–203
Hegemony
    defined, 48
    oppression and, 48–49
    unearned privilege and, 49–51
High-pitched frequency, 163
Hill, Christopher, 199
Hippocratic oath, 128
hooks, bell, 128
Humor, 98–99
Huxley, Aldous, 194

I

Ideas
    conclusion and, 120
    conclusions to provide review of, 120
    effect on listeners, introduction to show, 118
    for topic, brainstorming for, 70–71
    grouping, 113–114
    illustrate key, 96–97
    introduction and, 118
    ordering, 114–116, 119
    questions to generate, 71
    transitions to provide order for, 119
"I/it" relationship, 28, 51
Illustrate key idea or theme, 96–97
Impact statement, 81, 100–103
    audience and, 101
    credibility and expertise in, 103
    to advocate for transformations, 100–103
    to change the frame, 102–103

Impassioned public speaking, 170–189. *See also* Language
Implicit bias, 53–54
Impression management, 116
Impromptu speaking, 159–161
Inclusive language, 181
Inductive logic, 198–203
Informative speeches, 64–66
    attention-getting strategies, 93–100
    credibility and, 87–93. *See also* Speaker preparation
    focused attention and, 83
    pedagogy and, 82–83
    purpose of, derivatives of, 84
    shaped by speaker's credibility with audience, 85
    shaped by speaker's relationship and understanding of audience, 85–86
    teaching and, 82–83
Informed public speaking, 124–141
    academic integrity and, 128–129
    bias and, 138–139
    ongoing conversations and, 126–129
    supporting materials in, 129–138. *See also* Sources
Instagram, 37, 64, 217, 220
Interpersonal, 24, 25–28
Introductions, 116–119
    impression management and, 116
    primacy effect and, 120
    to draw listeners' interest, 117
    to establish credibility, 117–118
    to provide structural forecast of speech, 118
    to show effect of ideas or issues on listeners, 118
Invitational rhetoric, 181–182
"I/thou" relationship, 28

J

Jefferson, Thomas, 125
Johnson, Mark, 10–11, 12, 237, 238
Jokes, 98–99

K

Kaepernick, Colin, 233–235, 238, 240, 244, 245
Kamenetz, A., 244
Keller, Helen, 46, 126, 243
Kennedy, John F., 66
Key idea
    dramatize, 97–98
    illustrate, 96–97
Keyword outline, 112
King, Martin Luther, Jr., 185, 223, 234
Kirschner, Elliot, 138
Knowledgeable, introduction and, 117–118
Knowledge levels, 64–66

L

Lakoff, George, 10–11, 12, 237, 238
Language
    advocacy through, 182–186
    artistic appeals and, 14–16
    connotative meaning, 176–177
    denotative meaning, 176–177
    inclusive, 181
    invitational rhetoric, 181–182
    metaphorical, 10–11
    nuanced, 180–182
    poetic, 177–180
    rhetorical frame, 175–176
    rhetorical schemes, 178, 179–180
    rhetorical tropes, 178–179
    speaking situation framed through, 175–177
Lanza, Adam, 41, 59, 76
Lao Tzu, 48
LaPierre, Wayne, 59, 63, 76, 77
Lay testimony, 131
Learning styles, 90
Lincoln, Abraham, 35
Listeners/listening
    compassionate, 33
    conclusion and, 120
    critical, 33–34
    importance of, 32–33
    introduction and, 117–118
    reciprocity and, 34
Liu, Wenjian, 191
#LivingWhileBlack, 54
Loewen, James, 243
Logical reasoning
    analogical reasoning, 206–209
    causal logic, 203–205
    defined, 194
Logos, 14–15, 45
Lorde, Audre, 120, 134
Low-pitched frequency, 163

M

Mandela, Nelson, 13
Maslow, Abraham, 54
Maslow's hierarchy of needs, 54
McIntosh, Peggy, 49–50, 238, 239–240
Mediated cultures. *See also* Culture, mediated
Metaphor, 178, 184
Metaphorical, 10–11
Metaphors We Live By (Lakoff and Johnson), 10–11
Metonymy, 179, 184
#MeToo movement, 215–216, 220–222, 224–225

Milano, Alyssa, 216, 221, 225
Miller, Chanel. *See* Doe, Emily
MLA, 137
MLK Library, 74–75
Modes of address, 226–227
Modes of delivery, 154–161
    extemporaneous speaking, 154–157
    fully memorized speech, 157–158
    impromptu speaking, 159–161
    speaking from a manuscript, 158–159
Monologic communication, 26–27
Monroe's motivated sequence (MMS), 115
Morrison, Toni, 11–12
Most Valuable Player award, NBA's, 62, 63
Moynihan, Daniel Patrick, 125
Mythical norm, 49

N

Narration sickness, 28–29
National Rifle Association (NRA), 3, 59, 77
NBA, 62, 63
Necessary cause, 205
Need, in Monroe's motivated sequence, 115
Newsweek, 135
Newtown, Connecticut, 41, 54–55, 59
NFL, 233, 240
The New York Times, 76, 77, 135, 139
Nihilism, 241
Nixon, Richard, 66
Non-CMC forms of communication, 217, 218–220
Nonverbal communication, 144
Nuanced language, 180–182
Nye, Bill, 61

O

Obama, Barack, 41, 54, 59, 76, 143, 184, 195, 242
Olbrechts-Tyteca, Lucie, 197
Oppression, hegemony and, 48–49
Oral citations, to establish competence, 91
Oral communication, 151–152
Order, 114–116, 119
Organizational patterns, 108, 114–115
Orwell, George, 139, 182
Outlining, 110–116
    defined, 108
    full-sentence outline, 112, 155
    keyword outline, 112
    to develop speech, 111–113
    to group ideas, 113–114
    to order ideas, 114–116
    working outline, 112

P

Palmer, Parker, 33, 37, 43
Pantaleo, Daniel, 171
Paradoxical writing, 7
Paraphrasing, 137
Pathos, 14–15, 45
Pedagogical, 81–83
Pedagogy, 82–83
Pedagogy of the Oppressed (Freire), 24–25, 28, 47
Perelman, Chaïm, 197
Performance speeches, 142–169. *See also* Delivery
    communication in, 147–153
    defined, 144
    ephemeral, 153
    rehearsal and, 166–167
    social reality and, 144–147
Periodical sources, 135–136
Persky, Aaron, 100
Personal transformation, 236
Personification, 179
Persuasive appeals, 14–15
Persuasive speeches, 64, 66–67
Pew Research Center, 53, 134
PGA, 46
Physiological needs, 54
Pitch, 163
Plato, 13, 43
Plutarch, 100
Poetic, 177–180
Post hoc fallacy, 206
Power
    abuses of, 9, 215, 221–222
    hegemony and, 48–50
    public speaking and, 48–51
Praxis, 32
Precise language, to establish competence, 91
Precise thesis statement, 73
Presentational aids, 73, 88, 89, 90
Prestige testimony, 131
Preview statements, 118
Primacy effect, 120
Primary audience, 149–151
Primary orientation, 64–65, 66–67
Privilege, 238–239
Problem posing, 24–25
    agency and, 30
    reflexivity in, 31
    teachers and, 30
Problem-solution, 115
Protagoras, 13

Public speakers
    agenda set by, 82–83
    as advocates for specific transformations, 100–103
    attention-getting strategies, 93–99
    character of, establishing, 92
    competence, establishing, 91
    credibility of, 87–93. *See also* Speaker preparation
    effectiveness of, enhancing, 91–93
    role of, relative to audience, 84–86
Public speaking
    accountable, 190–213
    anxiety, 161–162
    as advocacy, 42
    as banking, 28–30
    as calling, 42–43
    characteristics of, 149–150
    communication as, 147–153
    constitutive, 2–21
    dialogic, 24, 27–28
    empowering, 232–247
    evolving, 214–231
    fear of, 34–37
    impassioned, 170–189
    informative, 81–84
    informed, 124–141
    interpersonal, 24, 25–28
    introduction to, 5–9
    monologic, 26–27
    performance speech and, 142–169
    power and, 48–51
    praxis and, 32
    primary audience in, 149–151
    relational, 11–16, 22–39
    respect in, 28
    responsive, 40–57
    specific to time, place, and purpose, 58–79
    structured, 106–123
    teaching and, similarities between, 30–31
    timeliness and, 152–153
Public speaking anxiety, 161–162

Q

Quality of sources, 132–136
Quantitative research, 96–97
Questions, as attention getter, 96
Quintilian, 15

R

Ramos, Rafael, 191
Rania, Queen, 107, 121
Rate, 163
Rather, Dan, 138

Reasoning
    analogical, 206–209
    appropriate use of, 192–194
    causal logic and, 203–205
    cause–effect relationships and, 203–206
    clarifying, to enhance an argument, 195–196
    deductive, 196–197
    defined, 191–192
    forms of, 194–209
    inductive, 198–203
    necessary, sufficient, and contributory causes and, 205
    situated, 209–211
Recency effect, 120
Reciprocity, 34
Reflexivity, 237–240
    advocacy and, 241
    becoming reflexive, 239–240
    concept of, 237–238
    defined, 31, 46, 237
    ethic of care and, 47
    in problem posing, 31
    persuasion and, 46
    practicing, 238–239
    privilege and, 238–239
Reframing, 166
Reframing fear of public speaking, 36–37
Regulative rule of communication, 226
Rehearsal, 166–167
Relational communication, 11–16
Relational public speaking, 22–39
    defined, 24
    interpersonal, 24, 25–28
Repetition, 48, 108, 110, 118, 137
Representation, communication as, 9
Researching sources, 133–134
Resilience, 244, 245
Responsive public speaking, 40–57
Review statement, 120
Rhetoric, 12–16
    as means of persuasion, 43–44
    critical thinking and, 12–16
    defined, 12–13, 43
    invitational, 181–182
Rhetorical frame, 175–176
Rhetorical schemes, 178, 179–180
    antithesis, 180, 185
    syllepsis, 179–180, 185
Rhetorical strategies, 183–185
Rhetorical tropes, 178–179
    metaphor, 178, 184
    metonymy, 179, 184
    simile, 178
    synecdoche, 179, 184
Rice, Tamir, 187, 233
Roosevelt, Eleanor, 162
Rowe, Carillo, 244

S

Sanders, Bernie, 63
Sandy Hook Elementary, 41, 55–56, 59
Satisfaction, in Monroe's motivated sequence, 115
Scaffolding, 75–76
Scope, 72–76, 88. *See also* Thesis statement
Scribner, M., 33
Security needs, 54
Self-actualization, 54
Sequentially, 115
Sharing source material
    approach to, 132
    bias in, 138–139
    direct quotes, 137
    paraphrasing, 137
    reality created by, 138–139
    responsibility in, 137–138
Shaull, Richard, 31
Simile, 178
Situated reasoning, 209–211
The Six Pillars of Self Esteem (Branden), 128
Slacktivism, 228
Slippery slope fallacy, 206
Snapchat, 217
Social constructionist model, 173
Social construction of reality, 173–174
Social media
    implicit bias in, 54
    #LivingWhileBlack and, 54
    #MeToo movement and, 215–216, 220–222, 224–225, 227–228
    name change and, 10
    persuasion and, 45
    relational public speaking and, 12, 23
    speaking occasions and, 60
    #takeaknee movement and, 233–234
Social reality
    audience participation in, 145–146
    construction of, 173–174
    creating and maintaining, 144–147
    intentionally, 146–147
Social significance, 16–19
Social transformation, 235
Sonic messages, 153
Sophists/Sophistry, 13

Sources
  anecdotal evidence, 131
  characteristics of, 133
  citations, 130, 137–138
  contextualizing, 136
  defined, 130
  descriptive/narrative evidence, 131
  empirical evidence, 130–131
  evaluating, reliable strategies for, 134–136
  expert testimony, 131
  Google Scholar, 134–135
  lay testimony, 131
  periodical, 135–136
  prestige testimony, 131
  quality of, 132–136
  reality created by sharing, 138–139
  researching, 133–134
  sharing. See (Sharing source material)
  testimonial evidence, 131
  types of, 130–132
Space, speech related to, 223–225
Spatially, 115
Speaker preparation, 87–93
  credibility enhanced through, 87–93
  defined, 87
  role as speaker, understanding, 88
  syntax structures, understanding importance of, 88–89
Speaker's claims, transition and, 119
Speaking contexts, 59–60, 88, 222, 223, 226
Speaking for, 41–42
Speaking from a manuscript, 158–159
Speaking from the heart, 37
Speaking occasions, 60–64, 72
  defined by relationship to community, 63–64
  deliberative speeches, 63
  epideictic speeches, 62–63
  forensic speeches, 61–62
  topic suited for, 70–72
  types and purposes of speeches considered in, 64–69
Speaking purpose, 60, 72
  deliberative speeches and, 63
  epideictic speeches and, 62–63
  forensic speeches and, 61–62
  informative speeches and, 83
Speaking with, 41–42
Speech development, outlining, 111–113
Stacks of labels model, 173
Stallman, Richard, 217
Statistics, to illustrate key idea or theme, 96–97
Structure
  benefits of, 108–109
  conclusions and, 120–121
  defined, 108
  goal of speech and, 108–109
  introductions and, 116–119
  outlining and, 110–116
  transitions and, 119
Style guide, 137
Subordination, 113, 114
Sufficient cause, 205
Supporting materials, 129–138. See also Sources
Syllepsis, 179–180, 185
Synchronous communication, 219
Synecdoche, 179, 184
Syntax, 88–89

T

#Takeaknee movement and, 233–234
Tactile messages, 153
Teaching
  informative speaking and, 82–83
  problem posing and, 30
  public speaking and, similarities between, 30–31
Teleprompter, 154
Testimonial evidence, 131
Text messages/texting, 82, 217, 220, 222, 226
The Courage to Teach (Parker and Scribner), 33
Theme
  dramatize, 97–98
  illustrate, 96–97
Thesis statement, 72–76
  argumentative, 75
  direct, 74–75
  elements of, 73
  precise, 73
  purpose of, 72–73
  to focus on important questions, 75–76
  unique, 73–74
The Today Show, 227
Time, 135
Timeliness, 152–153
Time, speech related to, 223–225
Topic, 70–72
  brainstorming for, 70–71
  defined, 70
  introduction and, 116
  narrowing, 72–76. See also Thesis statement
  selection, process of, 71–72
Transformations, advocating for, 100–103
Transitions, 119
Trump, Donald, 66, 125–126, 215, 221
Trustworthy, introduction and, 117–118
Turner, Brock, 100, 101
Twain, Mark, 126

Twitter, 64, 217
Tyson, Neil deGrasse, 28, 143–145, 150–154, 157, 159, 164–165

U

Unearned privilege, 49–51
UN High Commissioner for Refugees (UNHCR) reports, 121
Unique thesis statement, 73–74
United Nations, 19
U.S. News & World Report, 135
U.S. Religious Landscape Survey, 53

V

Variety, 90
Verbal communication, 144
Victim impact statement. *See* Impact statement
Video chat programs, 218
Visualization, in Monroe's motivated sequence, 115
Visual messages, 153
Voice, 162–164
    articulation and, 162–163
    dynamics and, 163–164
    effective use of, 146, 164
    pitch and, 163
    rate and, 163
Voice calling, 225–226
Vowel sounds, 162–163

W

Walker, Alice, 244
The Wall Street Journal, 135
Warren, J. T., 237
The Washington Post, 135
What does it mean to be White?: Developing White racial literacy (DiAngelo), 240
WhatsApp, 217
Women's March, 215, 221–222, 224, 227
Words
    abstract, 9–10
    ambiguous, 10
    arbitrary, 9
    connotative meaning of, 10
    denotative meaning of, 10
    in rhetorical schemes, 178, 179–180
Working outline, 112
Wyche, S., 233

Y

Yousafzai, Malala, 23–24, 36, 63

Z

Zuckerberg, Mark, 228

CPSIA information can be obtained
at www.ICGtesting.com
Printed in the USA
FSHW020603141120
75837FS

9 781516 525324